DEATH
BECOMES
US

DEATH
BECOMES
US

Pamela Skjolsvik

Book design by Maureen Cutajar
www.gopublished.com

ISBN: 1519147414

For Sonya Reed #878111

AUTHOR'S NOTE

Due to HIPAA regulations, names and/or identifying details have been changed to protect the identity of some people in this narrative. In certain other cases, if I have changed the name of a person or a place, I make note of that change in the text. While most of my interviews were recorded, those done at the prison were not, as I couldn't bring in a recorder or a pencil and notebook.

CONTENTS

"What do you say to a man who is being executed tomorrow? Did you say good luck when you left? I'm not trying to mess with you. That must be a strange thing to sit down in front of somebody you know is going to die and you'll ask me later what it's like. I'll tell you what it's like..."

—JIM WILLET,
FORMER WARDEN OF THE WALLS UNIT, HUNTSVILLE, TX

PROLOGUE

I t would be pretty awesome to brag that I confronted death in a brave and dramatic fashion, but that would be a lie. I would never have embarked on an exploration of my biggest fear had it not been for David Foster Wallace. It's not that Mr. Wallace was my literary superhero or that his books inspired me to question the meaning of my existence. Honestly, I didn't know he existed until September 12, 2008—the day he died. I was nervously waiting for my grad school instructor to call so we could discuss the future of my MFA thesis. She had recently received my first submission and I cringed at the thought of her slicing through my sentences with a red pen or cackling at my creative use of grammar. Not that she was a cackler, but she did intimidate me, and I wanted nothing more than to impress her. Like Band-Aid removal, I figured it was best to just get the whole uncomfortable conversation over with as quickly as possible. Ten minutes past our scheduled meeting time, I decided to take matters into my own sweaty hands. I found her phone number in the MFA directory and dialed it.

A funeral home answered.

"Oh, I'm sorry. Wrong number," I said and promptly hung up.

I dialed a second time without giving it much thought. This time there was a hint of agitation in the woman's voice.

"It's me again. Sorry," I apologized.

I felt like a pest for interrupting this poor woman at her dismal job. I triple-checked my instructor's number and slowly pressed each digit with paranoid precision.

Funeral home.

I hung up without a word, scared that I had entered the realm of prank calling and the phone authorities, whoever they were, would soon be pounding on my door. Perspiration trickled down the inside of my shirt. My interactions with teachers—or anyone in a position of authority—always brought on the nerves. Anyone could tell by my resumé or my laughable liberal studies degree from an underachieving state college that I didn't belong in post-graduate work among professional journalists. I was pushing forty and working in a dead-end job that involved proofreading ad copy for the phone book. And while I should have been grateful to be accepted into a writing program with such esteemed company, I simply felt like a fraud—a two-bit campfire storyteller with bits of marshmallow and melted chocolate stuck to my aging face. While my classmates tackled big-issue topics like murder, war and immigration, I played it safe and wrote about what I knew—my quirky, neurotic self.

While I waited for her call, I refreshed my inbox, eyed the clock, and checked my phone every few minutes to make sure there was still a dial tone. My two kids were upstairs glued to the television, but I knew that at the least opportune moment they'd get bored or want to eat lunch and Mommy's very important college time would be over. I tried to rehearse the conversation I'd be having with the teacher in my head so I could speed through it, but my thoughts kept returning to that funeral home. What kind of person would want to work there? Having recently been employed as a detention specialist in a jail, I thought I'd had a few strange jobs, but mortician made my former occupation look pedestrian. People at funeral homes touched dead people—and not just quick little taps with their pointer finger. They had prolonged contact with cold, decomposing bodies. What kind of person would subject themselves to that?

When the phone rang ten minutes later, it startled me. Instead of playing it cool and answering on maybe the third or fourth ring, I answered immediately without the pleasantries of 'Hello' or 'Skjolsvik residence.'

"Do you live in a funeral home? When I tried calling your house, I kept getting a funeral home."

From downstairs, I could hear that *Sponge Bob* was over and two sets of footsteps were approaching the stairs.

Diana laughed as if this kind of thing was completely normal. "For some reason, when I'm on the phone and someone else calls, it gets diverted to this one particular funeral home. I don't even know where they're at."

My kids, Nik and Lola, stared at me expectantly from the landing.

"Hold on a minute." I covered the phone with my hand. "Mommy's gonna be on the phone for about an hour and it's really important that I talk to this nice lady. Please go back upstairs."

"Can we have a snack?" Lola mouthed dramatically.

I nodded like a lunatic, knowing full well that both of my kids would use this phone call to their advantage.

Diana apologized for her lateness. She'd just found out that David Foster Wallace had hung himself. She was devastated by the loss of one of her favorite writers. I was confused. Woo-woo as it sounded even to me, it felt like this call was meant to happen the way it did. Death delayed her call, while mine was diverted there by some strange cosmic hiccup of the land-line phone system.

Despite the downer tone of our conversation, Diana also felt that reaching that funeral home was kind of a happy accident. I had originally intended to write about all the weird jobs I'd held, but since I'd already been there and done that, it didn't seem like much of an artistic leap. Death and dead bodies still lingered in my thoughts. Diana suggested that I explore professions that dealt with death. And because I admired my mentor and wanted to impress her almost as much as I coveted gold stars and future accolades, I contemplated tackling the most fear inducing assignment ever. But how could I admit to my brilliant mentor that not only was I afraid of death, I was also afraid of people?

My heart pounded. This was a turning point and I knew it. I could either play it safe like I always did or go big and fail spectacularly.

"Okay. That sounds like a good idea. I'll do it."

More than anything, I just wanted to end the call so I could go outside and smoke. It didn't occur to me that I had just agreed to my death sentence.

Part

I

"I'm not afraid of death;
I just don't want to be there when it happens."
—WOODY ALLEN

CHAPTER ONE

Meet a Stranger

The story begins, as all stories should, with a mysterious sticky note placed in the middle of my computer screen. A name, a phone number and 'Funeral Guy' is scribbled on it with a Sharpie. I recognize the handwriting and shuffle into my coworker Matt's office with the yellow piece of paper adhered to my pointed finger.

"George really wants to talk to you," Matt says in his usual dramatic fashion, like it is absolutely imperative that I call this morbid stranger immediately.

"Is he weird?"

I feel like Matt is trying to fix me up on a blind date with the elephant man. He mulls it over with his legs splayed in his high-dollar, super-fancy art director chair. I know he's trying to fuel my neurotic fire and/or make me blush. I try not to stare at his manspreading or the giant bulge that literally stretches to his knee. Assessing another person's weirdness is probably not Matt's forte.

"No?"

"Well, then why does he want to talk to me so bad?"

"I don't know, Pam. Maybe it's because you told me you wanted to talk to him about his job."

Oh.

George Liese and I agree to meet for coffee at the Steaming Bean. I arrive twenty minutes early and study each person as they enter the door of the café. No one looks like a body-building embalmer. I half expect someone with a pallid complexion and a dark, neatly-pressed suit to waltz through the door to the tune of *Amazing Grace*, but as the clock ticks past our meeting time, I worry that I have been stood up. It wouldn't be the first time. I call George and he answers on the first ring. While I cased the joint and built up a million different excuses as to why George wouldn't show, he was sitting at a coffee shop that I had never heard of, which is quite a feat in a town as small as this one. He apologizes and says he'll meet me as quickly as possible.

True to his word, in five minutes the bell over the door jingles as a tall, thin man in his late fifties enters, dressed in dark blue jeans and a burgundy button-down shirt. I rise from my table and approach him. His hands are quivering. Mine are sweating. I wipe them quickly on my jeans and shake his cold, trembling digits. We shuffle over to the counter and stare at the coffee menu like the secrets of the universe are hidden among the chalk text. As with every other social encounter I've experienced without the benefit of liquid courage, my mind wanders towards the catastrophic. *I don't know what I'm doing. I will sound stupid and unprofessional.*

I order a mocha-no-whip from the teenage barista, while George orders a "nothing fancy" black coffee. I pick up the tab, as it seems like the writerly thing to do— something that David Foster Wallace might do if he were still alive. When our order is called, there is no escape. George looks to me to pick our table.

The small café is hopping with Fort Lewis College kids. Beneath the din of the bean grinder, the cash register, and about twenty voices, an obscure Norah Jones song plays as we settle into a wobbly table in the front window.

"You're my first interview," I confess, hoping it will excuse my novice interviewing skills and the fact that I haven't exactly figured out my brand-new digital recorder.

"Really? Well, cool," he says with enthusiasm, like he can't believe how lucky he is to be questioned by a person who doesn't know what the hell she's doing. He crosses his long legs, leans forward, and sips his steaming black coffee while I fumble with the recorder. His hands are now steady. I place the tape recorder between us with my list of scribbled questions in front of me. I want to run to the restroom to wipe the sweat from my pits, but I know that at this point the only thing I can do is keep my arms down to hide the growing circle of wetness on my shirt. I stare at my questions, but really all I want to ask him is why he become an embalmer. Why out of all the possible ways to make a living would he choose to work with dead people? I hadn't done much research besides watching *Six Feet Under*, but The Society for Embalmers' website didn't make the profession sound particularly enticing.

> Embalmers come into direct contact with the body. They are exposed to blood and body fluids and infectious diseases such as AIDS, Hepatitis B and C, and Creutzfeldt-Jacob Disease. Some causes of death will be difficult for some people to see. Trauma, motor vehicle accidents, child deaths, cancers and the list goes on. For those who feel they want to ultimately be an embalmer, they will need to be able to face the challenges of the types of cases described here. It is not glamorous and requires hard work.

No glamour, hard work, and according to Salary.com, the median salary for an embalmer in the United States is only around forty-two thousand dollars. I've made that much working plenty of unremarkable jobs. Plus, I never had to touch dead people, look at anything gross—with the exception of the office refrigerator—or come in contact with any infectious diseases.

I open my brand new Moleskin notepad with the unlined pages. It looks like a small sketch book. I test the new black ink pen on the cream-colored virginal page. January 16, 2009. George watches me with interest as if some sort of magic is about to happen. I press record.

"So, George, when did you become an embalmer?"

"1980. I used to work at the Durango Herald as a graphic artist. What a change, huh?"

George chuckles and slaps his knee. He knows that I work in an art department with gym-rat Matt and a bunch of other graphic artists. And here we both are—two artistically inclined people chatting about death.

"That's where I met Harold Young. He owned the mortuary. And I talked to him. I had a fear of death and so I talked to Harold about it and he said to go talk to my minister. And the minister sent me back to Hood."

Since George's fear is apparently too big for God, Harold invites him to help out at Hood Mortuary on the weekends. Hood is the only funeral home in Durango and is situated on a high traffic corner of 3rd Ave. If you didn't know any better, you would think it was just another ornate historic home on a street where everyone, including me, wants to live. Unfortunately, you have to die to temporarily reside there. It doubles as the morgue.

George reluctantly agrees to help Harold out with the bodies. Within a matter of months, George went from an irrational fear of death, to driving people to the graveyard, to preparing their bodies for burial. I ask him about working with his first cadaver, which has to be the creepiest experience ever. George stares up at the ceiling.

"I remember it vividly. He was a Hispanic guy who'd died in a car wreck. And the weird thing was it didn't freak me out."

"Really?" A real journalist would press further. Naturally, I change the subject. "So what's your favorite part of the job?"

He leans forward and smiles, as if he has something terribly embarrassing to confess.

"Cosmetics. It's my specialty. I do the restoration, or restorative art is what they call it. It sounds kind of morbid, but I really enjoy it. I put people back together. It's a hard process."

I notice a young, hipster couple sporting ironic t-shirts staring at us from the couch. I ask George if he received any sort of special training in makeup application.

"No, but I've read a lot of articles." I laugh as if he is making a joke, but he's completely serious. He quickly reminds me that he is an artist by trade and an earnest one at that. I have a hard time accepting that being a graphic designer at a small town newspaper prepares someone for the gruesome reality of sewing a person's lips shut so they won't gape open during their wake.

"So, is there any special sort of makeup that you use?" I really want him to say something crazy like Mary Kay, a cosmetic company I dabbled in to make some extra money, but he says there isn't a particular brand. He prefers to use oil-based cosmetics, the stuff that stage actors use.

To achieve the best look, George explains that he has to keep the skin of the cadaver supple. To accomplish this, he uses lots of moisturizer and will 'work' the face to keep it as natural looking as possible — kind of like fluffing a couch pillow that someone is still sitting on.

As George explains the importance of moisturizer, I contemplate the physical act of kneading someone's cold gray skin with Mary Kay's Miracle Set. If more people knew about the odd stuff that happens in embalming rooms, they might find themselves leaning away from George's expressive hands and more towards the idea of cremation. Like me. But despite the creepiness of his job, he seems like a normal, nice guy who goes to the gym and drinks his coffee black.

"I wish more people realized how quickly they can go." George gulps his cooling coffee like a shot of whiskey. "We don't realize it, but a little accident, a fall and you bump your head and you're dead."

George punctuates this last statement by uncrossing his legs. The table jolts upwards and scares me even more than his last statement. He leans back in his chair and tells me that he has found dearly departed family members in his prep room, but he prefers not to work with them. I wholeheartedly agree with him on that. He has, however, embalmed friends, and finds it an honor to do so.

"I treat everyone like they're one of my relatives. I have a lot of respect for the dead."

When I ask him if most people he works with are on the shy, sensitive end of the spectrum, he reveals, "I'm shy. I'm very shy. But there's a few people I work with that are very... bubbly." Like George, I don't think I like bubbly. I have a hard enough time dealing with perky baristas.

When I ask what his funeral plans are, George admits that he doesn't really care what happens to his body after death. "It's really up to my daughter, but probably burial."

He wants to know who else I am going to interview. I tell him that I'm planning on speaking with some hospice workers.

He practically squeals about how amazing hospice workers are, but then reveals that the idea of hospice scares him. "I become attached to people." George doesn't have a problem with a dead body: it's the dying that freaks him out.

When I click my recorder off, George informs me that the average cost of a funeral is around seven grand. My jaw drops. I could buy a really nice used car for that amount of money. And that is for a standard, run-of-the-mill funeral—no bells, whistles, or piano-shaped coffins. A super-deluxe funeral will cost something akin to purchasing a small house in Nebraska — all to throw a party that no one wants to attend.

Later that night, I add 'cost of funerals' to my ever-growing list of fears. After a quick Google search, I find out that the state of New Mexico, where George works, will pay for my cremation if my family doesn't have the money to cover burial, but they will hold my 'cremains' hostage for two years. It's no wonder nobody wants to contemplate death. Not only is dying a drag—it's expensive.

*   *   *

I first realized I was going to die on August 17, 2000. I was not terminally ill with a respirator hissing by my bedside, nor was my body bruised and bloodied from a crippling car wreck. I wasn't even in a hospital. It was just my thirtieth birthday, which is a fairly monumental occasion—a day for celebration, a surprise trip to France or at least an all-day spa experience. Instead, I was in my living room at 6 am, dressed in a 42 DD maternity bra and nasty old pajama bottoms, with a striped breastfeeding pillow strapped around my fleshy midsection.

My husband Erik entered our living room like a chipper, dutiful waiter, setting a glass of water ornamented with a pink straw next to my new glider chair, as if this tiny gesture would somehow atone for the constant feeding, waking, changing diaper schedule. It was the big 3-0, and I fully expected something big and magical to happen. Only now do I realize that the big magical thing was right there in front of me.

"Do you want to listen to any music?" he said, digging through a stack of CDs on the floor.

I nodded a bleary eyed "whatever" as he pressed play and left me to feed our daughter for what seemed like the millionth time.

James Taylor's blanket-warm voice filled the annoyingly bright room.

I opened my eyes slowly and stared down at the wonder of my first child. She was dressed in an eco-friendly cloth diaper that had seemed like a wonderful idea at the time. Her pale pink body wriggled in ecstasy as her tiny hands reached towards the warmth of my body. Giant wet tears dropped from my eyes and landed on my daughter's exposed skin. She remained oblivious, perfectly content with our soft, cushy, milk-machine arrangement. But I was overwhelmed with feelings of uncontrollable panic. Where was the remote? I needed to hit the pause button on the new sound track of my life, but I was trapped in an extremely ugly glider chair that didn't match any of my other furniture.

James Taylor melted into the syrupy timber of Mama Cass.

I lost it. Strange guttural sobs melded inharmoniously with the easy listening lullabies. Erik bolted into the room like I'd just dropped our daughter and knelt by my side with a fixed, worried expression on his face. But unbeknownst to him, there was nothing he could do—no water, wet washcloth or fluffy pillow was going to fix this panic attack.

It could have been any number of things that set off this melodramatic state: post-pregnancy hormones, lack of sleep, James Taylor, the size of my butt, or the scope of my birthday. Thirty was just a number, but I seriously thought that by the time I reached it, I would feel like I'd graduated into adulthood. I didn't.

My unrecognizable reflection in the mirror didn't help. This was not how thirty was supposed to look. In the past nine months, I'd gained seventy pounds and now weighed twenty more than my husband. My once slender body had become soft, fleshy and foreign. All I needed was a bikini-clad Carrie Fisher chained to my leg to complete the look.

In addition to losing, or perhaps swallowing, my former physical self, I was now responsible for the health and happiness of someone whose needs were immediate and maddeningly indecipherable. Granted, I had the Boppy pillow, the glider chair, the crib, the pink clothes and the changing table—but no matter how many times I pored over the pages of the "What to Expect" books, nothing prepared me for the overwhelming need of a newborn baby. My day-to-day temperament leaned towards avoiding and/or leaving when people or situations became too messy. But you can't behave this way towards your new baby. All the parenting books say so.

And then there's the whole tenderness thing. No one prepared me for that. It sounds clichéd, but when I gazed down at my snuggly, peaceful daughter, it just didn't matter—I loved her like I'd never loved before. I didn't need fancy dinners, or flowers or chocolates to be wooed by her. I loved her without condition. At the moment of her birth, my primal instincts were awakened and sharpened with her first breath—I would do anything within my power to keep her happy and free from harm.

Days into my daughter's beginning, the question that no new parent or really anybody wants to think about arose—what if something happened to me? What then? At some point, I was going to die and there was nothing I could do about it. I had never contemplated my own death. To me, it was some abstract, ethereal ending that would happen way off in the future when I was geriatric, fast asleep, or too bored with life to care. I had never envisioned car crashes, slipping on a patch of ice, being stabbed by a psychotic serial killer or more realistically, suffering from some painful long drawn-out disease caused by my off-again on-again smoking habit. The world suddenly became a much scarier place.

The highlight of my thirtieth birthday was a shower. The day ended just as it began—in the ugly glider chair. After cake, Erik presented me with my birthday gifts. Like my current state of disarray, his gifts to me were unwrapped without any sort of frivolous presentation; two books about parenting. Somehow, I managed to keep the sarcastic remarks to myself. Lucky for him, motherhood, like life, is a terminal diagnosis that can suck the life out of a person both mentally and physically. I was too tired to make petty complaints about Dr. Spock or the lack of a Tiffany blue jewelry box. If I could die at any moment, I certainly didn't want my last words on this earth to be "My vagina is now the size of the Lincoln Tunnel and all you got me for my birthday was "What to Expect: The First Year?"

In fairness to my husband, it wasn't all that bad. If anything, I learned a valuable lesson: I had someone to live for, someone who needed me, someone who would demand more from me than I'd ever demanded from myself, and most importantly, someone I didn't want to fail by doing something silly like dying when she hit puberty.

But that hasn't been easy. I've got some bad habits.

I love to smoke, and I mean *love*. I'd quit the minute I knew I
was pregnant, but after I was done with breastfeeding, I picked
up right where I left off. I did not particularly like the taste of cigarettes or the butts that littered the floor of my garage, but I did
relish the escape they afforded me. In a somewhat socially ac-
ceptable way, I could hide from my job, my kids, a heated
argument, an awkward social event, or anything else that I
deemed too uncomfortable, gynecological exams excluded. It was
glorious. For almost twenty years, the cigarette was my best
friend. But by the time I hit my late thirties, that time when nature tends to give you the face you deserve, my best friend
betrayed me with tiny little lines above my constantly-puckered
lips. At thirty-eight, I decided to kick her ass to the curb.

I'd ditched her before. Like Mark Twain, I found it easy to quit
smoking. I'd done it a hundred times with the costly assistance of
nicotine gum, patches, lozenges, and an antidepressant disguised
as a nonsmoking aid. In one of my previous attempts at quitting,
I even ventured to see a hypnotherapist named Sonja who prom-
ised, "With six sixty-dollar sessions, you'll be smoke free." She
had testimonials, so I figured that this whole dysfunctional cigarette dependency would soon be over and I would be a tree
hugging granola girl with fresh pink lungs in a matter of days.

During our first session, Sonja suggested that we have a funeral
for my cigarettes. I'd only been to one funeral in my life, so it was
sort of a wacky, novel idea. As I sat in the reclined La-Z-Boy with
Sonja's soft monotone voice guiding me through the ceremony, I felt
my body tense. Granted, this experience was all happening in my
head, but as soon as I pictured my carton of Camel Lights being
lowered into the dark, cold, freshly dug earth, I wailed like a hungry
baby whose mother had just left the room. Caught off guard by my
own reaction, I contemplated diving right into that fresh grave,
greedily snatching my beloved friends, and lighting one so I could
contemplate the serious nature of this event. With calm reassurance,
Sonja kept on with the funeral proceedings. The wailing subsided as
my mind floated elsewhere, namely the Conoco station that offered

a three-for-two special on Camel Lights. But like all difficult things, there wasn't a quick fix for my nicotine addiction. I had to want the desired outcome, and at the time, I didn't. In fact, the minute I purchased a new pack of friends, I was more dependent than before.

After I met George at the coffee shop, I decided to quit smoking. Again. If I was going to pay attention to death, death might start paying attention to me.

*   *   *

After my short and surprisingly pleasant meeting with George, I feel emboldened to dip my toe further into the death pool. Dr. Carol Huser is the coroner in my town. She also writes occasional health-related pieces for the local newspaper. I figure we have the writing thing in common, so I shoot her a quick e-mail. I'm not expecting much, since Hood Mortuary never responded to my inquiry for an interview. Dr. Huser responds within the hour.

Because my only knowledge of coroners comes from *CSI* and old reruns of *Quincy M.E.*, I joke to myself that Dr. Huser is a crime-solving sleuth who can dissect a body and surmise from the wound patterns that the murder occurred in the library with a candlestick at the hands of Professor Plum. Meeting her is less jitter-inducing when I think of her that way.

On entering her office, I discover that she is not quite the character I expect. She is a petite woman in her early sixties with short auburn hair. Dressed in a green sweater with matching green loafers, she brings to mind Mary Martin as Peter Pan.

I take a seat across from her desk. Her office is small, orderly and without personal effects. Despite the fact that this is her lunch hour, the plain brown sack sits unopened on her desk. I'm amazed she can still stomach food. I feel guilty for imposing on her private time, so I cut the chit chat and place my recorder on her desk.

"Do you remember your first anatomy class?" I ask.

"Not particularly." She yawns.

Not the best start. "Do you remember the first time you had to dissect a cadaver?"

"I remember that I did. It's not something that stands out."

Seriously? I vividly remember the day I had to dissect a poor little fetal pig in 8th grade science class. I shift uncomfortably in the brown wooden chair, unsure of how to proceed. "So it wasn't like a rite of passage? Like, uh oh. Tomorrow's the big day."

"No. It was just another class."

God, I want a cigarette. *Yes, but it was a class with somebody's grandma or grandpa or mom or dad lifeless on a metal table and you were cutting them open with a sharp instrument.* "Have you ever had to perform an autopsy on someone you know?"

"Yes." She answers without an iota of feeling, like I have simply asked if she brushed her teeth this morning.

"Did you have a problem with that?"

"No."

That's when it hits me: I am talking to a very unusual person, a person who has no problem digging around in the bodily remains of the recently and sometimes not-so-recently deceased. She tells me her job is like solving a mystery. My face must be curdling because she admits that she isn't the least bit squeamish and that she has become desensitized to the sight of dead people. She says her sense of humor helps, but I'm getting the distinct impression that it's on hiatus today.

I briefly entertain the notion of asking if I could watch her work some time. But that would be a silly, futile pursuit. I can't finish a piece of chicken if I encounter a vein. I would most likely vomit during the autopsy and then it would be months until I was able to stomach food again. I haven't even seen George's artistically preserved dead people—how could I possibly handle watching someone get cut open and picked apart?

When I leave Dr. Huser to her sandwich, I feel like I haven't really penetrated the essence of what it takes to do her job. My meeting with her is like a dinner party conversation, something I don't imagine she or George get to engage in very often. Do acquaintances ask how their day went? Or do people remain silent about that part of their lives? There is fascination, but also repulsion. On my drive home, I wonder if they feel misunderstood or lonely because they can't share this part of themselves with others.

If anything, their roles are probably the easiest part of the death process. The embalmer and the coroner only have to touch the physical remains of a body. They have no idea if the person on the metal table liked guacamole (okay, maybe Dr. Huser might know that), or had grandkids or liked to watch *Dancing with the Stars*. To them, it's just a body.

*　*　*

I have no experience with dead bodies. At the age of thirty-eight, I have only dealt with the loss of one person: my Grandma Lola, who possessed none of the qualities of the annoyingly infectious "Lola" songs that bring to mind yellow-ribboned showgirls getting whatever they want, or men who dress like women. My grandma was a stern, religious woman with a short crop of curly white hair and a plethora of patterned polyester dresses, which she donned every day with rolled-up hose and heeled shoes. She did not wear pants. No sirree. Pants were for men and Lola was definitely not a man, at least not in this song.

My parents called it quits in 1974, after five kids and twenty-four years of marriage. In 1977, Lola moved to Kansas to live with us. She wasn't a doting grandma, enchanted by every little thing I did or said, but she was there, so she gets an "A" for effort. In addition to teaching me how to knit, she turned me on to bad TV, and we spent countless hours glued to the boob tube, watching *The Love Boat*, *Three's Company*, and *Fantasy Island*. For an old-fashioned woman in her 80s, she had a voyeuristic fascination with sexy shows. Every time I catch a glimpse of those old sitcoms on late night TV, I think of her sitting in her rocking chair, staring at the TV, her needles blindly clicking and clacking—knit, purl, knit, purl.

Although she would never say it, Lola was probably miserable living with us. My mom was either at work or out on a date, and I wasn't exactly the most pleasant teenager. In the winter of our discontent, December of '84 to be exact, my mom accidentally walked in on Grandma while she was dressing and discovered that her mother's skin looked like an old bruised pear. Lola failed to mention her curious skin condition because she didn't want to be a burden to my mother, whose own life was in a constant state of turmoil. After a frantic trip to the doctor, we discovered that Grandma Lola had advanced leukemia and wouldn't live much longer.

I did my best to lift my mom's spirits, as her own mother lay dying in the hospital. Because I didn't know what else to do, I put up our fake, flocked Christmas tree and decorated the house with plastic garlands and red bows. The few presents we had under the tree that year were all from Grandma. It was a strange, sad time, and it didn't help that every radio station assaulted us with "Grandma Got Run Over by a Reindeer."

Even though I was fourteen, my mother decided I was too young to visit Grandma at the hospital. She died four days before Christmas. We didn't discuss it. As my mom confirmed later, "we just got through it." And by all appearances, we did. I acted as if nothing had happened, by being strong, silent and stoic, just like Lola. Unfortunately, on a fourteen-year-old, that comes off as snotty indifference.

But I did care. I cared deeply. I just didn't know how to show it.

On the day of Grandma's funeral, three of my older siblings and I crammed into my mom's Olds Cutlass and drove to southern Illinois for the burial. For the first part of the three-hundred-mile trip, we sat in silence, staring at the back of the hearse. But then someone broke out in song. Within minutes, everyone in the car was belting out Beatles tunes. I felt choked and uncomfortable. I knew there had to be an appropriate way to mourn someone, and singing "I Wanna Hold Your Hand" as we drove to a funeral service wasn't it. When they broke into "She Loves You," I defiantly plugged my ears and regressed into "na na na na na na, I can't hear you, I can't hear you," which egged the others on to turn up the volume. I hated being the center of attention, especially at times when I didn't know how to act. I wanted to disappear and figure this whole death thing out on my own.

All I remember about the service is sitting next to my mom with her mink coat on my lap. I don't remember any particulars. I don't even remember where we sat. My mom tells me that there was an open casket, but for the life of me, I can't recall looking at it or into it. It's just an uncomfortable memory blanketed in mink.

On the drive back home, my siblings resumed their gleeful Von Trapp family tour through the Beatles discography. I pressed my face against the cool pane of the car window and glared at the barren winter landscape. A loud, off-key rendition of "Ticket to Ride" filled the cramped space. There was no escape. I could tolerate the discomfort or leap out of the moving vehicle. As a moody self-preservationist, I chose the former. As my body relaxed into the plush maroon seat, I unclenched my jaw, closed my eyes, and quietly hummed along.

On a gut level, I knew there had to be more to grieving. It was all so anticlimactic and confusing. What are we expected to do when we lose someone? How do we announce our grief or ask for some time alone to figure this stuff out? Wear black? It was 1984. Black was my wardrobe staple, accentuated with lacy Madonna-inspired hair-bows and rubber bracelets up to my elbows. Black wasn't mourning, it was Monday. But, if I gleaned any misguided information from my first death experience, it was this—ignore it. If you can, sing a happy song, but never, no matter what, look at it or talk about it or contemplate it. Death has the power to change everything.

CHAPTER TWO

Try Something New

Instead of pursuing hospice, like I bragged to George the embalmer, I sit at my computer and stare at a series of stark black-and-white baby pictures. In these photographs, a woman in her early forties cradles a newborn baby as her husband gazes down at them with reverence. In a second close-up, the mother kisses the child's forehead. In a third, the baby's tiny hand is shown inside his father's. These photographs are typical—but for these parents, they mean so much more. These images are memorializing the son they just met. He died moments after birth.

I don't even know who these people are, but tears stream down my face as another photo appears on my computer screen. I can't keep it together. The song that accompanies the slide show doesn't help my emotional state. It's beautiful and sad. My impulse is to walk away from these photos, but I'm forcing myself to look at them, to study their normalcy.

Death photography is nothing new. In the 1800's, it was a fairly common practice to take pictures of people who had just died, as it was less expensive than painted portraiture. In some of those photos, the person is posed as if he or she were still alive. Families were proud of these images and featured them prominently in their homes. But today there is no culturally normative response to postmortem photographs.

Which brings me to Carol Cardwell, a volunteer for Now I Lay Me Down To Sleep, a national organization that provides free professional portraits for families of babies who are stillborn or at risk of dying as newborns. Carol is just one of over seven thousand volunteer photographers. In the past year alone, she has photographed ten babies and their families. Out of these ten, the parents on my screen are the only ones who knew their baby was going to die at birth. The other nine families were unaware of their child's fate. One minute everything was going as planned, and then something happened, whether it was an umbilical cord problem or an undetected chromosomal disorder. But the end was the same—an end to a life that had never really begun.

Carol agrees to meet me for lunch at a small, busy Mexican restaurant. As usual, I arrive first and the hostess seats me at a window table, which seems to be the trend of my interviews so far—death on display. I set my recorder and notebook on the table to appear more official and study the oversized menu, even though I know I will order what I always order at a Mexican restaurant: cheese enchiladas. Carol, a middle-aged woman with reddish hair and a pleasant face, greets me warmly and takes the seat next to me.

After a bit of small talk about the weather and why I moved from San Francisco to Durango, I start the interview by telling her in sort of a juvenile manner, "I read the website and that is like, wow. That is something that I could NEV-ER do. I'd be too sad. (Long awkward pause) So, how did you get involved in this?" The tone of my voice implies I think she's joined the mafia.

She politely ignores my inexperienced interviewing skills and answers my question. "Well, another photographer in town had told me about it and it seemed like a great way to give back."

Once she began volunteering, she photographed three babies in one month and four babies the next. Between sips of water, she admits that she became depressed after encountering so many deaths and grieving families in such a short amount of time. She'd had several personal losses, but so many at once was overwhelming. She brings up her two nephews who died within months of each other. As she tells me the details, the waiter approaches.

"Are we ready to order?" he says, smiling at the two of us.

"Yes," I say a little too emphatically.

When he departs with our order, I ask how she enters the picture after a baby has died. She tells me that the nurses are key to procuring her services. If a "fetal demise," a term Carol dislikes, is imminent or has occurred, they will give the grieving family a brochure to explain Now I Lay Me Down To Sleep. Since professional photographs are not usually on the top of the family's priorities, the nurses will gently encourage them to consider it. As Carol says, "They might not be thinking about it now, but they'll care later."

"In your experience, are the families receptive to it?"

"I've only had one that wasn't."

Receptive might not be the right word. Carol admits she feels like an intruder, and has walked into rooms where the pain is so tangible she can't help but feel it.

"It's not so much the death that bothers me. It's the pain that the parents are going through. That's what's hard for me. Watching them hurt so badly because of the loss."

After a year, however, she is slowly learning to create some professional distance.

"What I learned after the first one is to not do the images right away. I let them sit for a couple of weeks because it's such an emotional thing. If I let them sit and go back to them, it's much easier to go through the process."

As we talk between bites of enchiladas, Carol's eyes well up with tears at several points in the conversation. It's mostly my fault. I ask her to recall her first volunteer experience.

"It was devastating. I was a mess. I was a mess for at least two and a half weeks after that." That's when she started problem solving. Part of that was bringing her adult daughter along, who acts as her assistant. They are able to decompress and support each other.

Her biggest issue now is whether the parents want to hold their baby. Some are so grief-stricken that they can't bring themselves to do it. Carol says that about a third of the families she's photographed have felt this way. She doesn't push them. At a recent training session, she found out that she herself could touch the baby.

She also saw images from another photographer in a larger city that horrified her.

"It was just like, here's a photo of your dead baby."

Like all the images I've seen on NILMDTS' website, Carol photographs the babies in black and white and uses a fair amount of photo-shopping to soften the image. She assures me that if she's going to do this work, she wants to do it well: to give the family something to hold onto and share. To her, a bad photograph is worse than none at all. I can't imagine what a bad photo looks like. Well, I could, but I don't want to.

As the waiter clears our plates, Carol asks me about the people I've spoken with. I rattle off my list, confessing my awe for everyone I've met so far. I'm kind of a wimp.

She shakes her head. "You're a very strong person and I can tell that just by talking to you."

For some reason, I get that a lot. More than likely, it's my height. Many people assume that a six foot tall woman is brave, capable, over the age of 21, and probably a basketball player. But while I might look like Ripley in *Alien*, I'd be too much of a chicken shit to go back and save the cat.

While we wait for the waiter to return with the bill, Carol tells me about the death of her ninety-five-year-old grandmother. She wants to talk about her experience, and since I'm the death writer lady, I guess she thinks I'd be a good audience. I too have lost a grandmother, so I naively assume I can offer some comfort. "Well, at least she had a long, full life," I say.

I'm such a nitwit.

I quickly pay for our lunch and walk with her outside, itching to return to the safety and solitude of my car. Although I don't feel comfortable with other people's sadness, I truly hope Carol retains her sensitivity and her quest for artistic perfection. The families she works with need someone who won't walk away from them during the most difficult experience of their lives.

And it is. It happened to my parents. In 1954, in her seventh month of pregnancy, my mother developed toxemia and almost died carrying her first child. While she was in a coma, the doctors were forced to induce labor to save her life. The baby, my oldest brother Bruce Allen Johnson, weighed 2 pounds, 14 ounces at birth. My mother found him dead in his crib when he was three months old. Losing their first child devastated my parents. To this day, my mom says it was the only time she ever saw my father cry. There are plenty of pictures of my four siblings and me, but none of Bruce. All of the photos they had taken of him didn't turn out: they were all distorted, blurred and eventually tossed away. Even though he lived for three months, he is lost to me, and to all of us who never knew him.

When I get home, I try to watch Carol's slideshow again, but I can't bring myself to do it. Because I have brought two healthy children into this world, these images are too painful to look at. I feel guilty for my own good fortune, yet I'm even more fearful that my children could be taken at any moment. This fear of imagined loss manifests itself in overprotection, which will probably come back to haunt me when they're dysfunctional twenty-somethings who can't figure out how to pay their phone bill.

It's funny, but when I was a kid, I'd play outside for hours till it got dark and my mom had no idea where I was or with whom I was spending my time. I'd come home with sunburns, mosquito bites, scraped knees, and it was no big deal. She had faith that I would be okay. As a control freak, I would never let my kids run all over the place without adult supervision. The instant availability of horror stories on the news and on the Internet has tainted my faith in people.

But the opposite is even worse—lack of communication or even information, which I'm encountering a lot more as I delve deeper into professions that work with death. I can't get people to return my calls. George, who was so gung-ho about meeting and talking with me initially, has stopped answering his phone. I've only tried to call him a couple of times about visiting him at work, but I'd like to think he'd have the courtesy to call me back. But maybe he's in the profession he's in because he isn't a social butterfly. After all, the dead can't get pissed if you fail to RSVP for their funeral service.

In addition, the only funeral home in town won't return my e-mails. It's clear that they aren't willing to talk to me until I've flatlined or am calling on behalf of someone who has. Whatever their reason, it's seriously getting on my nerves that the only game in town won't let me in. Thanks Jessica Mitford.

While I wait around for someone, anyone to call me back, I read my friend Susan's latest personal essay about suffering two miscarriages. In this early version of her work, her descriptions are clinical and devoid of emotion. She writes that people around her don't publicly acknowledge her grief because her baby wasn't really 'real.' Like Susan, I've had two miscarriages, but the weird thing is, I didn't regard them as deaths until recently. When they happened, well-meaning friends and family said, "It's a good thing it happened when it did," but not, "I'm sorry for your loss." Women who have experienced one don't talk about it much, if at all. Their silence could simply be due to the fact that a miscarriage is perceived as a failure to produce a baby. But for any woman who has ever wanted one, that baby is real the minute a blue line appears on the pregnancy test.

It was for me. I found out I was pregnant on the day of my wedding. My first, that is—first wedding and first pregnancy. My period was late, but I attributed that to pre-wedding jitters. It was bad timing on my part to take a pregnancy test on an already emotionally weighted day. When I showed Guy the stick with the two blue lines, the color drained from his face. He tried to keep it together for my sake, but his eyes revealed an inner horror, like he was in a tiny canoe heading over Niagara Falls. I wasn't too thrilled either. In the pictures from our wedding, we look like mannequins—stiff and uncomfortable with frozen, strained smiles. During the champagne toast, I felt guilty for even holding a glass of alcohol. While I did my best to hold back tears, Guy looked like he had a corncob firmly wedged up his butt. We waited a couple of weeks after the wedding to share the news with our family. Nobody was particularly thrilled.

Since we didn't have insurance, we reluctantly climbed aboard the public assistance bandwagon for prenatal care. At the age of twenty-three, I was working as a waitress in a popular breakfast cafe, while Guy made about ten bucks an hour in an office job. We barely made enough to cover the rent in our one-bedroom apartment, and now we were somehow going to have to support a child. Naively, I decided to share my baby news with everyone, including my regular customers at work. I thought that maybe they'd feel sorry for me and tip me more. They didn't.

In my tenth week of pregnancy, I was in the dressing room of a maternity store trying on pants to fit my expanding belly. I removed my skin-tight Levis and found bright red spots on my underwear. I grabbed some tissue from the dressing room and left in a panic. I called Guy from the mall and we met at the hospital. Since UCSF was a teaching hospital, and we were on the government's dime, several pre-med students stood around and watched as the doctor performed an internal (wand in the vagina) ultrasound, which was demeaning and torturous.

The head physician's eyes stayed fixated on the monitor. "I'm afraid the fetus has died. I can't find a heartbeat," he said.

My eyes turned to Guy, the only friendly, caring face in the room. He looked oddly relieved. More than anything, I felt embarrassed splayed out on the exam table with the medically termed 'missed abortion' still inside of me. As the doctor covered the lower half of my body, the medical students left the room.

"It's for the best," said Guy, patting my arm.

"I can order a D&C right now, or you can let it happen naturally," the doctor said.

The last thing I wanted was to break down and cry in front of Guy or that steely-faced doctor. I chose option two and fled from the hospital as fast as my unstable legs could carry me. The next few days were weird and tense as I waited for the fetus to expel itself. "It will be like a heavy period," the doctor had offered as some sort of reassurance.

When the cramping began, I sat in the bathtub, hoping the heat from the water would help to soothe my aching body. But it was unbearable. I was hurting, I was alone and more than anything, I wanted someone to walk me through this, give me comfort, or just hold my hand and say they were sorry. As I exited the tub, a spasm of pain overtook me and I fell onto the tile floor.

Guy ran to the bathroom and managed to get me into some clothes. He drove me to the nearest emergency room, which was located in a Catholic hospital, just a few blocks from our apartment. Contractions surged through my body as I approached the receptionist.

"Can I help you?" she asked.

"She's having a miscarriage," Guy replied.

"Oh."

She called a nurse, who quickly shuffled us into a private room. I was directed to remove my underwear and change into a gown. She then led me to a scale. Blood streamed down my legs onto the green tile floor. I was mortified by the spectacle my body was causing, so I kept my mouth shut. The nurse threw a large cotton pad onto the examination table, asked me to sit down and then stuck me about four times with a needle. Her unskilled intrusion popped one of my veins, resulting in deep blue bruising up and down my arm. Not only was I bleeding all over the place, I also looked like a track-marked junkie.

After thirty minutes of waiting and wondering, the frazzled ER doctor wandered in.

"How's your pain level?" he asked.

"Better," I said.

As he inspected between my bloodied legs, he asked the nurse for a pan.

"No wonder this was so painful," he said and removed the placenta, which was the size of a Porterhouse steak. Like an excited kid in a science lab, he pointed out the fetus to Guy, who relayed to me later that it looked like a slug.

That night, and for many nights after, I cried, slept, chain-smoked, and ate a lot of ice cream. I never went back to my waitress job at the diner. I simply wanted to pretend that it didn't happen. There was no funeral or public grieving over this thing—this slug. Everyone was complicit in maintaining the silence—except for my father, who broke it with his trademark grace and sensitivity. Holding my cousin's newborn baby, he said, "See what you missed out on?"

A second marriage, a second miscarriage. I told everyone I knew that I was pregnant. I reasoned that since I'd successfully produced one healthy baby, I couldn't possibly lose another.

At ten weeks, I went in for an ultrasound to see why I wasn't feeling pregnant anymore. The doctor gave me the news as if she were diagnosing a hemorrhoid.

"You can try again in about three months," she said and left the room.

Her demeanor was cold and detached. Erik squeezed my hand. As we stared at each other in disbelief, the ultrasound technician patted me on the shoulder.

"I'm sorry," she said.

At the receptionist's desk, I scheduled a "D&C" for the next morning. There was no way I was going to endure the natural option again.

The night after my procedure, a friend stopped by my house with a Pyrex dish of homemade lasagna and a bouquet of flowers. When I heard the doorbell ring, I panicked and told Erik I didn't want to see anyone. It was much easier to pretend it didn't happen and hope that others would follow suit. This was easy to do when I didn't have anything to show. Even Now I Lay Me Down to Sleep has a cutoff date for their services—the baby has to be at least twenty-five weeks old. It sounds cruel to say, but before then, it's not considered a real, viable baby, and it's certainly not photogenic.

Photo or not, my loss was real. But was my discomfort with others the only reason I never allowed myself to grieve and recognize these miscarriages for what they were—death? Was this withholding of grief affecting my life? Was it manifesting itself in ways that I wasn't aware of? All I know is that I'm uncomfortable when others are grieving. This is normal to an extent. I mean, I'm as much of a pleasure seeker as the next person, but I always took it a step further—I would avoid the person or the uncomfortable situation until everyone involved forgot about it. But this became more difficult as I got older. There were too many losses and situations I simply couldn't escape anymore.

One was my hairdresser. After six years of loyal patronage, I decided to divorce her. In the last year or so, I felt like she took my every-six-week appearance for granted. She'd abandon me under the heat lamp to chat with another customer, who inevitably had better hair or more fashionable clothing. I'd watch them jealously while the heat lamp shut off and cooled, feeling stupid and unattractive, a plastic bag molded to my damp, freshly dyed locks. I was beginning to feel like a redheaded stepchild with fake 3N hair. Since I despise confrontation more than a trip to the DMV, I did not inform Lisa Marie of my decision to end our relationship. Like an adulterer, I sought out someone younger, with better hair.

*   *   *

My new hairdresser's name is Heather and she's closer to my house, which helps to abet my adultery. As she secures the cape around my freshly washed hair, she asks me, "Do you have any animals?"

"Oh, I've got a dog, a cat and a couple of kids," I reply, thinking I am terribly clever and funny. "Do you have any kids?"

She pauses for a moment. "I used to."

In that instant, I am besieged by messy, sweaty, heart-pounding panic.

"What happened?" I ask in a tiny, sheepish voice, bracing the arms of my chair under the smock.

She hesitates. This is not a conversation she wants to have with a stranger. She is not alone. It is not a conversation I want to engage in either. Her hand trembles as she combs and cuts each section of my hair with long, sharp scissors. I eye her every move in the mirror, scared that she might accidentally cut my ear off. I can't keep still. I am so miserable in the presence of her grief, but there is no escape: she is cutting my hair. A trickle of sweat runs down the inside of my shirt as I stare at my ghostly white face in the mirror.

Heather sets the scissors down. "Last November, my son Tommy was at home with his dad. They were eating pizza for dinner and Tommy choked on a bite."

"Oh my God. How old was he?"

"Two."

"Oh, I am so sorry." I don't know what else to say.

She looks sad and nervous. I look like a heartless bitch. Heather picks up the scissors and resumes the cut. I don't know what else to talk about. Every possible topic seems trivial in comparison. To fill the awkward silence, I tell her that I am in school and writing about people who work with death.

"You should talk to my husband Dan. He's in school right now to become a paramedic."

"Really?"

I am so not ready to talk to this man.

As I drive the six miles home from the salon, I sob out all the fear and anxiety I held back in Heather's sad presence. While I agreed to meet with her husband, I know full well that I am not emotionally competent enough to talk with a person who has experienced the most gut-wrenching pain and loss imaginable. Heather and Dan embody my worst fear—I want to avoid them at all costs.

Avoiding Heather will be easy, but Dan is going to be difficult: EMTs are the next stop on my self-imposed death tour. In my town, there is only one fire station, and Dan works there. In order to ride along with the fire department and their EMTs, I am required by their Captain to attend a HIPAA (Health Insurance Portability and Accountability Act) class. The whole purpose of the training session is to remind me that I can only write about what I see with my own two eyes, and not what the EMTs tell me. If they talk about a patient with someone who is not involved in a patient's care, it can result in a hefty fine, firing, or both.

The class is held at the volunteer fire station in a fluorescent-lit room that is probably two degrees shy of a walk-in freezer. I take a seat in the back of the room to minimize the chances I will be called on if there's a pop quiz. There are about fifteen teenagers, two very buff women and an older gentleman with white hair and a beard who looks like an undernourished, yet very outdoorsy Santa Claus. Skinny Santa reclines awkwardly in a folding chair at the front of the class, apparently too cool to sit at a table with one of the obnoxious teenage elves. Despite the fact that they are essentially good kids volunteering to be firefighters, they are still teenagers, and act accordingly. I feel as if I've wandered into a high school cafeteria on pizza Friday.

As I wait for the instructor to arrive and stop the horseplay, I overhear one of the more astute young men in attendance proclaim, "How come you didn't friend me, bitch?" I glare in his direction, thinking he is trash talking one of the few teenage girls in the room, but I am wrong. He is sardined between three other young males on a grimy brown couch. These handsome specimens are all in the throes of hormonally-induced acne and look no more than twelve. Their laughing, joking and punching each other is getting out of control. Instead of feeling relieved by all the altruistic people in this room, I find myself frightened by this motley collection of volunteers. I was hoping to find tall, muscular men with six-pack abs.

The captain storms into the room. In a booming voice, he yells, "Everybody shut up and pay attention." The room quiets and the bodies stiffen. As he lumbers to the front of the class, he stops at my table to introduce himself. I must stand out with my tape recorder and pensive demeanor. It is quite apparent that I am the outsider—one who is becoming increasingly worried that one of these kids is going to be responsible for saving my life one day.

The class is quick and pretty self-explanatory, but that's the way bureaucracy works. I'm cleared to ride along with the fire department, which sounds like something that might finally earn me a bravery badge.

Since I'm cleared to ride along with the EMTs, I decide to revisit Heather. What doesn't kill me will make my stronger and all that. My hair hasn't been colored in months, and at the tender age of thirty-eight, my scalp is sporting a stripe of gunmetal gray. I make another appointment at Salon del Sol, but I still feel guilty for leaving Lisa Marie. I find out through my friend Katie that she has been wondering why I cancelled my last appointment and never rescheduled. How do you tell someone—and not in person—that you're a scaredy cat who doesn't have the guts to end a relationship like a normal, responsible adult? Hallmark doesn't make that card.

I arrive at my 9am appointment ten minutes early, determined to keep things happy and upbeat with Heather. I love going to the salon and I don't want to feel like the black cloud of doom every time I'm there. One of my favorite experiences in life is to have my hair shampooed. For some people, it may be climbing a mountain or eating a fabulous meal. For me, it's the simple act of someone washing my hair. I'm not a touchy-feely, huggy kind of person, so when touching is a responsibility of the person doing the touching, I'm perfectly okay with it.

As I wait for the salon to open, I feel that familiar fight-or-flight reaction. My heart rate climbs as my mind races with possible exit plans. I have hair issues, and this could be part of that, but I suspect it has more to do with Heather. She is a good stylist with a pleasant personality, but I long for the easy familiarity I had with Lisa. I also worry about making Heather feel sad by mentioning my kids. I'm clueless as to whether or not I should mention my kids. I don't know if it's okay to do so and I'm scared to ask. I mean, how stupid would that be? "Heather, can we talk about my children?" It's not like I babbled on endlessly about my kids with Lisa, but now it's like a giant pink elephant. Children, children, children. Don't talk about children.

Heather sees me enter the salon and motions me over to her station. Despite her pleasant demeanor, I'm pretty sure that I'm not destined to be her favorite customer. After our first awkward encounter, she must think I'm either a weirdo or a masochist. But I'm relieved that Heather doesn't mention the death stuff. We talk about my hair, styling products, and celebrity gossip. It's trivial and superficial: everything a salon visit should be. She does an excellent job on the color. It looks more natural than it has in years. As I pay the receptionist, Heather approaches and hands me a business card with a phone number written on the back.

"My husband Dan wants to talk with you."

Oh, crap.

It has been three weeks since Heather gave me Dan's number. In that time, several businesses have put up signs along the side of the road that read, "If we can't find you, we can't help you." Since I can't read the smaller print, I don't give it a second thought—until my daughter brings home a flyer from school. Next to a photo of a smiling tow-headed toddler are the same words.

In 2007, three-year-old Tommy Miller choked on a piece of food while eating dinner at home. His desperate father called 911 and began CPR. Unfortunately, his home address was not clearly marked. Tommy died that night as anxious firefighters searched the road for his family's house, passing again and again as he tried to breathe. In honor of Tommy, and so no family will have to go through the same tragedy, we want you to get a clearly visible reflective house number on your home.

I live in a rural community where a lot of properties aren't clearly marked. For many residents, that's part of the charm of living in the country. That is, until something tragic happens. I order the reflective number signs for our house, which would have been the perfect opportunity for me to talk with Dan, but I can't bring myself to do it. I can't figure out if it is his grief that scares me or just death in general. I try to think in practical terms. I'm a problem solver and I want this problem solved. Part of me thinks I need to get it over with and just talk to the man. But the reluctant part of me thinks I need to build up to that. This sounds crazy, but I think I need to see a body first.

That's going to be a problem. George won't return my calls and the local mortuary wants nothing to do with me. I contemplate crashing a funeral. Every day, I scan the obituaries, hoping that I'll find a funeral service with a viewing. That sounds so horrible, so Harold and Maude-ish. My husband Erik can hardly believe that I've only been to one funeral in my life. He's been to plenty of funerals; friends, a brother-in-law, a friend's mother who committed suicide and his own father's funeral when he was fifteen. He is familiar with grief and loss. But to me, those concepts are like a foreign country that I never want to visit. I've lost three cats, a grandma, and suffered two miscarriages. Out of those experiences, it was my cat Binky's death that really killed me. A cat. And if a small furry creature can wreak havoc on my emotional life, I'll never be able to handle the deaths of those I love most dearly.

CHAPTER THREE

Face the Pain

While I'm busy avoiding Dan and his grief, my coworker-friend Katie darts into my office, giddy with excitement. She juts her chin forward and brushes back her long blonde hair.

"Okay—where exactly is my thyroid?" She palpates the flesh of her pale neck.

"It's towards the bottom. Why?"

"My doctor says I may have a goiter. I'm going in tomorrow for an ultrasound."

This makes Katie happy because she thinks that a thyroid condition is going to erase the muffin top she's failed to lose after the birth of her son. When I was diagnosed with an enlarged thyroid in 2006, my doctor told me that the medication would help me lose weight and boost my mood. Neither of those things happened. It just made me sweatier.

I touch my neck to demonstrate the approximate location of the thyroid.

"It's at the bottom and kind of wraps around the wind pipe." I demonstrate like a flight attendant pointing out the emergency exits. As I'm saying this, I discover something round and hard at my thyroid, like a small pea. It moves when I swallow. "What the hell is that?"

After the nurse practitioner examines my neck the following day, he says he doesn't really know what that lump is. As I leave his office, he hands me an ultrasound order. I am now beyond nervous. The ice-queen receptionist barely looks at me when I approach the desk. She's not very friendly or helpful, which one would think would be the basic requirements of her job.

I hand her the order form. "Can you please tell them I want the first available appointment?"

She takes the form and casually drops it on her cluttered desk. "I'll call after lunch today."

I raise my eyebrows.

"We're really busy right now. I'll call you as soon as I make the appointment. You're all set."

I am so not set. I just want to stand there and weep to make her feel bad—but I don't like crying in front of people. My eyes fill with tears as I shuffle out of the office. There is the very real possibility that this little lump is nothing, but that's not how my mind works. I'm a worrier who's just been handed a fatal diagnosis.

That night, I sit on the edge of my bed, hyperventilating between sobs as Erik tries to figure out what the hell is wrong with me. I don't typically burst out sobbing, but the more I explore death, the less control I feel over my life. Death is all around me and for the first time in my life, I'm paying attention to it. I may even be attracting death, if that *Secret* book lady is right.

I think I need counseling.

My friend Susan, whose son Zane has been a hospice patient since the day of his birth, tells me I should talk to her grief counselor,

Kati Bachman.

As I sit in her small green office, with one lone chair and a box of Kleenex by its side, I am amazed by Kati's positive, kinetic energy. She reminds me of Tigger, ready to pounce on the sadness that at different times resides in all of us. As we talk, her right foot jiggles in sync with the rhythm of her speech. I envisioned a bereavement counselor as someone a bit more sedate, but maybe I'm making her nervous. Who am I kidding? I'm nervous. I feel as if Kati Bachman can see right through my bullshit exterior to the panicked child who fears loss and death above all else.

Loss and death are what keeps Kati employed. And just as it takes a village to raise a human being, I learn that it takes a small village of social workers, volunteers, clergy and counselors to support a person as they transition through death. Kati tells me that the whole purpose of hospice is to compassionately assist a dying person through their last developmental stage.

"Death is so normal, but we treat it like it is the most abnormal dark thing you can think of." While nibbling on her lunch of turkey and cheese sticks, she explains the normal yet transformative power of grief. "Kids die. So do babies. So do young mothers. So do young fathers. So do old fathers. So do old mothers. Everyone dies. We can't be guaranteed that we're all going to live into our nineties."

I think about all the cigarettes I've smoked in my life and the cancerous tumor that is surely growing in my neck as her mouth moves. I stare down at a blank page in my stupid unlined notebook. I feel as if I'm grieving something. As if Kati can read my mind, she says "People need to be in the presence of someone when they are deeply filled with sorrow, because it's the loneliest place. And it's rare to be with someone who doesn't run away when you're grieving. Because when someone runs away, what do you immediately think?"

She leans forward and points at me with her string cheese.

"That I did something wrong," I say, looking up from my notebook.

"Right."

In the short time I've been in her presence, I get the feeling that Kati doesn't run away, but keeps pace with you, maybe cheers for you, gets you an ice cold water and a protein bar. She leans back into her chair and pauses for a moment. "I've got the coolest job in the world. I get to see people heal from the...darkest, darkest, darkest thoughts and time in their life. I can see them heal and grow."

But I wonder: how can she just sit there and eat her lunch when her eight-hour workday is filled with grief and crying and sadness? "How do you prevent yourself from feeling sad?"

"First and foremost, you gotta remember: it's not my loss that I'm supporting people in. It isn't my loss. I don't have the same feelings that they do."

True, but if someone starts crying at my work, I'll usually disappear into my office or behind the locked door of the restroom. I never know what to say. And even if I did, I'm not so sure I could say it without sounding like a complete nincompoop.

"Do you find yourself putting up an emotional barrier?"

"I strive for presence. I strive to be as authentic and present with each client as I can. The day you stop feeling is the day you're not doing your job. Most people need just to be normalized and validated that what they're feeling is okay, and that there is no right or wrong way to grieve."

If there is one thing that Kati wants me to take away, it's the idea that grief isn't wrong.

"The better we get at dealing with our losses and the more familiar we are with those feelings, the walk isn't as unnatural. The walk isn't as unfamiliar. That's really what grief is about—it's about unfinished communication and the unfamiliar feelings. And that's what makes it so treacherous."

Kati explains that the average person only experiences a significant loss every nine or ten years. "You never get to practice those feelings. Most people want to forget about them."

Well, yeah. Who wants to master grief? Not I. I want to be spared. But since I know this isn't possible no matter how hard I wish for it, I feel myself being recruited into something that scares the living daylights out of me—volunteering for hospice. In addition to her counseling work, Kati is also the volunteer co-ordinator.

She assures me that the two-day training session will be inval-uable to me, and to seal the deal she says, "You don't have to be a volunteer after the training."

Bingo—those are the magic words. This sounds perfect. I'll get to experience hospice without anyone dying. To let her know what kind of person she's dealing with, I reveal that I have abso-lutely no experience with dying people. I also tell her how I stupidly tried to comfort Carol Cardwell about her ninety-five-year-old grandma's death. Kati shakes her head and takes another bite from her lunch.

"That is an intellectual solution to an emotional experience. And that doesn't work." But she assures me that it is quite nor-mal.

"It is so important that we support people with grief. Grief is normal. It is not a psychosis. It is not an abnormality in how your brain functions. It isn't that you had a mom that couldn't deal and locked you in a closet for three years. It's normal. It happens to all of us and it will happen to every single person that walks a hu-man journey."

Kati leans towards me and I meet her intense gaze. I feel like she's gently holding back my hand so that I can't cover my eyes during the scary movie. She knows what's behind the door, under the bed, or in the closet. She sees it every day. It's the thing that waits for all of us. And she wants me to see it.

"Part of grieving is learning how to love yourself and let peo-ple love you. And we don't do that very well."

Her phone rings, jarring me from this moment and the words that feel like they were intended for me. She checks the caller ID as I scribble *I need to get out of here* in my notebook.

"I'm so sorry Pam, but I need to take this. Call me," she says.

I mouth the words 'thank you' and hightail it out of there.

*   *   *

My discomfort, along with the potential for tears at every turn, stays with me at my ultrasound appointment. In the lobby, the technician calls my name, stumbling on its pronunciation like everyone else.

"How are you today?" she asks in a perfunctory manner.

"Fine," I reply as we walk back towards the examination rooms. I don't know why people ask that, especially medical technicians who aren't allowed to talk to you about anything they discover while poking and prodding you. *I'm not fine. I'm worried. I'm trying to remain optimistic about this whole thing but I've seen far too many movies where this doesn't go in the direction of a Walt Disney happily-ever-after and I'm terribly afraid that you are going to find an egg sized cancerous tumor in my neck and that I'm going to have to endure months of chemotherapy with the accompanying hair loss, vomiting and general misery. Then I will die anyway, leaving my mother heartbroken, my husband a widower and my children motherless.* "How are you doing?"

The examination room is dark. She instructs me to lie down on the paper-covered table, which makes me feel like a slab of beef at the deli. I'm trying not to tear the paper as I situate my body on top of it, while she props a pillow beneath my neck and tucks a white paper bib into the top of my shirt. After typing something, she drops a dollop of cold goop onto my throat and slides the all-seeing magical wand thing over the right side of my neck. She swirls and stops—click. Swirls and stops—click. Then she types. She seems to be concentrating on the right side of my neck. *The thing is on the left.* She moves to the left side. There are fewer clicks and less typing, which doesn't make sense. She remains quiet, which makes matters worse. I know she isn't allowed to reveal anything because she isn't a doctor, but the lady who performed Katie's ultrasound reassured her with "I wouldn't worry."

My tech's parting words are less comforting. "The radiologist will take a look at these today and send over a report to your doctor."

The nurse practitioner calls me the next day. "You have a nodule on the right thyroid which is about 15mm, and a complex cyst on the left that is a little smaller. These nodules are very common, but we'd like for you to get a biopsy."

Even though his voice is calm and reassuring, I immediately get a second opinion from Dr. Google. This is never a good idea.

Just when I think things can't get any worse, I round the corner into the deli section of Wal-Mart. Lisa Marie, my former hairdresser is there. In the six years of our professional relationship, I have never run into her outside of the salon. She pushes her cart towards me, but she isn't looking in my direction. My heart pounds in my chest and I think I should just let her walk past, breathe a sigh of relief and run from the store as quickly as possible. But I don't.

She sees me. I know she sees me.

I have to say something, but I can tell by the way she's studying the wall of juice across from me that she wants to avoid me just as much as I want to avoid her. Heat rises in my face, accentuating the fact that I feel panicky and weird.

Lisa Marie walks past me without even a perfunctory glance of acknowledgement.

I guess it's really over. Get me a giant scarlet letter, because she now has visual confirmation that someone else has been running her fingers through my hair. There's no denying this fact. My hair is now short and an entirely different color than it used to be—it's the handiwork of the other woman. I don't even like the new 'do. There I was, just chatting away with Heather, oblivious to the long strands landing on my cape as she informed me that she and Dan were trying for another child. This was an important conversation. It wasn't like I could say, 'Okay, that's great Heather, but do you think maybe you could watch what you're doing?'

I call out Lisa's name. She stops, turns towards me and looks directly at my hair. I instinctively brace for a verbal lashing.

"Hey, Pam. How's it going?" she says sweetly.

I'm a horrible person. "Pretty good. How are you?"

"I'm good."

Awkward silence.

"So, I um, well, I went to someone else last month." Like a Freudian slip of the hand, I touch my hair. She is silent. "It's not like I hate you or anything." Open mouth, insert size 11 foot.

"Of course you don't," she laughs. "Don't worry about it. She pats me on the shoulder. "Your hair looks cute short."

I don't believe her, but I accept the compliment. I feel like a steaming, stinky pile of dog-doo. We part ways amicably. I grab the remainder of my groceries with stooped shoulders, down-cast eyes, and the speed of a contestant on *Supermarket Sweep*.

In the parking lot, I breathe a sigh of relief, as though an emotional weight has been lifted. Maybe I'm growing up. Or maybe I'm feeling emboldened by this potential cancer diagnosis in my neck. Lisa wasn't dying in the middle of Wal-Mart or grieving the death of someone she loved, but I didn't run away from the situation when it would have been very easy to do so. Maybe now that I've ventured into bigger, but not necessarily better things, the smaller challenges of life won't seem quite so daunting.

It's probably the cancer.

To find out if it is the cancer, I check in at the hospital's diagnostic imaging department for my biopsy. I don't have any special instructions other than not wearing any perfume or lotion on my neck. Erik accompanies me for this procedure, which in my mind confirms that I will be dead in six months. He's not what you would describe as a sentimental coddler. And here he is, covered in dust from his job at the auto-body shop. He attempts to hold my hand, but I can't sit still and my palms are sweaty. There is a boy of about eleven with a horrible sounding cough waiting to be seen. His father walks him around the periphery of the large room. His strained attempt at catching his breath adds to my nervousness. The latest flyer sent home from school urges parents to get their kids and themselves vaccinated for pertussis, aka whooping cough. I flip through an old *Travel and Leisure* as a distraction. Each time the boy coughs, I wonder why he isn't forced to wear a mask so as not to infect all us tumor-riddled folks in the waiting area.

After the nurse butchers the pronunciation of my last name, I'm led into a small, well-lit room. It looks different with the lights on. The ultrasound tech is a woman in her late forties with thin sparkly strands of ribbon in her hair. She instructs me to lie down on the table. I tell her I need to use the bathroom and escape. Nothing comes out. I stare at myself in the mirror for the time it would have taken to pee. The color has drained from my face, which accents the darkening pit-stains of my white-cotton t-shirt. This is the moment of truth. A doctor is going to confirm or deny my fears. I don't know which is worse—the knowing or the not knowing.

I exit the bathroom and lie down on the table like a good patient. There is a TV monitor on my right that the tech uses, and another on the wall to my left for me. I keep my eyes closed for most of the procedure. It is much easier than I had anticipated. There is a bit of stinging as they numb my neck, but I don't feel the needle jiggle back and forth to collect the tissue.

To diffuse the situation, I crack jokes with the tech and the doctor. They are friendly and don't seem overly concerned. They can't confirm or deny anything till the lab results are in, but I take their casual demeanor as a good sign. I leave the hospital with a giant purple ice pack affixed to my neck. When I return to work, Katie questions me about the procedure. Unlike me, her thyroid is perfectly healthy. I show off my swollen puncture wounds to coworkers with a tiny inkling of pride. I survived.

While I wait for the biopsy results, I go to the salon for another color appointment. After my first couple of visits with Heather, I feel like I am suffering right along with my hair. I can't help it. I fear change—both emotional and follicular. In her defense, the latest 'do is growing on me, in more ways than one. Yet I still miss Lisa. She would do exactly what I wanted, even if it was the same thing every six weeks for a year. Sadly, I may even miss being ignored and unremarkable. Now, I have the self-inflicted pressure of being a witness to someone's life.

My appointment is at 5 PM on a Monday. The salon is empty save for the receptionist—who also turns out to be the owner. She offers me a drink while I wait for Heather to finish a pedicure. I want a soda, but I'm informed that they only serve coffee, tea or wine. I opt for tea and wait. And wait. And wait. Punctuality is a weird hang-up of mine, so I'm mildly perturbed by Heather's lackadaisical attitude towards our meeting time. It doesn't help that I'm not looking forward to this appointment. Heather wants to try a permanent color on me and I'm just not ready for that kind of commitment. It's 5:30 by the time she appears. I coldly inform her that I'm going to stick with my regular old semi-permanent color. Her face can't hide the disappointment. She fastens a cape snugly around my still achy neck and asks me how I like the new cut.

"I've gotten a lot of compliments," I say quickly.

And I have, but I don't say I like it. That would be stretching the truth.

"Oh, well, good," she says. "I'm gonna go mix your colors. I'll be right back."

The receptionist/owner turns up the music—a bastardized disco version of Don Henley's *Boys of Summer*. This same loop of songs plays every time I have an appointment. I don't know how Heather and the owner can stand this forced musical gaiety. For me, it's like Hell's lamest nightclub.

Heather disappears to the back of the salon. The setting sun blares onto her station, exaggerating every flaw of my makeup-free face and disheveled hair in her giant mirror. I look old, tired and stressed out. What I really need is a call from my doctor, some dim, maybe rose-colored lighting, and music that isn't quite so peppy. To add to my discomfort, a man enters the empty salon and quietly takes a seat on the couch in the reception area.

When Heather appears from the back, he approaches her, kisses her quickly on the lips and takes a seat next to her station.

"Pam, this is Dan. My husband." As she says this, she squirts a sizeable amount of brown dye onto my hair and massages it vigorously into my scalp, as if it were shampoo. A small dollop lands on my cheek. With my head at the mercy of Heather's hands, I nod awkwardly in his direction. In the mirror, I look like a half wet, angry cat. Heather wipes the dye from my face. "Pam's the writer. You haven't called her yet, have you?"

He shakes his head. I feel like Heather must really want him to talk to me, but this is the last place I want to have a conversation about his son's death. A salon visit should be pampering and stress free and fun, especially now, but here I feel like I'm on display.

"What's the name of your book?" Heather asks as a way to get the conversation going.

"Well, it's not actually a book. It's my thesis. I'm in a graduate program."

She stares at me expectantly.

"Um, I'm thinking Death Becomes Them."

They are both silent.

"Or maybe Somebody's Gotta Do It. I don't know. I haven't really written it yet."

Dan laughs. "I like that one."

Dan's face is sunburned and his eyes look tired. His arms sit firmly across his chest, indicating to anyone with a limited understanding of body language that he does not want to be staring at a strange woman getting her hair done. I try to keep the conversation light and funny, like I'm a circus monkey who can talk. I do not mention their son. I am relieved when Heather sets me up to sit under the heat lamp. I open a dog-eared copy of Us Magazine. I have never in my life been so interested in Jennifer Aniston's failed relationships.

When I return to the station, Dan has moved back to the couch. Heather dries my hair.

"I'm just going home. You don't need to style it," I say, and reach for my purse.

She hangs up the hair dryer with a sigh and follows me to the reception desk. I remain quiet throughout the transaction, fumbling in my purse for a pack of cigarettes that aren't there. I want to tell her I had a thoroughly horrible time. Instead, I hand her a tip and tell Dan that it was nice to meet him.

Everyone breathes a sigh of relief.

As I drive home, I notice in my rear-view mirror that I now have light orange roots and medium brown ends. A potentially fatal diagnosis can lessen the silly worries of life, so I'm not terribly worried that my hair is two colors.

A few days after my biopsy, I get a call from my doctor's office. The person tells me that everything looks normal. I'm fine. I don't have the C word. I feel as if I can finally breathe. I collapse onto my couch.

Ever since that first conversation with George the embalmer, I've felt that I would attract death into my own life. I was now looking at it and acknowledging its presence. Death happens all the time, every day—old people, young people, sick people, well people. Why not me? What makes me so special to think I could escape it? I wonder if other people feel this way—naively expecting that somehow they will get out of here alive.

*   *   *

"Do you all mind if I sit down? I get really nervous speaking in front of people."

Christie Moore's face is flushed and she gesticulates with her hands to keep them from shaking. I find her fear of public speaking kind of ironic, considering that she works with death on a daily basis, as a social worker for hospice. Out of the eighteen people who are here to become volunteers, no one raises their hands to protest.

I on the other hand want to escape as silently and invisibly as I can. Combined with a case of nerves, I am battling some kind of stomach bug. My gut, which is bloated to a pregnant-sized bump, gurgles at fairly regular intervals as I do everything within my power not to let-er-rip in this small, tastefully decorated hospital conference room. I've acquired my son's virus, if not his penchant for vomiting. That's not much comfort. How can I be fully present here when I feel like the contents of my bowels could expel at any moment?

Despite my discomfort, I am heartened to see so many people interested in working for hospice. Of the eighteen people in attendance, the majority are women, mostly in the over-fifty category. There are three men, two of whom are spouses. The unattached third man sits cross-legged in his chair and tells us during the introductions that he likes to "do good things." His hair is long, his beard is scruffy, and he wears an old pair of Birkenstock sandals with new wool socks. At one point during Ms. Moore's discussion about social work, I notice that he is asleep.

As is usual for me in large groups, I appease my social anxiety by remaining on the outside to observe. The gut problem doesn't help. I do not attend lunch with my classmates on the first day. Instead, I drive twenty minutes to my place of work to use the bathroom. We are closed on Fridays, which works out perfectly at the moment. When I arrive at my building, the parking lot is empty. I rush inside without locking the front door, but lock the door to the bathroom. Despite this little sabbatical, I'm watching the clock compulsively. I only have a ten-minute window and then I have to drive the twenty minutes back to the hospital. Inside the bathroom, I can hear someone's footsteps inside the building. This freaks me out —which does nothing for my progress.

I exit the restroom loudly, hoping it's another co-worker. I hear a woman's voice call out, "Hello, is anybody here?"

"Yes?" I answer, my voice peppered with resentment.

"Are you open?"

Yes, Ma'am, of course we are! We always work with the lights off. It's more productive that way. I stomp towards the direction of her voice. "Um, no. Not on Fridays. I'm just here to pick something up."

She holds a piece of paper and an envelope that is becoming more wrinkled by the second. "Um, my mother just died. I was out of town and this was the first time I saw my proof. I've been away. And-you-all-spelled-the-name-of-my-profession-wrong!" She is hysterical at this point. "You spelled acupuncturist with two C's. This is ridiculous! I-I-I'm not paying for this."

I've heard that one before. It's usually a grandparent. Relatives start dropping like flies whenever our customers miss our print deadlines. But this was my fault. "I'm really sorry, but I can't do anything today because everyone is gone. I'll definitely take care of it on Monday. Okay?"

She nods and walks out the door with the crumpled up piece of paper. I lock up and speed back to the hospital, thinking about how weird and random that was. I can't even escape to a bathroom in an empty building without being confronted by someone's death. Why does this stuff keep happening to me? Either I'm attracting it, or it's been around me all along and I wasn't paying attention.

On the second day of training, two grief counselors instruct us to write down ten people that we care about. This list is easy for me, as I don't have many to choose from. I wait for the more contemplative folks to finish up.

"Is everyone done?" asks the older female counselor.

We all look around the room and nod yes. She picks a folded piece of paper out of a bowl and reads it. "You've just received a phone call from the police. The number 2 person on your list has been in an auto accident and is dead."

My chest tightens. I stand and lean up against the wall. I can't catch my breath. Tears well up in my eyes and my jaw clenches to hold back an outburst. I can't believe I'm actually feeling like this. It's just a simple exercise, but I want to leave the room. I have to remind myself that it didn't happen. But it *could* happen, and I won't be prepared. Like now.

"Does anyone want to share who their number 2 is?" asks the male counselor.

I don't say a word because if I say his name aloud, it might come true. My number two is Erik—who is really my number one. I wrote "Mom" first, but losing Erik would be much more devastating. If Erik were killed in a car accident, I don't know how I'd handle it. Whenever he's late from work, my mind concocts that call, or the flashing lights of a police car at the door. I love him, but he's a horrible driver.

The two women seated to my left are both crying and wiping their faces with their shirtsleeves. I hand them the box of tissues in front of me, after grabbing a few for myself. My hand fumbles in my purse for my cell phone. I desperately want to call Erik—one, to make sure he's not driving, and two, to tell him that I love him.

At the end of the two-day training, the participants take a short quiz in order to graduate from the program. We are pretty much spoon fed the answers, so it's no big surprise when we all pass. Kati thanks everyone and instructs us to call her about scheduling an interview. She asks us to rise from our seats and join hands in a circle. My stomach lets out an angry rebuttal. I don't want to hold anyone's hand, especially now that I'm carrying some hideous gastro-horror, but I do it anyway. I feel the need to celebrate the fact that I'm not dead.

After hospice training, I look at everyone on my list as a loss that could happen at any moment—especially my aging parents. My dad, who is in his late seventies, is currently on a whirlwind driving excursion to visit all five of his children. In the two weeks since he left North Dakota, he has driven to Northern California to see my sister, down to Southern California to see my brother, over to Nevada to see my stepsister and now to Colorado to see me. He plans to spend four days with us and then he's off to visit another sibling who lives seven hours away. This kind of trip is not unusual for him, but it rarely involves visiting his offspring. It's usually a bridge or poker tournament that calls to him like a half-naked siren. I'm worried that this is his farewell journey.

He says he'll be here at 6 PM and he's rarely off by more than twenty minutes. The man is a professional road warrior. There are no leisurely pit stops at Cline's Corners to peruse the knick-knacks and T-shirts. If he didn't need gas, I'm sure he'd go the crazy astronaut route and wear a diaper.

I've rushed home from work to make, in my father's words "the best damn lasagna I've ever had." Only three things in life make my father happy: food, golf, and poker. Since golf and poker are not my forte, I do what I can with some noodles, mozzarella cheese and a bit of spaghetti sauce.

The phone rings, interrupting the culinary magic. "Pamela?" The female voice is friendly, yet serious. It sounds like a bill collector who can't pronounce my last name.

I respond like an irritated robot. "This is she."

"Hi, Pamela. This is Suzanne Dunbar."

Suzanne Dunbar is my doctor. It is 5:30 on a Thursday.

"Listen, did anyone from my office call you with your biopsy results?"

You mean the one I had months ago? "Well, yeah. They called a couple of days after. They said that everything looked fine, not to worry."

There is a long pause. "Well, um, there wasn't enough tissue present in that first sample, so I'd really like for you to consult with a surgeon."

I can barely comprehend the implications of what she is saying. This is so left field. "A surgeon?'

"Well, you could have another fine needle aspiration, but it might yield the same inconclusive result."

"Oh. Well, isn't the chance of me having thyroid cancer really rare? I mean, I read that it's like 5 percent or something."

She remains silent.

"So do you think I need surgery?"

"I'd really like for you to consult with Dr. Deaver. He specializes in the thyroid. I can't say at this point. I have his number for you."

I sense the urgency in her voice. "I can look it up," I reply.

"I'll get everything sent over to his office. Do you have a pen and paper handy?"

"Yeah."

"Here's his number."

I reluctantly write it down on an old envelope and hang up.

I'm speechless. Why didn't I ask her why they called my house months ago and said everything was fine when it wasn't? Why is it not fine now? Does she have a quota or something to fill with that surgeon? I am so angry and confused. How could they have not gotten enough tissue? The lab person was in the room preparing slides. Something isn't right.

I'm afraid, but I don't want to worry my father. He didn't drive all this way to deal with a hysterical middle-age child. Instead, we do what we always do when he's here: play Gin Rummy to keep us occupied till dinner. He doesn't seem too concerned with the state of my health, or at least that's how he's playing it for the two days he's at my house. He does tell me that when his life becomes less 'fun,' he's going to get a fifth of bourbon, sit in the closed garage and start his car. I ask if he'll at least call to let me know the day he does it so that we can retrieve his body. He agrees that that would be a good idea.

Because I technically already have a surgeon, I am not allowed to switch to Dr. Deaver. I have to stick with the man who removed my gallbladder a couple of years ago. Not that I have anything against him. The surgery went well. He was a nice enough guy.

But he's not the thyroid specialist. And I think I really need the thyroid specialist.

When he looks over my chart, I don't think he has any idea that the biopsy result he's looking at is almost three months old. He begins mentioning abnormal cells and lone nodules and I'm thinking, what—what—what the hell is he talking about?

I interrupt. "I thought I was here because there wasn't enough tissue?"

"We just need to do another biopsy to make a more definitive diagnosis. If I go in, I don't just remove the nodule. I'll remove the entire lobe. We're not there yet."

He rises from his chair and stands beside me to show me the biopsy report. I see the last few lines. "Part A: Cytology of the right thyroid nodule shows only rare nondiagnostic follicular cells. In Part B, dense lymphoid aggregates are present with rare Hurthloid follicular cells. These findings likely represent a lymphocytic thyroiditis, however lack of follicular epitheleum and a dense lymphoid infiltrate preclude exclusion of lymphoproliferative disease. Additional tissue sampling with resection or biopsy is recommended."

Resection, I learn, is partial removal of the thyroid. The doctor explains that he makes a lengthwise incision at the bottom of my neck, stretches the muscles, and takes out the thyroid. I'd have to be on medication for the rest of my life. I am so angry that I have to go through this again. It's not the knowing or the not knowing—it's not having the thing present in the first place. As much as I'd like to believe otherwise, I'm not immune to death. I think back to my list at the hospice training. Why didn't I put myself on it?

I'm even more nervous during my second biopsy, even though I know exactly what's going to happen: the insertion of the needle, the stinging, the repeated poking and jiggling, the sweaty palms, the cracked jokes. Or perhaps that's why I'm nervous. The doctor performing this biopsy is more skilled than the first one. He wields the magic wand while maneuvering the needle on his own, unlike the first guy, who depended on the tech to do it for him. There is hardly any stinging when he numbs my neck, and he apologizes in advance for leaning on my boobs for leverage.

"You can hit me if you want to," he jokes.

He thinks out loud as he proceeds. "This one is close to your windpipe, which is kind of tricky."

He moves the needle back and forth, eyeing the monitor but not my neck.

Please don't puncture my windpipe.

"This one is close to your carotid artery. Don't swallow. Do you need to swallow?"

Yes, now that you mention it.

"Okay, all done. I wouldn't worry. You're my fifth thyroid biopsy of the day. They're so common," he says.

"But this is my second biopsy. I'm a little scared."

"I know. They just need a better sampling. The first round was a lot of blood."

As I'm being bandaged up, Erik and the doctor talk cars. The tech laughs at the fact that these two men have totally forgotten the real reason we are all together. I take it as a good sign. The doctor isn't going to talk about his Corvette if I've got cancer or something. That would be wrong.

The surgeon calls me three days later.

"Once again, they couldn't find any cancer. We're probably looking at Hashimoto's Thyroiditis. I've ordered some blood tests for you, so if you could stop by the office and pick up the lab order, we can confirm that. Do you want me to send my results to your doctor?"

"Yeah. I guess so. So, are you going to call me with the results of the blood tests?"

"Yes."

My cancer crisis is over, but for how long? I smoked a pack a day for most of my adult life. I ate tons of processed foods. I drank to excess on innumerable occasions. I am a tumor waiting to happen.

CHAPTER FOUR

Exit the Vehicle

Working as a proofreader for the phonebook is akin to working in a death profession. Not only are we environmentally incorrect tree killers, we also leave annoying, cumbersome packages on your doorstep that are destined for the trash bin. It's glaringly apparent to anyone with a smart phone that the yellow pages are bound for a slow and painful death in the next few years. But for now, it's my job and I've got to do it. I stare down at the full page ad in front of me, looking for misspelled words or a dyslexically rendered phone number. It's a full-page, multi-color ad that mentions floods, fires, dirty carpets, and in smaller print—biohazard cleaning. I can't believe I'd never thought of biohazard cleaners before. While Durango isn't exactly the murder capital of the world, plenty of people die at home and aren't found for days. After these past couple of weeks, it's the perfect profession for me to explore; it won't be too dark, depressing or emotionally exhausting.

When I meet John Rivas, we settle into his cluttered, paper-strewn office. I find the messiness somewhat ironic, considering he's in the cleaning business. During introductions and getting to know you chit-chat, I discover that he's a fast talker. I don't know if that's his normal conversational speed or he just wants to get this conversation over with as quickly as possible. I take a deep breath and place my recorder on his desk.

"So, how long have you been the general manager at Best?" I lean back in the chair to give the impression of confidence.

"Nine years."

"And are you the person that they send to a biohazard cleanup?

"Yes. I try to go on every biohazard cleanup, every trauma scene cleanup, as we call it."

"How is it to deal with the families?" I say this as nonchalantly as possible, but it's the question I really want answered.

"It's tough. They're distraught... They're not all there. So you just have to reassure them and help them feel that they're going to be okay and that you'll take care of the mess. I always invite them to stay somewhere else for the next couple of days while we take care of whatever we need to take care of."

Taking care of what remains, I scrawl in my unlined notebook. "Do they typically just want to leave?"

"Yes, they want to leave. Or they're not even there. A lot of times I'll deal with a relative. Let's say it was a husband or a boyfriend. She can't even function, so I'll deal with a family member, a son or a daughter."

"Are you mostly dealing with suicides?" I look up from my scribbles.

"Most of the ones we've done are suicides. Yes."

I ask him if his company handled the cleanup of a fairly recent murder in an infamously shady local motel. He tells me they didn't, but then I silently wonder who did. Durango is kind of a small town.

"What kind of scenes have you had to deal with?" I'm hoping he'll elaborate on the nature of suicides without me having to ask how most people choose to end their lives. I don't want him to think I'm just a pen-wielding weirdo.

"Suicides. And death. People dying in the home and forgotten about."

"Like de-com-posed?" I stutter saying the word.

"Yeah. We did one recently up at Tamarron. A guy died in the locker room and it was a holiday weekend. Monday they found him. After a few days the body fluids start to run out. There's a little to clean up. Not much. I'd say most of the time it's just suicides."

"So...mostly suicides?" I want him to elaborate, but I'm too chicken to just ask the method.

He thinks for a moment, as if he's searching for the right answer on a game show. "We've also done jobs where deer have jumped through plate glass windows in the home and pranced around the house while they're bleeding to death."

For some reason this cracks me up. It's not something that the average American has to deal with, but this is Colorado.

"It's more common than you think. So, yeah. They see themselves and they charge head first into the plate glass. And they end up slicing their necks open. They're freaking out and they're stuck in someone's house bleeding out."

He's not getting the hint. "So with the suicides, is it mostly shotgun?"

"I have never done a shotgun. It's either small caliber or handgun or it's a hunting rifle. And the hunting rifles are hideous, hideous to clean up. A small caliber handgun is usually pretty easy to clean up. There's usually just one entry hole."

"So it's not..."

"I can show you the difference if you like."

Rivas swivels around to his computer and brings up a picture.

"Oh. Okay," I gasp. I don't really want to look at pictures, but here they are.

"I'll pull two different examples up." He clicks the keyboard with newfound purpose—to gross me out.

I feel like I'm at an awfully strange show and tell. I shuffle over to Rivas's computer screen to get a closer look. It would be rude not to. Like a macabre Jackson Pollack painting, shades of brown, pink and red are splattered across the white walls of the room.

"This is a high-power rifle suicide. And the results are, however big the room is, it isn't big enough." He points at the picture. "This is brain splatter from twenty five feet away." He brings up another photo. "And this is a small caliber. See? It's quite a big difference."

There is just a pool of blood on the couch and a small puddle on the carpeting below. It's gross, but as far as cleanup goes, it looks a lot less daunting than the first photo.

"How many of these do you do?"

"I say we do probably three trauma scene cleanups a year. Maybe four."

"Oh. That's not bad." It doesn't occur to me that I've just diminished the difficulty of his job.

"No, not that bad." He brings up another photo. "This is the one I did last month."

"Oh my gosh! It's everywhere."

"Yeah, and again, it's a high-caliber rifle."

The mundane photos of average living rooms and the parts that got blown away are horrific. I feel sickened and saddened by these images and what those poor families had to go through.

"The first few I went to were all small-caliber and I thought, oh this is gross, you know, a small puddle of blood on the floor. But that was nothing compared to the hunting rifles and the thirty-aught-sixes under the chin. Those are bad. It was a little tough. I mean, there's somebody's blood on the floor and brain on the ceiling."

I walk back to my chair and avert my eyes. "How much does it cost to have this kind of thing cleaned up?"

"We don't do a trauma scene cleanup for less than a thousand dollars, and it goes up from there. But most homeowner's insurance pays for it. That's one thing that the family members usually don't realize—that it's covered by insurance. It's tough to talk to them when you're at the job to do the cleanup, because they're already distraught. We just let them know that we'll take care of everything and we'll talk in a few days about payment."

"How many people go on these cleanups?"

"The less people the better. You don't want a whole bunch of people tromping around, especially if the family is still in the home. We go in with full Tyvek suit, which is white. And sometimes we get messy. The last thing we want is the family seeing us with their loved one's blood on us." He confesses that these scenes sadden him, especially when he knows beforehand what happened to the people involved, like a man who killed himself in front of his girlfriend.

"One minute she's cooking dinner, the next, she's sprayed with blood."

And I thought this interview was going to be easy. I want to go home and crawl under the covers for a week. I admit to John that I wouldn't want to know the specifics in order to keep that professional distance, but my incessant need to know the why of the situation would get the better of me. Whether we'll admit to it or not, most of us slow down at a car crash and crane our necks to get a better look—either from curiosity or for the mere confirmation that all is still well in our insular little world.

At the end of my questions, Rivas asks me about this project, curious to know the other types of people I'm interviewing. I rattle off the obvious: embalmer, coroner, and hospice worker. When I tell him about my plans to talk with Mike Graczyk, an AP writer who has witnessed almost every execution in Texas since 1984, he is intrigued.

He shakes his head. "Man, it's one thing to clean up after someone dies, but I don't think I could watch someone die."

I don't know if he realizes it, but lethal injection is clean and clinical and doesn't require a Tyvek suit or an enzyme solution to erase a human life from a room. The hunting rifle picture fades from the computer screen and is replaced by a screen saver of

John and his girlfriend. Their faces are squished together, beaming with happiness.

I close my notebook and place the recorder in my purse. I want to be brave, so I hand him a card. "I probably won't be the first person that will come to mind when you get another trauma call, but I'd like to give you my number just in case."

"You mean to ride along?"

"Yeah, if that's okay."

He tells me that it would be fine. With only three or four trauma calls a year, I may luck out and never have to see one.

*   *   *

What Rivas does is rare, at least in my small town. To get my head around this death thing, I need to be around people who witness the more common ways we exit the earth—heart attacks, car accidents, slip and falls, that kind of thing. There are three EMT crews that work on rotating shifts at the fire station. Today I'm hanging with the A crew. When I arrive, Dan Miller recognizes me from the salon and says hello. *He's probably thinking, "There's that weird lady again."* It takes me a minute to figure out how I know him. Last time I saw him, he was watching me get my hair dyed, and I did my best to avoid eye contact. Since that time, he has been hired on as a paid employee of the fire department. Because I still dread speaking with him, I'm secretly hoping this crew will be too busy to chat—but their lieutenant, Adolph Young, is quite pleased that I'm there and wants everyone to take a moment out of their day to speak with me.

Ian is the first person to talk with, as Adolph puts it, "the nice lady." It makes me feel old. Ian is lean, muscular, and his face is dotted with acne. He is 19 years old, a teenage boy with a buzz cut, encountering people and situations that would make your average person afraid to leave their house. My cat Spooky is older than him. Unlike my cat, Ian has been saving lives and putting out fires for almost fourteen months.

We sit on the front of the engine and stare out at the street in front of the fire station. Cars pass by and he politely waits until they've gone to answer my questions. He wants to be heard, just like every other teenager trying to prove his or her worth in an adult world.

I ask him about the first dead person he ever encountered. He thinks for a moment. "Besides family?"

I nod.

He tells me it happened in the middle of the night, a time that's supposed to be reserved for REM sleep. The guy "didn't have his seat belt on and his head had been out the window when the car rolled over him. It lopped off part of his head. That one kind of stuck with me for a while."

I raise my eyebrows as an indication for him to continue.

"Well, you're asleep. It's 2:30 in the morning and then all of a sudden it's right there in front of your face, just like something gross. You know what I mean?" .

I don't. I have nothing in the dark recesses of my brain that can even come close to the vision of someone's head being lopped off. I shake my head no.

"A car wreck. You don't have any time to wrap your head around it."

Yes, but that car had time to wrap around the driver's head.

By his eager expression, I can tell that he wants to clarify, to help me understand other traumatic scenes that he's witnessed.

"For me, they don't have to die for it to stick with me."

I move my tape recorder closer to indicate that I want to hear the story. He looks out to the street.

"There was this guy, totally flyin' high on meth, rolled his car and his kid was ejected. Dad's lying in a big pool of blood on the highway. The kid's on the other side of the car. Everything is broken."

Ian looks at me for my reaction, which I'm sure is registering a combination of disgust and sadness, then back to the street.

"That almost sticks with me more than some old fat guy who has a heart attack. It was pretty tough because there were kids involved. It was neglect. It wasn't an accident. It's not like a deer jumped out in front of that car. That kid shouldn't have been lying on the highway at three in the morning."

He is absolutely correct. That kid should have been at home, safe in his bed, sound asleep. Sometimes I find it rather—what's the word I'm looking for?—*odd*, that in this great land of ours, you have to have a license to drive a car or to own a dog, yet any ignoramus with a sperm count and a willing uterus can have a kid. Hell, Ian can't even legally drink a beer on his day off.

I share with Ian that in my youth I was pretty reckless behind the wheel, but now that I've had a couple of kids, I wouldn't dare get behind the wheel of a car if I've had something to drink.

His voice deepens with seriousness. "I've definitely gotten a lot more careful with operating my car, for sure. I think that's the one thing that's stuck with me is the seat belt thing. You know? I've never seen a dead person wearing their seat belt."

I guess a lot of people are recklessly optimistic: don't think about a car rolling over your unseatbelted head and it won't happen. Until it does.

What surprises Ian the most are the optimistic people who think that the appearance of an ambulance in their driveway is going to make everything okay. He says he has seen that with two recent calls.

"The other two deaths I've seen were elderly male patients. We showed up and both their wives thought nothing was wrong. The paramedics are here. It's going to be all right now. Only 3% of patients come back after we start CPR."

One woman checked her e-mail while CPR was being performed on her husband. Granted, this could have been her method of coping (something I am all too familiar with) but Ian felt that her nonchalance was strange. A part of me didn't think it was strange. Don't pay attention or accept death as an inevitable part of life, even when it's on the floor right in front of you.

I ask Ian what made him want to pump people's chests, breathe into their mouths and drive ambulances at breakneck speeds.

"I was a camp counselor and this kid that was in my cabin jumped off the top bunk and hit his head and went unconscious. Everyone was freaking out and for some reason I was cool and collected and was able to like—take charge of the situation. I realized I could probably do that for a living."

I ask how he copes with the pressure, the long stretches of nothingness, and the hair raising, lopped-off-head calls in the middle of the night.

"I work out a lot. If I don't, I get pretty stressed out."

When I pause for a moment, he adds, "It's kind of weird seeing how fast it can be over." He laughs nervously, like I've caught him trying to order a shot of Jack Daniel's with a fake ID.

Whether he realizes it or not, he is lucky. He's in on a very big secret: people can cease to exist in their bodily form at any moment, even if they wear a seatbelt, eat organic vegetables, practice yoga, volunteer at the old folks' home, and say their prayers at night. It's a sad, almost devastating secret, but I think the people who actually get it on a visceral level are at an advantage. It's one thing to paste a Carpe Diem sticker on your Prius. It's quite another to perform CPR for forty-five minutes on someone when you know full well that he or she is never coming back.

Despite his age, Ian's got about twenty years of emotional maturity on me through his experience at the fire station. I don't think I'd be the woman checking her e-mails, but I might be the one off in a corner peering at the devastation through splayed fingers.

When I finish talking to Ian, I try to avoid Dan, but it is impossible. He seems to be everywhere, and there are no calls. After lunch, Adolph says, "Why don't you talk to Dan?"

Because I don't want to talk to Dan.

I relent. That's why I'm here—to explore death. But with Dan, it feels personal.

It's absolutely freezing in the fire station, so I ask Dan if we can talk outside. There's more distraction that way. Dan sits next to me on the back bumper of the parked fire engine. A fresh wad of chew is packed firmly between his lower lip and his gum line. Stray pieces of wet black tobacco cling to his teeth. I can't bring myself to look at him. It has nothing to do with his habit. I completely understand nicotine addiction. Unlike cigarettes, which are all about the dramatic flourishes of the inhale-exhale action, chew is all about remaining tight-lipped. Dan wears black wrap-around sunglasses as we stare out into the dim, cool shade of the bay. My legs swing in front of me like those of a child sitting on a fishing dock.

To fill the awkward silence, I blurt out something terrible. The second it's out of my mouth, I want to stuff it back in. "So, um, I know the story of your son."

This statement alone confirms it: I must suffer from some mild form of Tourette's. I have no tact, especially when I'm nervous, which is pretty much when I'm awake. "So, is that what happened that made you want to become..."

Dan interjects. "Yep, yep, that was the pivot point."

I quickly divert the subject back to his job. What's the most surprising thing you've found out since becoming an EMT?"

"To me, mostly I found out what I was supposed to be doing in my life. I feel more right about what I do now than what I'd ever done before."

Dan used to work for a cable company.

"Of course we run into some things that are pretty rough, but I think that since I've gone through something comparably worse than a lot of the things I see, that I'm, uh... to me, losing a child was the worst thing that could happen."

I interrupt him. My voice starts out strong and fades into a whisper. "Yeah, well I think that's the worst thing that can happen to anybody."

Even though I'm compelled to know about his son's death, I'm afraid to really question Dan. If we talk about Tommy and how his death changed him, it could easily destroy my faith about how the world is supposed to work. Kids are not supposed to die before their parents, especially while taking a bite of pizza.

I don't press further. I know what happened to his son. I've read the paper and I've seen the signs around town. I don't think I can handle Dan's grief. Even though he wants to tell me his story, I feel like an inexperienced kid speaking with a world-weary adult.

Instead of asking about Tommy, I ask how he handles the life and death situations of people he doesn't know.

"The only way to get through something like that and probably one of my motivations for doing what I'm doing right now is... when I lost my son, I wanted to know why—and I wanted to know what I was supposed to do. So in that respect, you train hard and you really pay attention to what you're learning."

Even though he claims to be numbed up, Dan says witnessing the moment of someone's death is pretty heavy, whether he knew that person or not. "One moment you're communicating with the person and then five minutes later, they've died."

It's an EMT's job to save people, or at least get them to the hospital alive. It's what they're trained for. The death workers I've encountered find it easier when the person has already expired, or when they are simply transporting someone to the hospital. A death in their presence carries a heavier weight. Here's someone's life, and it ended right there—in a car, in a bathroom, or on the couch in the living room. What they face is an unceremonious, average, everyday occurrence, but it reminds them that no one gets out of here alive.

I ask him if he ever leaves a call feeling like he could have done something differently.

"If things go wrong, they go wrong. It has nothing to do with us. It was the circumstances we walked into."

I can't believe his levelheadedness. If I were in his position, I would be constantly second-guessing myself. I still have waitressing nightmares about not turning in someone's ticket, not knowing how the tables are numbered, or forgetting the daily lunch specials.

Dan doesn't seem bothered. "You'll always—if you did make a patient care mistake, I don't think you'll ever forget, and I don't think you'd make the same mistake again."

That's a hell of a difference from bringing someone Coke when they've ordered a Sprite. Dan tells me that they have a debriefing session on particularly bad calls. They have to leave at the end of the day knowing they did the best they could.

I ask him if he feels that he has to remain guarded with his emotions—to not get too close.

"I don't put a wall up between me and the patient. I don't feel like I need to."

Moving from cable work to saving lives is a huge professional leap. I ask him how it went down.

"After we got back from Tommy's funeral…Heather decided she wanted to be a cosmetologist and I decided I wanted to become an EMT. On our way home, I stopped by the admin building and I went in and said, 'Hey, number one, I want to thank you guys for everything you did. I just want to make sure that everyone who was on that call knows that I appreciate them for what they've done and for what we attempted to do there. And I'd also like to know how I could become an EMT.'"

Lieutenant Young pointed him towards a class in a nearby town and it was left at that. Later, the Chief asked Dan about an address-labeling program, and whether they could use Tommy's story as an example. He assured him that this project would come together when Dan and Heather were ready. It took them six months to give the chief a picture of Tommy. The photo was taken on Halloween, and in it, Tommy is dressed as a firefighter. He has blonde hair and giant blue eyes. His smiling face adorns all the posters around town.

All of a sudden, Dan looks at me as if he just remembered something really important. "I don't know if you know this, but Heather is pregnant."

"No, I didn't."

"She's not that far along," he replies.

My heart stutters in my chest. So much hope and emotion is wrapped up in that little tiny bundle of cells growing in Heather's body. My Tourette's strikes again when I tell Dan that I've had two miscarriages and that it was so weird dealing with that because there was nothing to show. I feel stupid for even saying it. What he's experienced is like a heart attack compared to what I've gone through. He held Tommy, loved him, took him for ice cream, read him books, and comforted him when he was sick.

I can't talk to him anymore. I check my cell phone and decide that it's the perfect time to go.

* * *

I'm not a church-attending religious person, but after Dan tells me the baby news, I start talking more to God. I've been asking him or her or whoever it is to watch over Dan and Heather and this little baby. I guess I'm trying to reason with the powers that be in the hopes that they would be spared them from experiencing another loss. *Maybe this new life could help them to forget the pain of losing Tommy.*

I decide to spend the summer with Dan and his crew, immersing myself in the life of an EMT. I feel at ease with them, and they appear to be comfortable with me around. Adolph is polite and funny and very host-like when I'm there. "Would you like coffee?" he'll ask when I arrive. Ian is young and constantly attached to his phone. Dan is sensitive and watchful, but he joins in on the good-natured joking around. He's the newest member of the crew. He volunteered for a year and a half, but he was recently hired as a full-time employee, along with three other guys. I've been at the fire station with Dan's crew twice now, and my presence seems to suppress all emergency calls. That's a good thing for the citizens of Bayfield, but it's bad for exploring death.

June 16, 2009. It is Dan's birthday, and Ian's is tomorrow. I bring a chocolate Pepperidge Farm cake to help celebrate. If I've learned anything about men, it's that they are a little more open to the presence of a strange woman when she brings them something to eat.

Dan thanks me for the cake by blowing a theatrical kiss from the kitchen. His cell phone rings. He answers it quickly, excited over the prospect of birthday wishes. It's Heather. He lowers his voice as he talks, but I overhear him say, "I love you too."

Ian looks at me and smirks. "He's a pro-b. He shouldn't even be talking on the phone, but we're letting him slide since it's his birthday."

I can't tell if he's serious, but Griego, another crew member, reassures me that he is. A "pro-b" is a person in their probationary first year of service. They have to prove themselves worthy by being the last to go to bed, the first to rise, the dishwasher, the drink-getter—basically the fire department's bitch. Ian has passed this stage, as evidenced by the continual beeping of his cell phone, alerting him to a new text message.

I am so thankful to be at the station tonight because it is allowing me to do exactly what I always do when things get tough or too emotional: I avoid. I found out today that my now twenty-year-old cat Spooky isn't going to live much longer. Erik took him to see the vet this morning because he's been sneezing a lot and his eyes are watery. The vet called and recommended that we test his kidneys.

I left work early and went to the vet's office to pick him up at 3:30. When I paid his bill, I was told that the vet wanted to speak with me. I could tell that this was not going to be a happy conversation about the awesomeness of my geriatric cat. When she entered the tiny examination room, she already had her serious, I'm-about-to-tell-you-some-really-bad-news face on. She probably expected me to break down, but I held it together. Spooky is old, so her telling me that his body was failing him was not particularly shocking. On top of that, I despise crying in front of people, even nice vets who have to deal with pain and sadness in pet owners' eyes almost daily.

But now that I think about it, I've had that cat for half my life. At nineteen, I moved back in with my mother after flunking out of my first year of college. I decided to get a cat to make me feel less pathetic and lonely. There was an ad in the paper that said in bold typeface, ADOPT or DIE! Inspired by this dire message, I drove over to check out the death row kitties. Like the men I was attracted to at the time, Spooky was indifferent to my presence. He was perfect and all mine.

After a few months, he traveled with me on a plane in a carrier on my big move from the suburbs of Kansas to San Francisco. He saw the dissolution of my first marriage. He was there for the birth of my children. He has been my constant companion, and in doing so has been a connection to my past. That cat is all that remains of my youth. Once he's gone, it's official—I'm old. Although we'll still have Kiki, our exuberant Blue Heeler, once Spooky dies, I'm never getting another cat. It's too painful to lose them.

As I sit here shooting the shit with Dan, Ian, and Griego, I realize that I'm just biding my time. All I do at the station is sit around, talk, eat, or watch them do training exercises. If we do get a call, I'm afraid that I'm not going to be cool, but then again I'm experiencing the life of an EMT—the whole 'hurry up and wait' thing. The difference is, these guys know what can happen. I don't.

As the birthday cake thaws on the counter, I'm doing my best not to think about my cat. Griego takes a picture of me at the dining room table—evidence of my existence at the station, I guess. I smile wearily at the camera. Just as I start collecting my things to drive home, their pagers go off in unison. The dispatcher's monotone voice dispenses information over a loudspeaker. I don't understand most of what she says— except for "fire." As the men run for the bay, their demeanors shift to serious within seconds.

"Here we go, Pam. Come on!" shouts Ian.

I grab my notebook and run after them. When I reach the truck, which couldn't have taken me more than thirty seconds, all three of them are dressed in fire gear.

Ian tells me to get in the far left seat and put the headphones on. I leap over the remainder of their stuff, fasten my seat belt, and fumble with the headset. Adrenaline surges through my veins as we pull out of the garage. Normally I ride shotgun due to occasional bouts of carsickness, but not on this trip. I don't want to change the way they do things and I definitely don't want to get in their way. *Gee, we were doing fine and then Pam messed everything up and the house burned down.* I try to remain as inconspicuous as possible. Hard to do when you're six feet tall and clueless.

Ian drives. Dan is on my left and Lieutenant Griego rides shotgun. The dispatcher's voice addresses them over the headphones and speaks in codes that I don't understand. She gives us the address of the shop where a fire is in progress.

As Ian pulls out onto the street, he says, "Can I get some music?" I'm thinking loud heavy metal to get them revved up for whatever awaits them, but I learn that 'music' is the cue for sirens. Even with the headphones on, the sirens are loud. Ian tells me to push the button if I want to talk. I can't find the button and right now I don't have anything to say. We peel down the road that I drive every day on my fifty-mile commute. Cars are pulled over on the side of the road, and the more I look out the window, the woozier I feel. Dan remains silent. Griego informs Ian whether he's clear at intersections. Ian is revved up and wants nothing more than to be the first crew on the scene.

His voice comes over the headphones. "Pam, are you okay?"

My fingers run over every inch of the headset trying to find the button to reply, fumbling like Helen Keller trying to discover the word for water. I turn to the front and give Griego the thumbs-up. This is not the time or place to discuss my nausea or my anticipatory grief about my cat.

Even though Ian drives fast and furious, we are not the first to respond to the call. Two engines are already on scene. The men jump out of the truck and make their way towards the shop, which is really just a large red barn. From where I sit, I can't see smoke or flames. For now, I remain inside the vehicle, which is still running, and watch as other engines pull up to the large gravel entrance. Two black labs and a collie mix run around the lot. Another truck arrives and blocks my view of the barn. I could correct this, but I'm too scared to step outside.

Everyone is dressed in heavy fire gear, even James Newman, the chaplain, who is walking towards the building, wearing a blue vest that announces his spiritual presence. The three mutts follow him, probably sensing that he's an okay, sensitive guy who might pat them on the head to quiet their dog fears. As I watch him, Dan opens the door of the truck and asks for the radios. I quickly grab them and hand them over. He's off without a word. There is no time for anyone to answer my burning question: "Where's the fire?"

A middle-aged man and a woman dressed in shorts and t-shirts appear outside the barn. A teenage boy has replaced 'Chappy' as the dogs' human companion. The situation must not be too serious, as the family looks relaxed. The firefighters from other crews stare at me with questioning looks as they walk past the truck.

After about thirty minutes of me just sitting there, the crew comes back. Griego opens the door and asks if I have any questions. I do. I jump out and he walks me towards the barn.

"You sat here the whole time?" he asks with an incredulous grin.

"Yep." I'm a lily-livered scaredy-cat. "So was there a fire?"

"It was a burnt out ballast on that old neon sign."

He points to the sign in question as we enter the shop. It is an antique Indian Motorcycle sign, which Griego informs me is worth about sixty thousand dollars. The barn is filled with old bikes in various stages of repair. What a response—twelve men in full fire gear, sirens and engines, hoses at the ready—all for a little old sign.

As the sun finally sets and the mountain air cools, I watch the responders slowly peel away from the scene. Erik, who is a gearhead, will like the tale of my first call, but I feel embarrassed that I've shown Dan and his crew my true, yellow-bellied colors. I couldn't even make it out of the truck without someone holding my hand.

*   *   *

At home, it's back to real life. In addition to his more serious ail-
ments, Spooky has a bacterial infection in his mouth from old,
rotting teeth. The vet prescribed an antibiotic that I must administer with a dropper twice a day. It seems sort of cruel to put him
through this when his life is going to end shortly anyway, but I
do it more for my sake than his. I have to feel as if I can somehow
make him better, or at least make his life more comfortable. But
as any cat owner knows, administering medicine is not an easy
task. My daughter Lola watches me intently as I attempt to squirt
the white liquid into the side of Spooky's mouth. He hisses and
tries to escape.

"Why are you giving him medicine? Is he sick?"

As Spooky leaps from the couch to hide from the dreaded
dropper of doom, I look at my daughter, whose eyebrows are
now scrunched together in a look of concern. I take a seat, sigh
heavily, and wipe at the white dots of Clavamox sprinkled on my
chocolate brown couch. Lola scoots up closer to me and watches
my pitiful attempt at a poker face.

"Spooky isn't doing too good," I say.

Lola's face goes full on scrunch. "What do you mean? Is he going to die?"

Her words are choked and choppy. Her eyes dart around the
room, looking for our cat's whereabouts. She is eight years old
and still saddened by the loss of our other cat, Binky. Lola and I
share the same emotional sensitivity when it comes to all things
small and furry. I'm afraid she is going to inherit the two thick
worry lines between my eyebrows, especially when her own dog
Kiki dies.

"Yes. He's going to die. We're all going to die at some point.
It's part of life."

I feel like I'm spouting dialogue from some ancient ABC after-
school special where everything is neatly wrapped up in an hour.
These words do not console her. Part of me wants to jump right in

and have a good cry with her. I don't know how to behave. Am I supposed to be modeling strength through adversity, or am I supposed to show that it's okay to be sad and cry? I'm sure there's a book about this somewhere, but I don't have the time to read it.

"Why do people have to leave?" she wails.

Shit, this isn't just about the cat. This is about something bigger: grandmas and grandpas and mom and dad and anybody she's ever loved. People.

"I don't know," I answer. I hate that I have no control over this situation. Nik, who is five, is oblivious to her crying. He runs past the couch with straws between his fingers. "Ching-ching," he hollers at us. Right now he's Wolverine, impervious to pain.

After six days away from the fire station, I realize I need to go back. I don't want them to think I'm a total wuss. It's also important that I talk to Dan about the night of his son's death, and that won't happen if I just sit on my couch and feel sorry for myself. It's June 25. No one is inside with the exception of a man installing a security system. Ironically, he doesn't question who I am or what I'm doing in the building. I step outside. The mechanic, Jim, is working on one of the engines. I've had very little interaction with Jim, due to the fact that he only works during the day. He doesn't acknowledge my approach.

"Are they out on a call?" I ask with a certain amount of exasperation.

"I don't know. It's not my turn to watch them."

All righty then. I turn and trudge back into the station feeling like an unwanted intruder, and plop down into the brown pleather recliner. Farrah Fawcett died today. This makes me feel sad, not to mention borderline geriatric. As soon as I open the book I've brought, my phone rings. It's my friend Katie. She's frantic.

"Michael Jackson just died."

"What?"

"He had a heart attack. Oh my God, Pam."

As this news hits me, Dan's crew enters. They've been at a training session.

"I gotta go. I'll call you later." I hang up the phone and blurt out, "Michael Jackson died!"

Dan says "really?" as if I'd just told him the time. That's pretty much the station consensus. I can't believe it. This is huge. I blab on and on and on about how "Thriller" was the first LP I ever bought, how I would go to my friend Amy's house to watch MTV just so I could watch his videos. How my mom bought me a vinyl Michael Jackson jacket at Venture, along with one silver, sparkly glove. Basically, I reveal that I'm one of those nut jobs that reserves space in their brains for the goings-on of famous pop singers. Michael Jackson's death feels personal and scary. If the King of Pop can die, what chance do the rest of us have?

"Why do people care about Michael Jackson? They don't know him. Hell, there's people dying in Iraq every day and you don't see people getting all messed up about it," says one of the volunteers.

"They don't know them. People from all over the world loved Michael Jackson's music. He meant something to them." He meant something to me, and now he's gone.

Another one of the volunteers quips, "I bet a bunch of ten-year-old boys are going to sleep a lot better tonight."

I feel horrible. Not only has a big part of my youth died, but I also feel ashamed, stupid, and trivial for caring about it.

As we sit down to dinner, Ian says, "Man, I shouldn't have made fun of Michael Jackson's death. One of my buddies just died."

"What happened?" I ask.

"His Humvee was hit in Afghanistan."

I don't know what to say, except "I'm sorry."

Despite my plans, I can't stay at the station tonight. I need a compassionate ear and I'm not going to find one here. Their indifference to celebrity death is overshadowed by the fatalities of everyday people whose lives only matter to a few.

A week later, I reluctantly return for another round of nothing-ness. As I settle into the chair to kill time, a female voice rattles me from my Saturday morning complacency.

"Upper Pine, please stand by for a medical page." It's 10 AM.

"Here it is, Pam," says Adolph on his way towards the bay.

This is it—my rite of passage. It will be the first time I see someone in need of the kind of care that requires a call to 911.

I jog to the ambulance and slip into the 'captain's chair' directly behind the gurney. I buckle my seatbelt, clutch my notepad to my chest, and the ambulance takes off. My heart races as we rush off into the unknown. All I have to do is watch what they do. I don't have to insert an IV or assess someone's mental state, but I feel anxious about the unknown. What if the person dies? Whatever happens, this time, I intend to step out of the vehicle.

Dan drives the ambulance as the engine follows us with lights flashing and sirens wailing. As he turns corners, I clutch the counter to keep my balance. The drive takes two minutes. Dan parks directly in front of the entrance to our town's poor excuse for a grocery store, while Kyle grabs the medical bag. I follow the four of them inside and stand off to the side by the carts. Ian sig-nals me over, but I'm hesitant. Max, a tiny, frail man with high-waisted black pants and a white shirt, is seated in an office chair in front of a stainless steel freezer. His companion, a man in his late forties, answers Ian's questions. He doesn't seem particularly concerned. Max, who has urinated on himself, stares off into the store, seemingly unaware of the four men around him.

Max appears to be in his late 80's. He can't hear very well, so his companion repeats what the EMTs tell him in a loud, animat-ed voice. Kyle, one of the A-crew members, kneels down to the old man's level and speaks one notch below shouting.

"Max, can I put this oxygen mask on you for a minute?" Kyle places the mask gingerly on the old man's face. "Take a deep breath, Max. As deep as you can go."

The nephew repeats the instructions, but the man wants noth-ing to do with the piece of plastic covering his nose and mouth.

Within a minute, he pushes it off his face like he's swatting at an irksome bee. Ian informs Max that he's going to take his temperature by sticking something in his ear. It is at this point that a man—one old enough to know better—taps Ian on the shoulder.

"Can I squeeze in there and get some ice?"

Ian looks back at him, perturbed by the interruption. Then, without looking at him, he opens the cooler and hands him a bag of ice.

The man taps him on the shoulder again. "I need four more."

Ian hands over four bags of ice. I can't believe the man's audacity. Can't the picnic, barbecue, boat ride, whatever, wait? I mean, really. Let the nice people do their jobs. Several people enter the store and gawk at the scene unfolding. Their eyes don't linger very long at the stranger in the chair. He isn't bleeding, he's older than dirt, and he's just sitting there. It's very anti-climactic compared to the big red shiny vehicles with the flashing lights outside the store. Most people grab a rickety cart and push past me—off to buy their 3-2 beer, milk, eggs, charcoal, or whatever.

Kyle stands up. "Max, we're going to take you to the hospital."

I stare at the back of Max's head as we drive to the hospital. The white skin of his scalp is freckled with age spots, delicately covered by long, sparse strands of what my mom would call frog hair. Adolph determines that this is a non-emergency transport, so we drive the speed limit without sirens. Ian and Kyle attend to him.

"Do you know where you're at?" Ian asks, like a concerned parent speaking to a child. He looks at Max intently.

Max answers in a hoarse whisper. "It's a secret."

"Max, I'm just going to stick you real quick." Before he can protest, Ian starts the countdown, "One, two, three," contact. He places the lancet on the counter and announces "sharps" to alert us that there is a contaminated needle that has not been placed in the sharps container. After he tests Max's blood, he leans over my chair and places the needle in the clear plastic box.

As soon as the blood glucose level is recorded, Kyle says loudly, "There's going to be a big poke in your arm, Max." Kyle attempts to draw his blood, but the old man's vein bursts when the needle is inserted. "Are you all right, Max?" he asks.

Max nods slightly. Kyle uses his cell phone to call the emergency room to give them the heads-up. Due to HIPAA regulations, radios are problematic when discussing the patient's name or condition. There are too many people in our small community who have nothing better to do than listen to scanners.

The drive to the hospital takes a good twenty minutes. A burgundy new-model Subaru Outback tailgates the ambulance and attempts to pass, but is interrupted by a solid yellow line and oncoming traffic.

"Do you know where you're at, Max?" asks Ian, trying to assess his mental state.

Max pauses for a moment and says, "Colorado."

"Do you live in Denver?" continues Ian.

Max remains silent.

"Bayfield?"

Max raises his arm and nods his head in recognition. "My mouth is dry," Max whispers.

Ian leans in closer.

"I like beer," Max says, as if there's a cooler full of ice-cold Bud under the gurney.

"Did you have any beer this morning?" asks Ian.

"No."

"What's your favorite kind of beer?"

"All kinds. Beer is beer."

Max and my husband should hang out. This is a good sign. If a patient's sense of humor remains intact, they're probably not critical.

When we finally arrive at the ER, Dan and Ian wheel him into an empty room. I follow the gurney like a lost puppy. A short, brunette nurse eyes me suspiciously when Max is wheeled into the room. I watch from the door. Max looks me in the eye, probably wondering why I'm there. His eyes look old and tired, like those of a bloodhound. He waves his finger at me, as a sort of acknowledgement. Ian and Dan lift Max's frail body from the sheet on the gurney to the hospital bed.

"That's pretty slick," says Max and smiles. He looks at Ian, the youngster of this crew of men and says, "You're next."

Four hours after we leave Max at the hospital, we get a second medical page. I can't believe it: it's either feast or famine, and I'm actually psyched to go. When Ian hears the address over the intercom, he informs me that we're heading to the home of a 'frequent flyer' — a person who calls 911 on a regular basis. When we arrive at the tiny white house next to a trailer park, we are greeted with a warning sign on the door: oxygen is in use and smoking is not permitted. Cigarette butts litter the muddy, makeshift porch. We enter.

Planted on a love seat that faces the front door, the elderly woman's body resembles an avocado seed in a jar of water, her skinny arms and legs like toothpick appendages. Her eyes are red, panicked and wet with tears. All four men gather around her like she is the most important person in the world. They know her name and greet her like a dear old friend. Dan crouches before her to place an oxygen monitor on her finger. She grasps his gloved hand. He reciprocates her touch and asks how she is feeling. She whimpers, which is not good when you're trying to catch your breath.

Her daughter, a large, scantily-dressed woman in her early thirties, paces around the small living space as she answers Adolph's questions.

"We've done everything the ER said to do and she still can't breathe. I want her to fight!" The woman lifts her arms up in frustration. Her abundant breasts spill forth from her ill-fitting yellow tank top. I can't bring myself to look at her. It is fairly obvious that what her mother needs is a little calm, compassionate kindness.

Adolph decides that we are going to transport the mother to the hospital. The gurney won't fit through the door, so Dan retrieves an orange chair from the ambulance. Ian helps ease the woman's body into the chair, and they proceed to fasten belts and buckles around her. Her tiny, bare feet dangle as they carry her out the door like a bride at a Jewish wedding.

As she is transferred to the gurney, her daughter tells Adolph that she'll be at the hospital in a couple of hours. She is aware of the tests her mother will endure and knows how long they will take. Mother and daughter communicate for a moment in Spanish. Adolph looks towards the daughter, whose face registers surprise. He wants to know if she has communicated anything of importance.

"A mother never leaves her children. That's what she just said," the daughter stammers.

My eyes tear up.

On the drive to the hospital, the woman's blood pressure decreases as we administer kindness, concern and oxygen.

*   *   *

After spending two months with this crew, I've only witnessed three calls. It's not because they don't get calls—it is because I am the 'white cloud'. The residents of my small hometown remain safe and protected, as long as I am at the station. When I leave, the calls resume. They should put me on the payroll to hang out. I've already missed several traumatic accidents, strokes, heart attacks, and young men dying in their sleep.

I spend my last day with them on a Friday. While they train and check the rigs, I watch TV. At 9 PM, we decide to play a game of Texas Hold 'Em, with every tea bag in the station as our chips. Every so often I say, "it sure is quiet," which I've been told is the magic phrase to bring about a call. It doesn't have the effect I'm hoping for. Kyle and Dan duke it out as the two remaining players, while the rest of us plop down on the multi-sectional couch to watch more television. At 11:30 I look over at the others. Adolph is sound asleep with his arms resting behind his head. Ian is dressed for bed in sweatpants, with his shoeless feet propped up on the coffee table. As Kyle removes his work boots, I rise to leave. Ian looks up at me and says, "Where do you think you're going? I need to sleep."

CHAPTER FIVE

Confront the Unknown

Knowing my track record of avoidance, I may never get up my nerve to speak with Dan about the night Tommy died. All I know is that I'm leaving for my school's summer residency in a month and I need to write. All this waiting around for death to happen is depressing me. I need to feel uplifted, or at least reassured that my soul will go on to someplace better and that death really isn't the end. This might be a good time for me to discover religion, but the universe has a different plan. During our lunch break, Katie informs me that Lisa, my former hairdresser, was told some very specific and important information by a medium named Annee Jawor who lives in Pagosa Springs.

"She talks to dead people, Pam. She's perfect for you," Katie jokes.

I figure she will at least be interesting, so I look her up online. She has a fancy website with tons of testimonials assuring skeptics that her accuracy and insight are amazing. A credit card processing device is placed prominently on her contact page. A one-hour reading with Annee will relieve my bank account of three hundred dollars, which means that she makes more per hour than your average physician. I whimsically e-mail her to ask if she'd be willing to be interviewed. She replies a few hours later in a clipped, Spock-like way. She agrees to meet with me and signs the e-mail, "With enlightenment of love." Later, her assistant TJ sends me an email with directions to her house, which lends an air of authenticity to her operation.

When I arrive at Annee's house, I am greeted by TJ, a tall handsome fellow, who shakes my hand officiously and then quickly darts out of the room. Annee enters, dressed casually in an appliquéd peach-colored tank top, faded jeans and white sport socks that are dirty on the bottom. She asks if I need to use the restroom. I probably do and she knows this because a) she's psychic and b) I just drove for an hour to her house, but I decline. She offers to fetch me some water and shuffles off into the house. I wonder why TJ isn't doing that.

I cautiously take a seat in a slim wicker chair with multiple pillows in varying shades of peach. A white Tiffany-style lamp sits on a glass table beside a pink box of tissue.

Anne returns with the glass of ice water and informs me that she is going to record the interview. I reply that I've brought my own device, but she insists that she likes to use her interviews on the website. "It will be anonymous," she assures me. Apparently I am not the first person to interview her. She presses buttons, looks at the computer screen for a moment, and then takes a seat next to me. I lean forward and open my notebook to my illegibly scribbled questions.

"So, tell me about your gift."

"I'm an interdimensional translator. That would be someone who is able to communicate with people who have passed over into that place of interdimensional."

I'm already confused.

"So as a medium, and as a gift as you refer to it, coming in as a child there was always hints of it. For me it was like not so much seeing the things that I saw, but what was so unusual to me was that others couldn't see the things that I would see. And so this created, as I got older, to realize that I was different."

I shift in the uncomfortable wicker chair and nod in her direction like I totally understand what she's saying.

She explains that she connects with those that have passed with a "vibrational change within her." She likens it to lucid dreaming.

"So what are the most common questions that people ask you?"

"Why am I here or what is my purpose?" She tells me she likes these inquiries because they imply that people are aware that they are here on this earth for a reason. As anyone who has watched the *Wizard of Oz* knows, the solution to the things we seek is already within us. Like the wizard behind the curtain, Annee just helps point those things out when all hope seems lost.

When I tell her about my fear of death, she dismisses it as a common, societal fear of darkness, or the unknown.

"The challenge of death and dying is not for the one who passed—it's for the ones who have been left behind."

She reassures me that all is well in that interdimensional place. "Life goes on. It doesn't end. Death happens to the human body but not to the spirit that resides within."

As I drive the hour back home, I still feel confused, yet oddly comforted. If Annee is correct, my spirit won't expire when my body does. I'll get to hang around people I love and see what happens to them, or I'll get to come back to earth for another round. I don't know if it's because she's given me a sliver of hope or what, but my visit with her emboldens me to turn into the fire station on my way home. Like the Cowardly Lion, I find myself saying, "I do believe in spooks. I do. I do. I do," as I try to muster the courage to speak with Dan again.

I'd heard through the small-town grapevine that the 'A' crew has had quite a few unusual calls on their last shift. This is my excuse for an unplanned visit. When I arrive, Dan and Ian are wearing helmets and performing a training exercise that involves a giant ladder. As I approach them in the bay, they look in my direction and say in unison, "You missed it!" There is a strange glee in Ian's voice as he relays all of the calls I missed on Wednesday: a pulmonary embolism, a fatal car crash, and a DOA 'stinker.' I listen intently and feign disgust at my horrible timing. But this is not the reason I'm here. I've put it off long enough. "Dan, I need to talk to you."

Ian smiles, punches Dan playfully on the arm and says "Uh oh," as if I'm about to send him to the principal's office.

"I need to talk to you about the night your son died," I clarify.

"Okay."

"Not here. I mean. Not now."

"We're not busy or anything. It's okay," he says and sets his helmet down.

And they won't be, as long as I stay inside the building. There is no escaping it. We're not in a hair salon, or cracking jokes around a dinner table. It's time for me to bear witness.

"Why don't we do this on the bus?" he says, and opens the ambulance door.

I follow him in. Dan takes the captain's chair and I take a seat on the side bench. I really feel like flopping down on the gurney so I don't have to look at him. The heat of the day is overwhelming inside this tiny sterile space; sweat trickles down my side as I fumble with the buttons on my tape recorder. Before I press the 'on' button, I tell Dan in a wobbly, unassertive voice that I want to know everything. But maybe want is the wrong word. I need to know everything. I need to know how this horrible, life-shattering event transpired and how he managed to live through it.

He relays the events of that night.

It was November 10, 2007. He and Tommy were eating pizza in the living room and watching a Nebraska Huskers football game. He was in his easy chair and Tommy was in his highchair. Dan's tone is conversational, so I sort of relax on the bench. Just when I think this isn't going to be so bad, he leans forward and clasps his head between his hands.

"This is the bitch," he says under his breath and lifts back up in his chair as if he's about to confess something. His hands clutch his knees.

"I told him to take one more bite and we're gonna take a bath." His voice rises and cracks. "And he took another bite. And then he started shaking."

My mouth gapes open. I can't look away or stare at my notebook. I look directly into Dan's sad eyes. I take a deep breath and uncross my legs to brace myself.

"He heaved forward—back—and his wrists went in like this. And then he just *woomph*."

Dan demonstrates how Tommy collapsed in the chair.

"Like that. I jump up and say, *Tommy, Tommy, what's wrong?* and I took the top off the high chair and get him unbuckled. Got him down on the floor. And he's looking. His eyes are open. And he's looking up at me. And I say *Tommy, what's wrong?* and I start doing back blows on him. And turned him back over to see if anything was happening. Nothing. I tried abdominal thrusts. Nothing. Rolled him back over to do a back blow and I could hear him just..."

Dan demonstrates a deep, wheezing breath.

"Like that. Real agonal type breathing and uh, I tried another back blow. I turned him back over and nothing had come out and then I saw him kind of disappear from his eyes. He was looking at me and I said *Tommy, stay with me, stay with me.* And then his eyes closed. And that's when I started towards the phone, but I didn't know how I was going to try and do CPR and call 911 at the same time. So with one hand I had him on his back and I started doing chest compressions. I dial 911 on one hand. I need an ambulance, gave them my address, told them exactly how to get there and hung up. I use both my hands and tried to give him a breath. The first breath went into his stomach. But I did compressions again and his stomach let loose and he aspirated out. I turned him on his side to get that out. I turned him back over, tried to get him another breath. That one actually did get into his lungs, but he was not responding back to me at that point."

Dan relays these events with urgency, like it's happening all over again. When he speaks that last sentence, he slows down, emphasizing each word.

"I checked for a pulse and felt a really weak pulse. All the time I'm saying, *Tommy stay with Daddy, stay with Daddy, Daddy's right here, stay with Daddy!*"

It's dusk. The ambulance has a hard time locating Dan's house. After fifteen agonizing minutes, the EMTs finally arrive at his house. When they take over, Dan realizes that he hasn't called Heather. He frantically phones her at the friend's house and says, "Heather, Tommy's not breathing, you've got to come home," and hangs up. She is twenty-seven miles away.

The EMTs remove Tommy from the house and work on him in the ambulance. They shock his heart and start artificial breathing as Dan stands outside.

Watching.

Praying.

"Hail Mary full of grace."

Pacing.

"Help me God!"

A helicopter is on its way from Mercy Hospital in Durango. The EMTs continue working on him in the ambulance. Precious minutes have passed. Dan can't remember how long.

Then one of the EMTs, the one he can't remember, looks out the back of the van and said, "We've done all we can do. We can keep trying, or you, you can put him in your arms. He's gonna die."

"What's the helicopter coming for then? I mean shit, the helicopter's landing! It's right there! What are we thinking? Let's get him in the helicopter and get him to the hospital."

The highway near Dan's house is blocked off for the landing of the helicopter. Dan walks down into the ditch, feeling the utter hopelessness of the situation, and screams at the top his lungs. "Why God, why?"

Tommy is flown to Mercy and then flown to a children's hospital in Denver. It is there that he dies in Heather's arms.

I am drained and on the verge of tears. Dan seems okay.

"Is there a tissue in here?" I look around the ambulance for something, even a paper towel to wipe my eyes.

"No, sorry. We've got band-aids," he jokes.

I wipe the escaped tears with the back of my hand and step out of the ambulance. I want nothing more than to rush home and hug Nik and Lola. I thank Dan for sharing his story and leave the station in silence.

Since I finally faced my fear by talking with Dan, I feel sad that my time at the station is over. I feel like we shared a moment, a real painful moment. Before, being in his presence was like a chore for me, a dance of avoidance. Now I want to know more. Tommy's death was just the beginning for Heather and Dan. What happened afterwards? How did they cope? What gave them the faith to move forward and to have another child? I want to find out.

I have nothing that even comes close to Heather and Dan's pain — just a geriatric cat with one little black paw in the ground. There is no comparison. But my response to the impending loss of my only cat scares me. What's going to happen when it's my mother or Erik or, God forbid, Nik or Lola? I don't think I could make it. I already find my behavior with Spooky changing. I'm withdrawing from him as a way to soften the impact of his eventual death.

I find it increasingly difficult to be around him. He's so skinny and sad looking. I'll scratch his head and brush him, but his sorry physical state only reminds me that he's dying. I want the old cat back, the sleek, black one with shiny fur and a crazy, spastic demeanor. I long for the days when he would chase a super ball around the house or roll around in a catnip induced stupor. But now he is stinky with dreadlocked belly fur, watching me with filmy eyes.

Is this the reason people put their loved ones in nursing homes? To keep them in a faraway place, so they aren't daily re-minded of their own mortality? Is it too difficult to witness someone who was once young and vibrant diminishing? As much as we'd like to deny it, we don't remain the same. We change. We slump. We lose our teeth. We lose our glasses. Some of us lose our minds. Maybe that's why our society clings to youth. If the outside remains shiny, young and vibrant, maybe we can cheat death. It's not me you're after, Mr. Reaper: it's my next door neighbor who never flosses her teeth and drinks cheap beer.

My wish for Spooky is for a peaceful death in his sleep. Yes, it will be shocking and scary to find his lifeless form curled up by the heater or on the couch, but I don't want to play God with him. I want him to die on his own terms. If he's in a lot of pain and he doesn't want to eat anymore, then I guess we'll have to visit the vet for the final goodbye. I'm hoping we won't have to.

*   *   *

Most of us don't know the exact day when we're going to die, even if we're terminally ill. It happens when it happens. Only people who commit suicide or someone who is being executed by the state knows the exact date and time of their death. It seems like a crazy idea, but I want to speak with someone who knows the day he/she is going to die. I figure we'll write a couple of letters back and forth and that will be the extent of it.

I search the Texas Department of Criminal Justice website to find someone with an execution date in the next six months. My only requirement for this person is that they not scare me. After reading the inmate's booking cards, most of the men do. There is only one man who doesn't seem particularly evil. While he did kill someone during a burglary, he didn't kill every member of his family or taunt the police with tattered pieces of their bloodied clothing. He just seemed like a young kid with a gun. His name is Khristian Oliver. The summary of the crime is on the TDCJ website, along with his mug shot, education level, height, weight and eye color. Before I can change my mind about contacting him, I compose a letter.

Dear Mr. Oliver:

You don't know me, but I'm writing you in hopes that you will let me interview you. I am writing my graduate thesis about end of life issues. I understand that you have a scheduled execution date of November 5. 2009. I would like to get your thoughts about this process, how you're preparing yourself, and anything else that you might want to share.

I want you to know that I do not judge you. This piece is not about the crime you committed. My own brother was in prison for twenty years. If you don't want to talk, I'll understand.

Sincerely,

Pamela Skjolsvik

I mail the letter along with my return address. I have to. As I stare at the blue box, it hits me that anyone with a limited understanding of Google could find me. Great. What if I piss him off and he sends someone on the outside to off me? I guess the joke's on him as I'm leaving for my summer residency for two weeks.

I entrust Spooky's care to Erik while I'm gone. Nik and Lola are off to Grandma and Grandpa's house. I'm kind of hoping that Spooky will die while I'm away, both for my sake and for the kids. Other pet owners have told me that my absence will make it easier for him to go. That's the plan, anyway.

*   *   *

After a day of airplane travel, with all the inherent headaches of switching planes, overpriced airport food, and waiting for what seems like days to arrive somewhere— anywhere— I finally land in Baltimore. I lug my two mismatched suitcases, a giant purse and a computer bag through the automatic doors of the airport. The thick, humid August air assaults my skin and frizzes my hair upon contact. I dart towards the Super Shuttle, eager for some respite from the sauna. No such luck. The blue van is packed and my hotel will be the last stop. Despite all assurances on the van and the driver's sweat-ringed polo shirt, the ride will not be super.

My hotel is nestled between the college campus and an up-scale mall. The rooms are large, the bedding is soft, and I don't have to share a bathroom with strangers. The true selling point, however, is that my fantabulous room ended up being cheaper than the dorm. But when I check in, I get the feeling there might be a reason for the steep discount.

There are two men at the front desk when I arrive: I am greet-ed formally and sincerely by the younger one in the blue suit. His manager is dressed in a brown suit without a nametag, and eyes his junior's every move. I hand the younger man my driver's li-cense and credit card, and he proceeds to massacre my name like everyone else on the planet. I correct him with the usual "like Dr. Scholls with a 'vik' on the end." I tell him I'm there for two weeks. He fumbles at the computer for a few elongated seconds, and then looks woefully towards the manager.

"I'm having some difficulty finding a room. She'll be here two weeks." The agony of defeat is in his voice.

The manager takes over at the keyboard, his fingers tapping a quick, loud rhythm as he stares blankly at the screen. "I can find something," he says with a devilish grin. And with that, his fin-gers stop.

That was fast. The man in blue hands me my room key with a smile. I open the flap and see that I've been placed on the tenth floor. I decline assistance with my luggage and head towards the elevator with a sense of impending doom. Normally, being on the tenth floor wouldn't be a problem. There's a view. Rooms at the top of hotels tend to be nicer. Still, I already know that something terrible and tragic happened in one of those rooms. A man named William Parente killed his two daughters, his wife, and then him-self in one of the rooms on the tenth floor.

My breath turns shallow as I lumber down the long hallway. I feel as if at any moment, the twin girls from *The Shining* will ap-pear and ask me in unison to come play with them. Towards the end of the hallway on the right, I find it: room 1023. I swipe my key, open the door and cautiously step inside. It doesn't look like the setting for a murder-suicide. There is a neatly made king bed with a navy blue bed spread and an artfully displayed stack of white pillows, as well as two burgundy chairs, a couple of nondescript paintings bolted to the wall, a wooden desk, a matching dresser, and a flat-screen television. I wander into the bathroom. The walls are dizzyingly papered with navy blue and white stripes. Above the marbled sink is a large mirror. The tile floor is clean—maybe too clean. The shower curtain is closed. Behind that white waffled fabric could have been the final resting place of a man who killed his entire family. I sweep it back quickly, like the first idiot to get hacked to death in a horror film. Nothing but a package of Bliss soap and a neatly folded bath mat.

There should be a law against Google overuse. Immediately after finding out about the murder-suicide at the hotel, I surfed the Internet to read all the gory particulars. I learned that the two girls and his wife were killed with blunt force trauma and asphyxiation. Mr. Parente purchased a knife at the Crate and Barrel at the mall across the street, and then killed himself with it in the bathroom. After the family failed to check out, the hotel staff discovered the horrific scene.

The gruesomeness of this case did not deter me from booking my stay here. Mr. Parente wasn't some random hall-wandering serial killer looking for a lone female traveler to torture and kill. He did that to the people he was supposed to love and care for. And what were the chances that I'd be in that particular room? Slim. But I sprint down the hallway and back down the elevator to the reception desk. The two men are still standing around waiting for guests to approach. I saunter over to the counter in a "hey there, buddy, old pal" way. I intend to charm them into giving me the dirt. This isn't the best of plans, because I am not particularly charming.

"So, I'm sure you guys get asked about this all the time—"

Both men look at me with pleasant expectation.

"—but I was wondering if you could tell me in what room the murder-suicide happened on the tenth floor?"

The guy in blue exhales a long and drawn out "Uhhhhhhhhh" while looking to the manager for some sort of lifeline.

The manager steps forward.

"Ma'am, we're not at liberty to discuss those particular details with you. But just so you know, the room in question is out of commission."

"Oh. Well, okay then." I smile, turn and head back to the tenth floor. Despite the manager's assurances, I have a sneaking suspicion that he isn't being completely truthful. Why would a hotel permanently lose money on a vacant room? That's a lot of lost revenue. Terrible things happen in hotel rooms every day: murder, suicides, extra-marital affairs, boredom, bad food, you name it. Where do they draw the line?

Everyone I tell at school about this "am I in the room" conundrum is shocked to learn about what transpired at the hotel. I get questioned about it repeatedly. For two days, I feel like I'm in some sort of weird soap opera where people I don't know are awfully concerned about how this is going to turn out. It's surprising that more people haven't heard about the murder. It made the national news for days. Baltimore. Murder. Suicide. Ponzi scheme. It was a big, horrible deal. After the inevitable questions from my much braver classmates, I am put on a mission to find out the room number. This is death, after all, but really, I just want to make sure I'm not in the room. I am now a firm believer in spooks and bad energy, not to mention books and movies with writers being driven to madness by prolonged hotel stays.

I meet my floor maid on the first morning. She's pleasant and says "Good morning" like she actually means it. But that's all I'm going to say about her, because I don't want her to get fired for talking to me. It is abundantly clear that management has instructed the employees not to say a peep about the murder. I do not ask her if she is the maid who found the Parente family. I do not ask her what room this gruesome discovery was made in. No, absolutely not. That would be too easy. I instead question her about the free water in the room.

"Is it really free?"

"Why yes it is," she replies. She hands me two refrigerated bottles and an extra packet of coffee for my room. I inform her that I'll be there for two weeks and hand her a ten.

Just as I'm about to crack the case wide open by further questioning of the maid about the hotel's choice of personal hygiene products, my teacher emails me to say that the murder took place in 1029. It's no surprise that my teacher, a Pulitzer Prize winning investigative journalist, beats me to the punch. I feel sort of let down when I realize the drama of not knowing is over. The next morning, I peek my head out of the door to make sure the hallway is clear. I proceed to the next two rooms. 1025 and 1027 follow in logical order on my side of the hallway. But the very last room, the one that should be 1029, has been relabeled 1028. Yes, 1029 is out of commission—the number, that is. But the room is right there. I decide it's time to find out the truth.

The first person willing to talk is Deanna, which is not her real name. I recognize her from the Starbucks coffee station near the hotel's restaurant. While I attempt to dog paddle in the pool, she attempts to divert the attention of the handsome lifeguard with a plate of pink cupcakes. It is obvious by the way she stares at him while he watches my pasty white body for signs of swimming distress that she is smitten. I crab walk over to their side of the pool and introduce myself, interrupting their flirtatious exchange. She tells me that this is her last day of employment. Eureka!

"So, Deanna, what do you know about the murder on the tenth floor?"

She leans forward as I bob in the water below her.

"I was working the day it happened."

"Really? Do they not want you not to talk about it?'

"Yeah. They told us to say we didn't know anything."

"Hmmm. I'm just asking because I'm writing about people who work with death. Is the maid who found them still here?"

"I don't know. I don't really know the maids."

"What about the room? Do they still rent it out?"

"Yeah. I was really upset when they did that. Who would want to stay in that room?"

"Not me," I say and let go of the pool's edge.

Since I've opened the morbid floodgates, Deanna reveals that she attended Virginia Tech and was on campus the day of the shootings. She doesn't seem terribly concerned with murder and mayhem in her environment. She returned to classes and finished out the semester.

After my fingers start pruning, I leave the two lovebirds to their cupcakes. I give Deanna my card and ask if she could find out the name of the maid for me. She said she would, but she never called.

The second loose-lipped person is the shuttle driver. I'll call him Aaron, an affable twenty-something who drives me the half mile to campus every morning. During the first couple of rides with Aaron, we talk about the hot, humid weather and school. Because I am the only person in the van, I feel comfortable enough to ask him about the room situation.

"So, I'm sure you've been told to keep quiet about this, but do you know anything about the murder-suicide on the tenth floor?"

"Yeah." He looks back at me, maybe to make sure I'm not a hotel detective, and sighs as if he's been carrying around a heavy weight.

"Well, I'm writing about people who work with death. That must have been horrible for the maid who found them."

"Actually, it was the manager who found them. They didn't check out when they were supposed to. Whenever that happens, they send a manager up to the room to wake them up or whatever needs to be done."

"Really? Is he still here?' The Baltimore newspaper said a maid found them and that the manager called 911.

"Yeah, but he doesn't like to talk about it. He took like a whole week and a half off of work after that day."

Is that it? "Man, I would too. It's hard to erase that kind of image from your brain," I say, as if I could even imagine the horror.

"He bought a flat screen TV and a PlayStation."

I laugh because I can totally relate to wanting a distraction. I hop out of the van and thank Aaron for the ride.

The next morning I run into the nice maid, who is gathering trial-sized toiletries from her cart.

"Hey. Thanks for the coffee."

"You're welcome. Are you enjoying your stay?"

"I am." I approach her instead of my room to see if the paper or if Aaron is telling the truth. "Were you the maid that found the people in room 1029?"

This startles her. She looks down at the neatly stacked bottles of shampoo and conditioner on the cart.

"No, I wasn't," she says with relief.

"Is that maid still working here?"

"Yes. Yes she is, but not on this floor. Not anymore."

"Oh." So was it the manager or the maid? I'm totally confused. "That must have been really hard on her."

She nods in agreement and turns towards the room she has to clean.

"I just don't understand why that man would do that here," she turns and says. "Why not at his home?"

I nod my head in agreement then motion down the hall towards room 1029. "So is that where it happened?" I say as if it doesn't matter one way or the other.

"I really don't know," she says.

"Oh, okay. Well, have a nice day," I say and leave her to do her job.

The different versions of this story are like a game of telephone where the message and the truth become distorted as it goes through the chain of people. Maybe the hotel has really strong-armed these folks into silence. Or maybe this particular woman doesn't want to know the room. Who could blame her? She has to clean it every day and sometimes bloodstains, real or imagined, remain in the psyche long after they've been wiped away with an enzyme cleaner. When I ask Aaron about the room, he says that it has been converted into a supply closet for house-keeping. Maybe it's better for the employees if no one knows the truth.

The next day, I get a strange voice mail from Katie.

"Hey Pam. Dillon was in a car accident. You know Dillon, right? His parents are going to pull the plug." And then the call dropped.

My immediate thought: who is Dillon? Not as in who was he, like his fears, wants, needs, loves, etc, but who the hell was he? I replay the message, hoping for clarity. Katie's tone sounds casual. "You know Dillon, right?" It takes me a minute, but I finally make the connection.

Dillon had worked at our office for maybe three months. He was just a shy kid, straight out of high school, with bad skin and a wardrobe full of baggy shorts. I didn't have any meaningful in-teraction with him. He would just reach his arm into my office and grab my recycling bin. When I said "hello" or "thanks," he'd quickly nod and move on to the next office. I was just another meaningless middle-aged paper-pusher in a dead-end job.

I try to call Katie back, but she doesn't answer. When I get back to the hotel, I read about the accident on the Internet. A bunch of boys were driving over Wolf Creek Pass on their way home from a concert. It was early morning when it happened. Five boys were in the vehicle, and only two of them were wearing seatbelts. The driver fell asleep at the wheel.

The following day, I call my employer and the receptionist tells me that Dillon passed away. She also tells me that our boss held a moment of silence for Dillon at the company barbeque. After paying his respect for the dead, he encouraged all staff members to attend the funeral by telling them that they didn't have to time out. I guess that was his idea of increasing funeral attendance.

I call Katie and she tells me that several of my office mates were at the service. The room was packed—standing room only. Dillon had an open casket, several people spoke, and there wasn't a dry eye in the church. I question why I wasn't there. It would have been a perfect opportunity for me to attend a funeral, to be in the presence of people grieving—and yet I'm stuck in Baltimore for another week. I know it sounds ridiculous, maybe even selfish of me to think it, but I should have been there.

The next day, I receive a letter from Khristian Oliver, the death row inmate. My husband scans it and sends it in an e-mail.

> *Dear Ms. Skjolsvik,*
> *I am sorry that I can't let you interview me for your thesis paper. My attorneys would not approve. Because of this I must respectfully decline your offer. I hope you find someone willing.*
> *Best Wishes,*
> *Khristian Oliver*

I am disappointed that he turned me down, but at the same time relieved. I write him back and thank him for his courteous reply. I don't search for another person on the TDCJ website to interview. I take it as a sign from the universe that I don't really need to interview a death row inmate, much less (as one of my classmates suggests) attend his execution. I can't even handle the thought of the vet putting an animal to sleep.

* * *

When I arrive home from Baltimore, Spooky is still alive and I'm happy that I didn't get my wish. Within days, it is my 39th birthday. To honor this occasion, if not my credit card balances, I decide to buy a reading from Annee Jawor, the medium. The reading is not cheap. I could have had a spa day getting rubbed and scrubbed and massaged and polished with no crying or thinking involved. Instead, I make Annee's log cabin a pit stop on our six-hour drive to Denver, where Erik and I plan to attend a Green Day concert—another credit-crunching birthday treat. Erik drops me off and takes the kids for an early lunch at the Golden Arches. I ask him to be back in an hour.

I knock twice at Annee's door. She answers immediately, as if she's been standing right on the other side waiting for me.

"Hi Pamela. How are you?" she says and swings open the door. The room is dim with soft music and a scented candle burning on her desk. I guess it is kind of like a spa visit. As before, she is dressed casually in jeans, a tank top, and white socks.

"I'm fine. And you?"

"I'm doing well," she responds.

"Can I use your restroom before we get started?"

She points to a room down the hall and I quickly retreat behind the safety of the closed door. There is another scented candle burning. I'm thinking this place could burst into flames at any moment as I wash my hands and stare at my face in the mirror. I am unsure of which towel to use. This is an after effect of my mother's fondness for decorative show-towels far too nice to actually be used. I wipe my hands on a crumpled bath towel hanging from the shower door and take a deep breath. I'm nervous. Annee might know more about my life than I do, and that's a scary thought.

Annee searches for a CD on her desk to record our session. Unable to find one, she looks around in a closet and says calmly, "Pamela, your heart is beating really fast. Please try and relax and enjoy this, because it makes my heart race too." Oh, hell. How does she know that? On the surface, I look calm and relaxed. At least I did in the bathroom. But maybe I don't. Maybe my cool façade is as transparent as the veil that separates Annee from the spirit world. I take another deep breath, try to relax into the pillows of the wicker chair, and laugh nervously. I'm not fooling anyone.

Annee locates a stack of disks and inserts one into the hard drive. She takes a seat in the matching wicker chair and informs me that she needs to be quiet for just a minute. The table with the Tiffany lamp and a box of pink tissue separates us. I stare at my hands and try to suppress the nervous giggles that want to bubble up out of my throat. It's not that I think this is funny—I just want to fill the uncomfortable silence.

"First of all, you have someone linking in immediately. Once again, I need you to relax. When your heart beats, my heart beats. I feel some shakiness there."

A burst of laughter escapes. I cringe. She continues. Her speech is brisk and filled with explanations and questions. She asks me to respond.

"You are a tremendously busy spirit, a bit unbalanced they say, but that's not an insult from spirit. They want to talk to you a little bit about that. There's so much that came through for me in premeditation this morning. Now just one moment."

The first person to come through is Erik's father. I never met the man. He died when Erik was fifteen. Because Erik's parents were divorced, and the grass is always greener on the absentee's lawn, he idolized the man. The two of them look almost identical in pictures: tall, blue-eyed and wiry, with straight noses and dirty blonde hair. His father chain-smoked and mixed lead paint with his bare hands. He died at 52 from the dreaded C word. No surprise there. Ronald wants me to relay to Erik that, "He loves him and is very proud of him." Annee modifies this with, "Those words weren't spoken very much."

Annee continues. I answer her barrage of questions with a yes or a no, as instructed.

"You have two children? Did you have a miscarriage or abortion? I see you have more than two children. I see them all. A grandma just came in. Is that your mom's mom? She's embracing you today.

She says you are very much like her. She has a great deal of love for you. And you and your mom are close. You understand? She's happy for that because she says there is nothing stronger than a mother-daughter bond. It wasn't always like that, she said. Boy were you stern in your position in life when you came in."

I start to cry, grab a tissue and dab my cheeks. My responses become shorter and higher pitched. I need a breather, but when I only get a high priced hour of Annee's time, I feel kind of stuck here in this chair. I guess I could leave this room, but I don't want to. She sees the people I've lost. Grandma. And the children—the people—that died before they were born. Annee recognizes them for what they were. Why couldn't I?

Annee changes the subject, perhaps to give me a breather, but she makes an odd choice. "Is your dad okay?" she asks.

This question throws me for a loop. "Physically?" My voice creeps into high-pitched dolphin territory.

"I don't know. 'Cause I got his father linking in, your grandfather. I feel as if your father maintains the silence in the family. I really appreciate your dad. He reminds me of my own dad. You and your mom are so much alike, but you never want to recognize those things in each other."

I love my mom. I talk to her every day without fail. My dad? Not so much. To say that he maintains the silence in the family would be a pretty fair assessment, unless you happen to get him on poker, football or golf—three things I know nothing about. My dad speaks in a loud, booming voice. He is practically deaf, yet refuses to get a hearing aid. Whenever he opens his mouth, it always sounds like he's yelling. I've gotten used to it over the years and have forgiven him for the stretches of silence that could span the Grand Canyon. I see him maybe once a year. I constantly try to gain his approval by telling him about a pay raise, or a writing victory, but he's never impressed.

My mother always excused my father's parental inadequacies because both his parents died when he was young—his father of encephalitis and his mother of a brain aneurism. He was shuffled off to live with a cousin at sixteen. He joined the military two years later. It was there that he discovered he could make a week's wages with one lucky night at the card table. None of the men at the air force base could read his poker face. It helped that he had a mind for numbers and statistics. My mom found his silence alarming, but Grandma Lola reassured her with, "Still waters run deep."

My parents divorced when I was four. Growing up, I thought my dad didn't like me because he left, and was hardly ever around when I'd visit him in the summer. There is a picture of my dad and me that perfectly represents our relationship. It is the day of my baptism. In the photo, I am a wee little baby in a white dress. My dad is dressed in a blue suit. I am propped on his lap like a wobbly-headed pillow. Instead of holding me, his hands clutch the arms of the chair. I could have toppled over at any minute, but he seems almost oblivious to my presence.

He looks at the camera wearily with just the slightest hint of resentment in his eyes, like "I didn't sign up for another kid."

There was a poker game that he really wanted to be in and wouldn't you know it, my wacky mother wanted her last child to be 'united with Christ.' He was angry and it showed. I was a baby and didn't know the difference, but now I'm an adult, and I have photographic evidence that I wasn't wanted. No wonder I'm so well adjusted.

"They're saying you've established a different relationship with your father, and you've come to terms with a lot of things. That is a good thing, they say."

I guess. No need to pine over imagined hurts. I've accepted him. He's my dad. Even though it upsets me, we will never communicate our feelings. It just won't happen. I imagine that silence will make his death all the more painful.

From there, Annee moves into my exploration of death. I interviewed her about it, so it's not a big revelation when it comes out in the reading.

"They say that this book is a healing book. This thing you're creating is helping to heal your own spirit. In this lifetime, you have fears and you are overwhelmed by these fears. And that's why they're taking me back to your past lives. In your past two lives, you died rather tragically and suddenly."

Oh boy. Now it's getting a little too out there. She reveals that I killed myself in my last life and I made a contract to explore death in this one. Now why would a depressed suicidal person want to explore death in their next life? Wouldn't they opt for door number two, as maybe a super model or a game show hostess?

She also says that I fear losing my children. This resonates and I'm crying again. Annee tells me that I need to stop doing this. She tells me that the children I lost are here. It makes me uncomfortable that she mentions them. They weren't real children. They were never born.

"Do you want to know their sex?"

"Sure." I uncross my legs and lean forward. *How could she know this?*

"You have a boy and a girl now, right?" Another thing she knows that I haven't told her. She seems confused about the order of the children, and works it out with whoever is relaying this information to her. She mumbles "okay."

"Well, the first one was a girl and the second one was a boy. He is your son's spirit guide."

It finally hits me in a psychic's office in Pagosa Springs on my birthday: I have a lot more experience with death than I'd originally thought. I lost two children. I don't know what a spirit guide is, but I feel strangely comforted that the boy I never got to know has decided to stick around and watch after my son. Annee discusses my kids. "They're very happy and very well adjusted," she says.

Grandma Lola interrupts Annee to inform me that "I'm a really good parent." That's reassuring. I think I'm adequate, but I wouldn't nominate me for Mom of the Year—at least not this year. I've been off exploring death. While I've tried to make time for my kids and discuss what I'm doing, I certainly wouldn't want their friends or their friends' parents to know what I've been up to.--*So what does your mom do, Lola? --She's writing to death row inmates and she's gone all the time at the fire house.*

Everything I learn during my reading is oddly comforting and well worth the money. If Annee is correct, the people we've loved and lost watch over us. They are interested in our lives. They want to communicate with us. They will hang out with us when we die. That is all well and good, but I secretly hope they're not watching me shower.

As I leave, I tell Annee that I want to witness the birth of Dan and Heather's child, but I haven't asked them yet. She asks me if the baby is a girl. I say I don't know. It's too early in the pregnancy. As I gather my purse and Annee hands me the CD, she says that hospitals are powerful places, filled with portals for spirits to either enter or leave this world.

CHAPTER SIX

Be Present

Last night I dreamt of a giant spider. It was crawling with its black spindly legs on my bedroom floor while I cowered on my bed. I knew I'd never be able to shut my eyes and go to sleep until it was gone, but I was too afraid to catch it or kill it. This is a common dream of mine. Whenever I feel anxious about something, whether its public speaking or a plane ride among strangers, along comes a spider that sits down beside my subconscious. Right now, I'm afraid to talk about Tommy with Heather, but I have to. Heather holds the secret to what I've wanted to know all along: how does a person who has experienced the worst possible loss go about living?

I arrive at the salon at 3:40 for our 4:00 meeting. Heather is cutting an older woman's thin, graying hair as the woman's husband sits at the next station and watches.

"Do you have an appointment?" the receptionist asks.

Heather interjects proudly from behind her station. "She's interviewing me."

"Oh," the receptionist sniffs.

Heather finishes the woman's hair and removes the smock from around her neck. Like me, she doesn't want her hair styled. Heather walks over to the reception desk carrying a large tin box and places it on the counter. "It's in there," she says to the receptionist and waddles back to her station. In her fifth month of pregnancy, she now has a real live baby bump beneath her maternity shirt.

"What's in there?" I ask.

"A huge spider. I opened my cabinet to get the dryer and it was just sitting there."

I shiver and wish I was still dreaming. Out of the corner of my eye, I spot something floating down from the ceiling. I turn quickly, bracing for the spastic spider dance that will ensue should it land on me. It is a tiny white feather. I turn towards Heather, suddenly more afraid than I was. "Are you just going to leave it there on the counter?"

"Jan is going to take it outside."

A tall woman with a severe ponytail saunters up to the desk, grabs the box and steps outside. I can't muster the courage to watch the giant spider's release into the natural world. I just pray she doesn't do it anywhere near my car. If there is one thing that could make me lose control while driving, it is a wolf spider skittering across my dashboard and onto my lap.

The husband, even though he doesn't have an appointment, asks Heather if she wouldn't mind cleaning up his hair. It is already our meeting time, but Heather agrees. I don't mind the delay, as she could probably use the cash. Dan told me that their insurance wasn't going to pay for Tommy's life flight to Denver and those flights aren't cheap.

Staring at myself in one of the mirrors, I see that the gray is peeking out again. "When was my last color appointment?" Maintaining the façade of youth is becoming an expensive pain in the ass.

"It was the day before I had my car accident"

"Your what?" I shout into the now quiet salon. "Is everything okay?" *God, please let everything be okay.*

"Well, my car isn't okay. My stomach hit the middle console, so they backboarded me and took me to the hospital." Heather stretches her back and pats her belly. "I found out I'm having a girl."

Despite the excellent news and the correctness of Annee's prediction, I am not okay. I wish we could just talk about Tommy at the salon. I'd be more at ease here, but Heather wants to have this conversation at her house.

Instead of her sensible Subaru, Heather now drives a huge white truck with a wooden bed. She looks tiny and vulnerable as she climbs inside. I pull my Toyota up behind the truck and follow her towards the house. She drives a bit over the speed limit, as do I—normally—but today I have to remind my foot to press on the gas pedal.

When I pull into her driveway, I notice a prominent black-and-white address sign posted on a pine tree. The further I traverse the long, winding driveway that leads up to the house, the more my foot wants to abandon the gas pedal. I pull my car up next to the smashed body of Heather's Subaru and step outside into the cool fall air. Broken glass from her windshield litters the ground.

"Be careful," she says as I tiptoe among the glass and gravel towards the house.

I remind myself to tread carefully as I step into her sunny, wood-paneled kitchen. I am greeted by photographs of Dan and Tommy that decorate the fridge. Everything is neat and orderly, unlike my house, with its sink full of dishes and stacks of paper that sprout from every level surface. I plant myself at the kitchen table as a silent declaration: I don't want to venture too deep inside. Nobody cries in the kitchen.

"Would you like some tea or coffee or water or something?" she asks.

Actually, a vodka tonic would be nice right about now. I stare at the boxes of tea stacked on the stovetop and look for one with a calming effect. My heart is racing. I'm grateful that Annee isn't here to call me out on it. "Chamomile lavender sounds good."

Heather dons a heavy brown sweater before filling the teakettle. As always, I remain armored in my black hooded sweatshirt. The room is chilly, but I can feel the buildup of nervous sweat in my armpits. I place the recorder on the wooden table and dive headfirst into the most difficult question as we wait for the water to boil. "What I really want to know is, how you got through the death of your son."

"People I love in my life helped me through it." She dips her hands into the pockets of her sweater. "And I became more spiritual."

I look up from my notebook. My facial expression must imply *what do you mean?*

"Well, spiritual things started happening. For instance, at his funeral, Dan and his folks were in the car. We were all bawling. All of a sudden, all of us went quiet. We had the windows up but we could smell this intense smell of lilies in the car. So Dan and I, both at the same time turn to see if there are any flowers in the back of the car. And there weren't. Dan's mom said, 'Do you smell lilies?' And Dan and I were like, yes. Then all of us started laughing uncontrollably. We were so full of joy at that moment. And we just knew that he was there with us. That Tommy was there. That he would always be with us. And that one day, we would be with him. It was kind of a little bit of a weight off of me. Not that that million pound weight was completely lifted."

My eyes fill with tears as the kettle begins to steam. I'm determined not to reach for the fresh pack of Kleenex in my purse as Heather fills the mugs. She seems calm and relaxed. I'm the one off kilter.

"There have been other things that have happened like that." She warms her hands on the mug and looks toward the ceiling. "Feathers upon feathers upon feathers would appear out of nowhere. A couple of days after he died, we asked Tommy to send a feather, because we wanted to know if he'd crossed over and if he was okay. We had three little white feathers appear."

I suddenly remember the feather floating down from the salon ceiling. She explains that feathers symbolize guardian angels. I don't know what to say. Maybe Annee is right. Maybe we've got these spirits that hang around and help us out when we need it.

Heather tells me that after Tommy's funeral, they took a road trip to help figure things out. One of Dan's fantasy football league friends, a man he had never met personally, offered up his house in Port Saint Joe, Florida. Because of Heather's interest in symbols, I later look up Saint Joseph on the Internet. It turns out that he is the patron of the dying and—some sites indicate— of 'dying a happy death.'

On their way to Florida, Dan and Heather stopped in New Orleans to visit with a friend of Heather's mom, a woman by the name of Pam Johnson. Pam Johnson is my maiden name, and as she's telling me this story, I'm thinking about how weird that is. I feel like I'm meant to be sitting here. Pam is a medium, and she wanted to give Heather a reading. To prove that she was able to communicate with the spirit world, Pam said, "I talked to Tommy and he wanted me to tell you that he was buried with a really fuzzy blanket and a one-eyed monster stuffed animal." And he was.

Although the medium was correct about the blanket and the stuffed animal, I have to remind myself how ordinary it all is. Pam Johnson is a really common name. Birds and down coats are always losing their feathers, even at the end of summer. Lilies were most likely at the funeral and maybe an arrangement had been put in the car.

As Pam told Heather, "Tommy wanted us to realize that he was okay, and he was happy where he was, and the only sadness he ever experienced there was ours." Then the spirits spoke through Pam. Heather noticed a change in her voice. They told her that she and Dan "needed to choose the path together or move on our separate ways. But we needed to decide right away."

I don't want to, but I ask if there was a question about whether their marriage could survive. I'd read somewhere that divorce is eight times more likely when a couple loses a child.

"At first, I felt like maybe I couldn't go on with him. But then I knew we needed to be there for one another."

I blurt it out because I've wanted to ask this question from day one: "Did Dan feel responsible?"

She looks down at the table then back up at me. "At first, but he no longer feels that way."

"It was an accident," I offer. "Did you two get counseling?"

She says that they did, but it wasn't what helped them. "The biggest thing that has helped us through it is each other."

Having met them, I would have to agree. Both of them are honest and open. They want to move forward. They want to help people. Hell, they want to help me, a complete stranger, understand. That takes courage. I realize that Heather has done her best to make sense of her son's death in a senseless world. What parent wouldn't? I would probably go over every minute detail to see what I did wrong. What if I did this? What if I didn't do that? But it was an accident.

"It was such a strange day. We did whatever Tommy wanted. If he wanted to read a book, we read a book. If he wanted to go outside, we went outside. He sat on my lap for about an hour and a half and just cuddled. It's like he knew ahead of time and he was saying goodbye to me. He wouldn't take a nap that day. He would not eat a thing with me. He wouldn't eat till Dan got home. Every time I tried to feed him, he'd refuse. He'd tell me he was hungry and I'd go to feed him and he wouldn't eat."

That night, Heather went to visit her best friend for a night of movies and cards. Dan and Tommy stayed home to watch the game.

"This was the first time I had ever left my cell phone at home" she tells me.

After several attempts calling her uncharged phone, Dan dialed her friend's home number. His only words to Heather were, "Tommy's not breathing."

Heather sped towards home. "I'm just screaming and praying the whole time, yelling at God, screaming, crying, saying 'Take me right now. Please don't take him."

When she got near her house, a helicopter was sitting in the middle of the highway.

"There were cars backed up for a mile or so. I just went around the cars and got in the oncoming line of traffic and a volunteer firefighter stopped me and she said, 'Ma'am, ma'am, you can't' and I said, 'That's my baby!' Tommy was in the ambulance being, um, they were still trying to resuscitate him and as soon as I jumped on the ambulance, someone said, 'I think it's time we called it.' And I said 'No! Get him in that helicopter right now and get him to Mercy.' And so they said okay and they put him on the helicopter and flew him to Mercy."

"What was Dan doing?" I ask quietly.

"When I got there Dan was totally calm. He was on the ambulance holding Tommy's hand telling him to 'stay with us.' But he said prior to that he'd been screaming and lying in the ditch. He told me that later. So they're loading him up on the helicopter and we just have our arms wrapped around each other and we have the chaplain with his arms around us praying over us. And the next thing I remember we're in a car with our landlords and they're driving us to the hospital. The next thing I remember is screaming and sobbing on my way into the hospital and some bitch nurse says to me, 'You need to calm down.' The next thing I remember, I'm in the hospitality room and Dr. Zemach is coming in. He comes in and he has this look on his face and I just start freaking out all over again, saying no, no, no, no, no, no. Just no! He comes up to me. He kneels down and puts his hands on my lap and gets real close to me and he just says, 'Okay, shhh. Settle down. We need to talk about this,' and he said, 'We were able to get Thomas' heart beating again. We gave him some drugs, but the thing is, he can't breathe on his own and he keeps needing to be resuscitated over and over again.' And he said, 'We have two options. One is to unhook him from the machines and you sit and hold him while he dies or—even though he wasn't breathing for a very, very long time and oxygen wasn't getting to his brain for probably about 45 minutes or longer—you can hope for a miracle and fly him, flight for life him to Denver to the Children's Hospital, or you can sit with him and we can unhook him.'

Despite the direness of the situation, Heather hopes for a miracle. Dan has left the hospital to retrieve her purse, pack a bag, and to get their insurance information. She is alone.

"This man comes out of one of the emergency rooms. I don't know who he was there with or what, but he comes up to me and he puts his arm around me and he pulls down his shirt and he has this big scar and he just takes me in his arms and says, 'you need to pray for a miracle.' He said, 'I died for 50 minutes and I came back and I'm fine, so there is such a thing as a miracle happening. You are so right to get him on that plane to Denver, and you need to do that.' That made my decision right then and there."

Tommy was flown to Denver. Heather accompanied him while Dan drove. Shortly after arriving at Children's, Tommy died.

After New Orleans, where they met Pam Johnson, Heather and Dan drove to Graceland, a place they had never been. In their living room, they have a picture, kind of like an Andy Warhol rendition of the 'King', that Tommy would look at and say, "Hi, Daddy." Tommy's middle name is Blue. Heather explains, "I knew he was gonna have big blue eyes and I wanted to choose a name out of the blue. With Elvis, the color blue is often associated with him."

When she says this we laugh and start recalling the blue songs of Elvis: *Blue Christmas, Blue Eyes Crying in the Rain, Blue Hawaii, Blue Moon, Blue Moon of Kentucky, Blue River, Blue Suede Shoes.*

"The next day after leaving Graceland, we turn on the Sirius XM, and there was a song on there, *Daddy Don't Cry* by Elvis. The song is about a child whose father is grieving over the loss of his wife. One of the lines is "Daddy, you've still got me and Tommy." Dan was driving at the time. He pulled over on the side of the road and lost it."

Heather reveals that the second year has been harder than the first. "I don't know. Maybe it's because it has finally sunk in. All I know is I had a hard time crying in the first year. Initially I cried a lot, and then I felt like my tears dried up."

"Maybe it's because you're pregnant," I say. "I know when I've been pregnant, I used to cry all the time." The minute this sentence escapes my lips, I realize I'm trying to solve her grief, make it more understandable, instead of letting her experience it.

"I cry about him constantly." Heather looks so small and vulnerable as she says this. Dan is on a trip up to Denver today. She is joining him tomorrow, but I worry about her being alone in this house tonight. She admits that she feels more alone since she's become pregnant. Friends aren't as quick to come around or call.

I can relate. Pregnancy is hard with all the body changes, the weepiness, and the fact that you can't do anything fun like smoke or drink a pot of coffee if you're tired. Hell, there are books out there that tell you not to think bad thoughts or they will affect your unborn child. This generation is so spooked about bringing babies into the world. Sure, there are things that are bad for baby, like heroin, crack or too much alcohol, but then I think of my own mom who said, "I used to drink 7&7's when I was pregnant with all my kids. We just didn't know any better."

I ask if they've picked out a name.

"Her name is going to be Marion. We're still arguing about the middle name. I would like her middle name to be Grace."

"For Graceland?"

She laughs. "No. I thought I was gonna lose her in that accident. But by the grace of God, she's still here."

As I prepare to leave, Heather hugs me and says, "This was really helpful for me. Thank you."

I have a hard time believing that my presence has been helpful, but what do I know? Maybe the simple act of listening is more of a gift than I realized. Despite my track record, I didn't run. I didn't change the subject. I just listened and tried to keep my mouth shut. I wish I would have asked about being present at the birth, which I'm hoping is the happy ending to my journey, but this conversation wasn't about me, and it was going so well that I didn't want to change the subject. It's a big request, and both Dan and Heather should probably be present when I spring that question.

*   *   *

Just when everything seems to be going well, Spooky decides to stop eating. The last two mornings, I have placed a fresh can of his favorite wet food in his dish, but he would just sniff at it and walk away. By the end of the day, his food became an untouched, hard crusty mound.

Most of his days are spent behind the television. I read somewhere that cats like to hide when the end is near. Since they are prideful animals, they don't want anyone staring at them as they struggle for their last breath. There may be a more Darwinian explanation to that—the animal is weak and needs to protect themselves from predators—but I prefer my own version. Cats do whatever the hell they want and they certainly don't want to fetch, sit, roll over or play dead. They just croak when nobody is looking.

I wake up knowing that this is going to be the day. Busy schedule, work demands, kids' karate lessons will all have to be postponed. Spooky needs my help to go home to that big catnip/tuna farm in the sky. I hop on the treadmill at 5:30 as I usually do, but a fit of uncontrollable crying gets in the way. I stay on for 20 minutes, running, crying and gasping for breath.

I wake Erik at 6 with a cup of coffee and a pained expression. "We need to do it today."

Erik knows that I am not a part of the "we" in that equation. I was present with our last cat, but this time, I can't bring myself to be there. It's too painful. I want to remember Spooky how he used to be, not cowering at the vet's office. I dislike emotional scenes in front of strangers as much as cats dislike shots. Death is such a private and personal event. For me, that is the appeal of hospice: dying at home. If a vet would make house calls, it would take so much fear and anxiety out of an already horrible situation.

Erik brings Spooky to the Humane Society, a place that is actually pretty far from being humane. They kill animals all the time, whether they're sick or not. Our vet was booked, and Spooky will end up there anyway, as they also house the county crematorium. Call me crazy, but I don't want any of my cats to decompose with yogurt containers and coffee grounds in some dumpster or landfill. I will now have four tin can urns with all my cat's names labeled on the side. At some point in the future, we will plant a tree in our yard and co-mingle their ashes in the ground. This is sort of for my own benefit, as none of my cats were tree-climbing, outdoor-loving types. They liked it on the deck when it was sunny, in front of the heater in the winter, or near my head while I slept. But I'm not going to memorialize them in any of those places. I already have enough cat remnants throughout my house: a leather love seat that was loved the minute it was brought into the house, the faint smell of urine in certain areas of the carpeting, and vomit stains that will never go away.

All my cat friends have died. I'm crushed.

* * *

I am seated in the hospice office, waiting for Pat Amthor, a hospice nurse, to show up for work. As usual, I'm early. Nancy, an office assistant who wears many hats, informs me that I am "going to have a lot of fun with Pat." Fun? Fun is not a word I would use to describe visiting the dying.

Just as I'm contemplating my own ideas of what would constitute a fun outing on a Friday morning, Pat walks up to me with a big grin on her face. "You must be Pam." She shakes my hand vigorously. "I have to do a few things before we can get going." And with that she's off like a tornado of goodwill.

Since I'm in no rush to get to the nursing home, I relax into my chair and observe. She stops and greets everyone in the office, either hugging them or gathering their papers, sometimes both. She even flirts with the chaplain. She is a multi-tasker who manages to pay attention to people and their needs. It's quite obvious she cares and that people like being in her presence.

On our drive to the nursing home, Pat tells me that she became a nurse in her 40's. "I really wanted to be a librarian, but my mom thought I'd make a good nurse."

She is now 63, but she doesn't seem, dare I say it, old. She styles her short gray-and-white hair in a stylishly messy, spiky 'do. Silver horses dangle from her ears, while a long turquoise necklace nestles in her cleavage. She wears a dark purple t-shirt with new black jeans and high-tech orange walking shoes.

Our first stop is the nursing home. We are there to visit an older female patient. I ask Pat what the woman is suffering from.

"She's got a terminal case of old age."

I crack up as we head inside. Five elderly people in wheelchairs have been planted around a well-stocked aquarium. Three of them are asleep. This scene is so sad, I can hardly stand it. I pray to God I don't end up being boarded at a nursing home to stare at a fish tank until I die.

Pat checks in at the front desk and then leads me down the hall. Her patient's room is empty.

"Let's check the activity room." Pat stops and talks to several people along the way, their faces lighting up when they see her. "Yep, there she is." She zips into the funny-smelling room, bringing it a desperately-needed dose of life.

I peer through the window as Pat retrieves the woman from a large circle of people listening to a group leader as she speaks in a loud, booming voice about "dog week." I had no idea there was such a thing. Despite this being the activity room, half the people are passed out. Some heads are bent forward, resting on their chests, others lean back with their mouths open, and some are tilted to the side. They should rename this place the communal snoozing room. It's 9 in the morning. Shouldn't people be peppier?

Pat leads the woman into the dining hall and we all take a seat at a Formica table. Pat informs her patient that she has brought a volunteer. The old woman extends her bony hand, and I shake it as lightly as I can.

"You have cold hands," she whispers. A line of oxygen is affixed to her nose.

"You know what they say: cold hands, warm heart." *Or maybe it's poor circulation from too many cigarettes.*

The woman smiles and turns to Pat. "Where are you from?" They've met before, but I assume that the woman has dementia.

"I'm from Colorado. What about you?"

"I'm from Pennsylvania. *Sprechen sie Deutsche?*"

"Oh, are you German?" Pat touches the woman's hand.

The woman pauses and thinks about it. "No. I'm Polish."

"Do you feel pain anywhere?" Pat checks the woman's ankles for swelling.

"No."

"Do you like pierogies?"

The woman replies with a smile. "Yes," she inhales, as if she can smell them.

"Did you used to make them?"

"No. My mother did." Her cloudy blue eyes wander off to the right.

Since I don't know what else to say, I tell the woman that her hair looks nice. And it does: white and full and softly curled. I hope my hair looks that good when I'm suffering from old age.

Pat listens to the woman's heart and her lungs as a top forty song plays over the loudspeakers. I find this music selection kind of odd. It must be for the staff, since Benny Goodman, Elvis or maybe Hank Williams might be more fitting for the clientele. When Pat finishes, she holds the woman's hand and tells her that she'll be back to see her on Monday. She wheels her back to the activity room, where the loud woman is still talking about dogs.

Our next stop is a private home. This particular home is beautiful, resplendent with every amenity you can imagine. I'd give you more detail, but I'm bound not to give away a patient's identity with particulars. Some I've changed. Like this one: a sweet yellow lab greets us as we enter the fabulous house. An equally-sweet woman in her late forties soon follows. Her mother is in need of Pat's care. The daughter has lots of questions, and seems breathless and worried.

We pad quietly toward the patient's room. Her hospital bed is situated near a window that overlooks a beautifully-landscaped lawn sprinkled with aspen trees. Family pictures from younger days sprinkle the shelf. Bottles of medication line the dresser like sentinels. The mother is peacefully asleep under a thick fleece blanket, but the daughter attempts to wake her. "Mom, Pat is here."

The mom opens her eyes slowly. The room is so bright that I want to shield her eyes or lend her my sunglasses. The daughter smiles down at her ailing mother with a look of gratitude.

"Good morning," the daughter says sweetly. "Would you like something to drink?"

The daughter adjusts the height of the bed, and then lifts a glass of water to her mother's lips. She drinks slowly from the straw.

"Do you want some coffee?"

The mom nods. I could use a cup myself, but I keep my pie-hole shut. I think the daughter is a little freaked out that I'm here in her private home. I can't say that I blame her.

Pat places her hand on the woman's wrist to check her pulse. She then listens to her heart and lungs and tells her to "take a big breath." I stand by the doorway, out of the patient's line of vision. Pat checks her legs for bruising, checks her ankles for fluid, and pats her on the arm. "How are you feeling?'

"I've felt better." Her voice is barely audible.

The dog sniffs my hand as I watch the three women in front of the window. He knows something is up in this room and wants permission to enter. I look down at him, smile and pat his golden fur.

Pat lets her know that she'll be by on Monday to visit. The mom nods and turns to the window. Outside, the aspen trees are losing their bright yellow leaves across the green lawn.

"Looks like winter's coming," says Pat.

"I know," the mother says, and closes her tired eyes.

As Pat pulls into the hospital parking lot, I feel giddy that I've conquered a fear—I've spent time with the dying. As I exit her Jeep, I thank her profusely for letting me tag along. I ask if she would be open to me riding along with her again. She says it would be fine with her and she's off. Since I've got two hours to kill before I have to be home, I drive to the local funeral home to confront yet another fear. The dead.

I dial several people for moral support as I watch the front door of the funeral home. The street is jam-packed with cars—a sure sign of a funeral going on at this very moment. A woman dressed in black exits the front door and strolls down the street. I feel like a stalker just sitting here. Finally, I reach my friend Audra, who convinces me to get out of the car and go inside like a normal person.

"Just do it. What's the worst thing that could happen?" she says in her thick New York accent.

I can think of a lot of things. But I hang up, exit the car, and walk in with a sense of purpose. When I push the door open, a youngish man in a suit greets me.

"Well hey there," I say, a bit surprised.

"I saw you coming."

"Are you the owner?"

"Yes, I'm Ryan," he says with a hint of trepidation, despite the smile on his face. He probably thinks I want to sell him something.

I give him the whole run-down: I contacted him months before in an email (his preferred method of communication), I'm in graduate school, and I want to talk to people that work with death.

He looks at me wearily and says, "So what exactly are you wanting?"

"Really, I just want to hear your story. Like, why you became a funeral director? That kind of thing. I'm not writing an exposé on the funeral industry or anything. I just want to know why you got into this line of work and what your day-to-day life is like." The fact that I've barged into a funeral home uninvited is so unlike me. What's even more unlike me is that I'm not going to leave Hood Mortuary until he shows me around.

"Oh." He relaxes.

After giving him my contact information to relay to the staff, I ask if he'll give me a tour. He agrees and I follow him through the house, mesmerized by the rich, dark wood and fabulous ornate detail on every window and door. He points upstairs and informs me that he lives with his wife and daughter on the third floor. The other two floors hold a chapel, small conference rooms, a casket room, an urn room, and several bathrooms. There are boxes of tissue on every level surface. When we reach the prep room, he tells me that he can't take me inside because they are performing an organ donation at that very moment. I quickly scan the clipboard on the wall and see that it is an eye donation.

When I get home, I check the obituary page. A young woman died the day before, so I figure she must be the donor. I think of my friend Katie, who says that she'll donate her organs, but she wants to keep her eyes.

"For what?" I asked her.

"I don't know. I guess so I can see Heaven."

Whether or not we get to keep our vital organs in the afterlife, in the here and now, we still look towards the Heavens for something more spectacular than our earthly concerns.

CHAPTER SEVEN

Dig a Hole

The crisp leaves of Colorado aspen trees crunch beneath my feet as I walk to my communal mailbox at the bottom of Forest Lakes. It's a beautiful autumn day. Halloween decorations cover the 'Don't Feed the Bears' sign affixed to the side of the mailbox shelter. I turn the key and pull a solitary letter out into the daylight. The standard envelop is adorned with block capitals—Khristian Oliver's handwriting.

My hands tremble. It's been months since I received his polite refusal to speak with me. I walk solemnly to my car, get in and lock the door out of habit, and carefully open the envelope.

10/6/2009

Dear Pamela,

Did you ever find anyone to help you with your thesis? If not, I will, I know I declined at first but today my attorney says I don't stand much of a chance of getting any relief and my execution date is for Nov. 5th. So if you'd like, send me a list of

questions you'd like answered or whatever you had planned. If
you don't need me that's cool too, just thought I'd offer. :)
   Take Care,
   Khristian Oliver

Tears stream down my face, and I'm afraid someone will tap
on my window to see if I'm okay. I want to hide or zoom off in
my tiny Toyota, but I'm paralyzed by a sense of impending doom.
I don't know what it is—the obvious lack of hope, or the fact that
Khristian ends his devastating letter with a hand-drawn smiley
face. I can't believe how callously I boasted to anyone within ear-
shot that I planned on attending his execution—not because I
wanted him to die, but because it seemed like something a real
writer would do.

I will never fully grasp the gravity of his situation with the exchange of a few letters. I have to go to Texas.

Meeting him will be problematic on several levels. First there's
the matter of bureaucracy in prisons. The Polunsky Unit is a max-
imum security death row facility, not some podunk county jail
that might bend the rules if I bribe the front desk person with a
pie. I'm not on Khristian's visitors list and I'm pretty sure that
they won't let him change it at the last minute. Last, but certainly
not least, there's the matter of my own finances. My credit cards
are maxed out, and I don't have an hour of vacation time at work.
It would be impulsive, not to mention stupid, to just fly off to
Texas without anything in place. I don't know how I'm going to
make it work—but I do know that the longer I wait, the more expensive it will become.

During the drive up the mountain to my home, my mind races
with possibilities. I dash through the front door, grab a legal pad
from the mound of books, bills and notes littering my desk, and
retreat upstairs to the cleanliness of my kitchen table. I scribble
questions to Khristian without much thought, just urgency. The
words flow onto the page as fast as my pen can write them. Only
now that I'm writing this book do I wish I'd composed this letter

on my computer, so that I'd have a written record of what I'd said to him. At the time, typed words on stark white paper seemed too impersonal. After a nondescript close, I call my mom, the only person who won't think I'm crazy for feeling sorry for a death row inmate. She can't believe it.

"I have to get to Texas, Mom. It's the only way I'll get to talk to him before he dies."

"How much are the tickets?"

I race down the stairs and check flights from Durango to Austin on my computer. Houston would be closer to Huntsville, where Kristian will be executed, but I have to fly in to Austin. Jenny, my best friend from junior high, just happens to live there—and there is no way I can make this trip without a friend nearby.

My answer appears. "Two hundred and forty dollars. That's pretty cheap, considering."

"You better get it now before it goes up. Do you want to borrow my card?"

I am both overwhelmed and guilt-ridden over my mother's generosity. It seems totally crazy and premature to buy this ticket, but that doesn't seem to stop me lately. Khristian has his date, and now I have mine: I fly out on November 3.

While I wait for Khristian's response, I try and figure out a backup plan—people I can interview so that this trip won't be a complete waste if I'm not allowed visitation privileges. My immediate thought is the executioner. I wonder how he—and I guess I'm being a total sexist here, because I assume the executioner is a man—feels about his job? Especially now that there are so many people exonerated after DNA evidence has proven their innocence. But I know even before I contact the prison that the executioner will be off limits. If the general public knew his identity, it would disrupt the machinery of death. The person pulling the switch or pushing the button is taking part in the most pre-meditated murder possible. How could that one person be exempt from the ramifications of their actions? They can't. So nobody knows. And that's the only way it can work: veiled in secrecy.

I imagine this person walking around the prison in a black hooded cloak with a voice-changing apparatus. Kind of like Darth Vader. No one dares to look at him as he stalks the bleach-scented hallways of the death house—not out of fear, but relief: *thank God it's not me that has to kill someone.*

Days pass without a reply. I am beyond antsy. The man is dying. Couldn't they let him call me? To make some headway, I pitch a story idea to the Houston Chronicle as a way of securing a media pass to the prison—the only other option for meeting Khristian should I not make his visiting list. One of the reporters I speak with says that if I manage to get an interview with the executioner, he wants to be present when it happens. He's kidding, of course, as it's never going to happen. My naïve optimism probably reminds him of his younger reporting days. As it turns out, the Chronicle isn't interested in a story about Khristian, or at least not one told from my perspective.

I've been so consumed with Khristian's upcoming execution that I forgot to pick up Spooky's ashes from the Humane Society. I think I've finally reached the point where I won't break down because he's dead. It will still be weird when some random person hands me his unrecognizable remains. I don't know how I'll react.

I venture in on my lunch hour and instead of stopping at the front desk, I breeze on in to the main cat room to see the real, live cats. The tiled room smells of urine and heavy duty cleaning products. Most of the kittens meow and beckon me with their paws stuck through the metal wires, while the older cats slumber or stare out of their cage with stoic indifference. It is heartbreaking to witness so many animals in need of a forever home. Like the men and women on death row, their days are numbered. This is a kill shelter.

I stop in front of the kitten cage, which is occupied by five black cats and a grey tabby. The black cats clamor for my attention, jutting their tiny front paws with razor sharp claws between the wires of the cage. If only they knew that this behavior is more of a deterrent than an attraction. The lone tabby sits on a carpeted ledge and eyes her crazy cage mates below. She looks wearily into my eyes and blinks. As I move to the next cage, she jumps from her perch and joins the bustling, whining crowd at the metal gate. I return to the crazy kittens and study her adoption card posted above it. The shelter has given her the name Fifi—a name befitting a pampered poodle, not a fierce feline with amber eyes, large ears, stripes and random dots that cover her like a leopard/tiger mix. Her tiny belly is shaved, but she looks too young to be fixed. I open the metal gate and grab her while attempting to push the remaining fevered felines towards the back. An older woman steps over to help me.

I take "Fifi" to the corner of the room and settle in to one of the metal chairs. Her delightful fur is as soft as a rabbit's, and she allows me to cradle her in my arms like a baby. She is calm and snuggly, kneading my arm with her paws. *You're mine*, she's telling me in kitty language. I'm a sucker for small furry things that need me, and if she plays her cards right, she might be able to escape the chaos of her young life. It has been fifteen years since I've adopted a kitten. Twenty since I adopted my first cat, Spooky. I'd forgotten how tiny and adorable they are. I don't want to put her back in the cage and debate about going back to work. I want to save her. A vet tech enters the room, looks at the two of us and says, "Awwww."

"I want to adopt her. What do I need to do?" The words just escape me. My intention of a cat-free existence is now over. Erik will just have to deal with it. I adopt Fifi and call him after the papers have been signed to inform him of our new family member. He is not particularly pleased, and thinks it's not the best decision to bring another cat home. Not because of the heartache that will eventually ensue when she dies, but because I've finally stopped needing my asthma inhaler at night. I convince myself that Erik will be swayed once he meets her. When we met, I had four grown cats with personalities and allegiances set in stone. He never got to witness their evolution or be a part of their young lives. With Fifi, or whatever we end up naming her, I am absolutely certain that he, along with our dog, will fall in love. That's my plan, anyway.

Even with the exciting allure of our new feline family member, renamed Judy, my thoughts are never far from my trip to Texas. Since an interview with an executioner is out, I decide to pursue the only other people who are inside the death chamber at the time of the execution: the warden and the state-assigned chaplain. An author who has written extensively about prison suggests I speak with Jim Willett, the former warden of Huntsville. After a little Internet research, I find out that he is now serving as the director of the Texas Prison Museum there. I call the museum, expecting to be transferred to a voice mail with a possible return phone call a week later, but Willett answers immediately. His deep resonant voice has Texas written all over it. His phone manner is pleasant and friendly. He is so accommodating to my interview request, even requesting a time in the afternoon so that we've both had lunch, that I have to remind myself that he took part in 89 executions. He agrees to meet on Wednesday, November 4th.

The state assigned chaplain isn't quite as easy. I leave a voice message, send an e-mail, and it is mid-October before I hear back from Richard Lopez, one of the two men who offer spiritual support for the men and women facing execution in Texas. He is hesitant and says he needs to get my request cleared with someone above him. He promises to call me back in a week. Since he's in the business of promoting God, I have faith that he will be true to his word.

I, however, am not a churchgoing person. The following Sunday, I take Lola into town to look for a car. I want to trade in my Toyota in hopes of lowering my monthly payments for something used and less expensive. Snow is in the forecast and I can't face another winter driving a car that has the heft of a roller skate. Besides, nothing is clinically proven to treat anxiety like 300 horsepower and all-wheel drive. I discover that Durango is a dry dealership town. No one is open. Angry, I drive the thirty miles back home, bolt up my driveway, and call to Erik, who is cutting down a tree across the street from our house. He can't hear me over the buzz of the chainsaw, so I retreat inside to tackle a little cleaning.

As I wash the last dish and place it in the metal rack, Erik bounds up the stairs and into the kitchen. He motions for me to follow him downstairs.

"Why?"

"Just come on." He is insistent—and whatever it is, he doesn't want the kids to see. Lola is engrossed in a drawing at the kitchen table and Nik is glued to Nickelodeon. I slowly follow him down the stairs, afraid of what will meet us.

"What is going on?" I say, clutching the handrail.

Frantically, he waves me towards our front door, exasperated by my stubbornness. At this point, he knows I won't take another step until he tells me what's up.

"It's Kiki."

"What happened?"

My heart races. With squinted eyes I slowly walk towards the garage, bracing myself for the worst. Kiki is in her normal spot, but a dark puddle of crimson is pooled beneath her body. Her belly is ripped open and her back leg is broken. She looks up at me with mournful eyes, eyes that say, *look what I've gone and done now.* I can't bear to meet them. She attempts to rise to her feet as I sprint back into the house. Erik follows me in. Lola is on the other side of the door.

"What's going on?" Lola asks.

"Kiki's hurt real bad," Erik says.

"Is she okay?" Lola cries. Kiki is Lola's dog.

Erik looks down at Kiki. She was running loose and got hit by a vehicle while he was busy cutting down a tree. Somehow she made it back to the garage. "I'm going to take her to the vet." His voice is calm and serious. Our daughter's reaction will be influenced by our own, so I try to hold it together. He takes Lola's hand and they walk out to the garage together.

I watch from the window as Erik scoops Kiki into his arms and places her gently into the back hatch of his car. When Lola comes back into the house, I do my best to sound optimistic, but I know in my heart this will not end well. Erik drives slowly down the steep incline of our driveway, literally carrying the heavy burden for both of us. I feel horrible that I didn't comfort my dog. I didn't even say goodbye. This whole year of trailing death has been a waste. I can't face death. I did exactly what I always do: panic and avoid.

Erik arrives home two hours later. He removes his blood-stained shirt and begins to dig a hole in our backyard. I don't know what to say or do, so I just stand there and watch. Nik and Lola join us.

Erik hands me the shovel. "I can't do this by myself. Kiki was a member of our family. I think we should all help dig her grave."

I scoop as much as I can and hand the shovel to Lola, who is amazingly composed. Nik can barely manage the shovel, so Erik helps him. As Erik finishes, I run upstairs and gather the four tins that contain the ashes of my cats. If we're going to bury Kiki, we might as well honor the other animals we've lost. We gather near Erik as he places the industrial-strength trash bag that contains Kiki's body into the ground.

As he buries her, I place the four small tins in the hole. I take Lola and Nik's hands in my own. This is a moment that both of them will remember, and they look up to me for guidance. How do we grieve? Do we cry? Can we be mad at our dog for chasing a truck? Can we be mad at ourselves for not having the two thousand dollars it would have taken to save her life? Yes.

With all the strength he can muster, Erik pushes a boulder on top of the soft mound of dirt to prevent wild animals from disturbing her grave. He digs in his jeans pocket, pulls out her collar and places it on top of the rock. Lola sobs, and I hug her close to my body. Snot is running from my nose, but there's nothing I can do about it now. Nik and Erik complete the circle of sadness.

I breathe deeply and try to come up with something profound to say, something one might say at a funeral, but words fail me. This loss is so unexpected. All I manage is, "She was a good dog."

*   *   *

Three days later I receive Khristian Oliver's response to my letter.

Dear Pamela,

I don't know if I'll be allowed to call you or not—we're supposed to be allowed phone calls but I haven't had one in 8 or 9 years. I would love to visit with you on Nov. 4th. If you come as media you can visit from 12 to 5 but if not I'll put you on my visitor's list and you can come from 9 to 12. I'll put you on my list just to be on the safe side. I have room.

While I'm at it I'll answer your questions but feel free to ask them when you come see me. Just know that I likely have no profound answers for you.

How does it feel to know the date of my death? Well, it's kinda scary but also exciting. I believe in the Lord so I have faith He'll be there to welcome me on the other side. Spiritually, I don't want to lose any part of myself—I want to retain my soul as it is now. (Just without the body)

Am I doing anything differently? No.

Have I retained hope that my ruling will be overturned? Not at this time, its still a little early, I won't know anything until the 5th of November.

Am I religious? No—but I am spiritual, I don't care for church dogma.

Have I given any thought to the after life? Of course.

Have I experienced any loss in being close to a fellow inmate who was executed? No—I try to keep to myself in here. Seeing people come and go so much has numbed me to the carnage going on.

Who did I pick to be at my execution? My parents, my sister and brother and niece.

Are they having a hard time of it? Yes, but they hide it well.

Why did I pick them? Because they've been with me from the beginning.

Well, I hope you no longer give up on your thesis. I'll get this in the mail to you.

Sincerely,

Khristian Oliver

While I am relieved that my visitation with Khristian is now confirmed, I can't bring myself to think about him for too long. It's too much sadness on top of everything else. I need to focus on my family, especially Erik. When he crawled into bed last night, I could smell that he was in the clutches of nicotine again. One of us is now off the wagon and if history repeats itself, it won't be long before I join him.

October of 2009 is turning out to be a horrible month. First Spooky, then Kiki, and now one of my greatest fears is coming true. Huge clumps of dyed black hair collect in my shower drain every morning. I pull the evidence out of the tub, wrap the disgusting black flurry clump in a wad of toilet paper and bury it in the trashcan. I don't want Erik to see the evidence, although it's becoming apparent by just looking at me. Even Heather pointed out that my hair was getting thinner at my last dye appointment. "But it's just in the front," she said, as if that made it a better, more tolerable kind of balding pattern. In an effort to cheer me up, she thought it would be fun to color my strands a blue-black, semi-permanent tint. The result isn't very fun. It just makes the hair loss that much more noticeable against the whiteness of my scalp.

In desperation, I book an appointment with a dermatologist. She scrutinizes my head like a mother chimp inspecting her flea-ridden offspring.

"Your scalp looks good."

As she rakes her bony fingers through my hair, I watch in horror as strand after strand falls to the floor.

"It comes out pretty easy."

I stare up at her blankly as she tugs and pulls at my hair.

"But it's quite normal to lose about a hundred hairs a day," she says. She stands back and evaluates me. "You know, to me it isn't noticeable, but then you know your hair better than I do."

I don't know if this is the doctor or the woman in her speaking. But yeah, I do know my hair, and it's falling out of my head at an alarming rate, especially now that she's messed with it. She hands me a brochure on hair loss. My options are some sort of steroid injection into my scalp, Nioxin, or I can try to relax and wait it out. She asks if I've had any stressful events happen in the last six months. I rattle off the death of my cat, the death of my dog, entering into odd situations with strangers and confronting my fear of death.

"I think it's safe to say this loss might be a result of life events."

Or it could be the hair dye at the new salon. I ask my friend Katie if she would call Lisa Marie for me. I want, or should I say, I need an appointment with her. I feel guilty as hell for doing it, but I long for the easy familiarity I had with my former hairdresser. My hair needs a cut, and so does my stress level. Katie gets me an appointment for the next day, which is akin to a miracle.

Walking into the old salon feels surreal. The young, hip receptionist greets me as if it has only been six weeks, not six months, since I last stepped foot inside the door. I decline her offer of a drink and plop down on the couch as Lisa Marie blow-dries another client's hair.

When it is finally my turn, my sense memory kicks in, and I feel as if I've never left. The lighting is good. Eighties music plays in the background. Lisa Marie is chipper and chatty. After securing a cape around my neck, she inspects my hair, lifting and sorting through different areas of my head. A concerned look crosses her face.

"Your hair's really dry, Pam. Has she been using a permanent color on you?"

"I think she said it was demi-permanent."

She lifts a lock and rubs it between her fingers. "No, this is permanent. Look how dark it is at the ends."

I believe her. She's been working with hair for almost twenty years. As she cuts my sparse strands, she explains that what I have been given is a standard straight-out-of-beauty-school cut that doesn't really work with my hair texture.

"See the difference, when I cut it like this?" She swirls my chair around to show the receptionist, who agrees. And she's right. When Lisa finishes fussing with my hair, it looks more like its old self. I pay for the expensive cut and book an appointment to be back in six weeks. I feel guilty for abandoning Heather, but now more than ever, I need confidence. I will meet a dying man in less than a week.

Part

"The fear of death follows from the fear of life.
A man who lives fully is prepared to die at any time."
—MARK TWAIN

CHAPTER EIGHT

Surrender

The day before I leave for Texas, I receive another letter from Khristian.

Dear Pamela,
Please call ***-***-**** to contact my family to schedule your visit on the 4th with their visit. I put you on my visitor's list. :) I look forward to seeing you!
Sincerely,
Khristian Oliver

Oh, great. Now, why would he make me call his family? Does he actually think I know what I'm doing? *Hello, my name is Pamela Skjolsvik and you don't know me and neither does your son, but he agreed to talk with me the day before the state of Texas kills him, so um, can I take the 9 to 10 slot or would you prefer if I spoke to him later in the day?* Talk about an awkward conversation.

Before I can chicken out, I dial their number. Thankfully, it's an answering machine. I state my name and that I'm a graduate student who is writing about Khristian for my thesis. I also say that I'll be visiting with him on Wednesday for a brief time. I'm hoping that I sound somewhat official so they don't freak out. *Yeah, right.*

When I first picked Khristian off of the TDCJ website, I had no idea about his family, nor did I think it would matter. But now that he's agreed to meet with me, Googling his name brings up articles about his parents, who are both artists from Waco, Texas. His father Kermit still moonlights at the United States Post Office while spending his days designing scarves for Hermes of Paris and painting ornate works of art that sell for the price of a nice new car. I was expecting Khristian to come from a broken home, but from what I've read, his family appears normal, practical and creative. They are also notably reclusive. When I finally see a picture of his parents, I am surprised to find that they are both African American. In all the pictures I've seen of Khristian, he appears to be white. Even his booking card on the TDCJ website lists him as Caucasian.

The following day, Erik drops me off at the airport. He hugs me, not like a lovesick suitor saying goodbye to his sweetheart at the airport, but like a parent hugging his scared-as-hell kid going off to summer camp. He knows that this trip to Texas won't be easy, and for most of it, I will be alone.

"Call me when you get in," he says, and kisses me quickly on the lips.

"I will." I pick up my suitcase, which feels terribly heavy for only four days of clothes, and lug it through the automatic doors. The tiny airport is served by only three airlines, but is bustling for a Tuesday. I take a seat in a far corner. I don't feel like making small talk or responding to inquiries about my travel plans. Instead, I call my Graduate mentor, Tom.

I'm a little taken aback that he answers immediately. Usually I get his voice mail, so I was mentally preparing a quick message. *Off to death row. I'll call you if I have any questions.* As usual, he is chipper, like a cheerleader, which wouldn't be such a bad thing for those of us who like to sit alone and write. After his pep talk, he reminds me to "get the name of the dog," which is writer-speak for taking notes, especially about the little stuff that we don't think is important at the time.

I arrive into Austin at 7:00 PM, feeling tired yet jittery. The anxiety of travel coupled with recycled air and too much coffee usually has this effect. Even though I'd like to stop by and see my friend Jenny before my drive to Huntsville, it's too late to swing by her house. Besides, there is nothing she can say that will prepare me for tomorrow. What I really need is a good night's sleep. The sun has already set, which doesn't bode well for my drive. I'm night blind with one hundred and sixty flat, foreign Texas miles to go.

As I wait in line at the rental car counter, I pull the printed directions from my purse and study them. My hands are shaky, and the argumentative couple in front of me doesn't help. The car they wanted isn't available, and they behave as if it's the end of the world. I know they're putting on a show to get a discount or something, but I don't have the time or patience for it. I reach into my purse, almost reflexively digging for a pack of cigarettes that aren't there. I can feel myself rolling off the wagon, but for the time being, it's a good thing. If my mind is fixated on obtaining a pack of cigarettes, it is temporarily off the fact that I will face a dying man tomorrow morning.

Along with my red Pontiac Vibe, I rent a GPS. I've never used one before, but at the moment I don't mind being told what to do, where to go, and how to get there. The robotic voice startles me at first, but in the darkness of a desolate Texas highway, I don't mind the company. After about twenty minutes, my technological companion goes silent, which adds to the creepiness factor. The full moon isn't helping. I turn on the radio to the first notes of "Don't Fear the Reaper" — as if chosen by some all-powerful DJ especially for my ears. It's amazing what our minds will do to reassure us that the world is exactly as it should be.

By the time I check in at the motel, which looks nothing like its picture, I'm pooped. The front desk lady, who appears to be more interested in going back outside to smoke another cigarette, assigns me to the back of the building with all the truck drivers. The air is thick and wet and smells of diesel fumes. Three doors down from me, a shirtless man sits on his bed with his door propped open and all the lights on. I can't help but think he's waiting to strangle a prostitute. The minute I enter my room, I bolt the door and secure the chain. When I turn on the light, cockroaches scatter up the wall by the microwave. Normally, I would scream and dance around the room like a maniac, but I don't need any attention from Mr. Night Owl. I stomp to the bathroom as if I really mean business, grab a mound of toilet paper, and squash them as fast as I can.

After the mass extermination and water burial, I gingerly sit down on the edge of the bed with the heavily patterned coverlet—the one that hides the blood stains, semen and crawling bugs—and call the front desk. It takes a couple of rings before Old Smokey picks up.

"Hi, um, I'm the lady that just checked in. There are a ton of cockroaches in my room."

"Oh, it's the weather. Whenever it gets colder they like to come inside."

I remain silent, hoping that she will somehow attempt to redeem herself by offering a new room.

"Since you prepaid for your room on Priceline, I can't offer you a refund. But just so you know, we have an exterminator that comes out here about three times a week."

"Oh." *Well that does me a lot of good.* It's late, I'm tired, and this woman has no clue about customer service. I ask for a 5 am wake-up call and hang up. I wash my face, squash a few more roaches, fling back the sheets to check for any errant strays, and crawl into bed with my clothes on. As I set the alarm clock, because I don't trust the wake-up call, I peek down at the floor by the nightstand. It hasn't seen a vacuum in over a year, if not five. My night is filled with paranoid, fitful sleep beneath scratchy, bleach-scented sheets. I don't need the wake-up call, because I never manage to fully fall asleep. At 4:30 am, I surrender to the day.

The motel's one redeeming quality is a Starbucks across the street. I order an extra-large latte to go and drive the forty miles to Livingston, where the Polunsky Unit is housed. As I cross the bridge over Lake Livingston, the early morning sun dances over the water. I wonder if Khristian Oliver will notice its beauty as he is transported to impending death.

I make a pit stop at a grocery store near the prison and try to use the ATM. The machine is broken, and they won't give me cash back if I use my debit card. I want to buy Khristian a soda or a candy bar from the vending machine, but it looks like I'll be visiting empty-handed.

And that's what finally pushes me over the edge. I purchase a pack of Marlboro Lights and a red lighter with a stupid Ed Hardy design. The minute I exit the store, I rip open the pack and smoke one while I still have coffee to wash away the horrible taste.

When I reach the Polunsky Unit, a guard stops me before I can turn into the parking lot. He is the quintessential fat happy Texan. In a 'what we have here is a failure to communicate' twang, he tells me to pop the hood and the trunk. I have no idea how to pop the hood of my rental car. Frantic, I run my fingers along the underside of the dashboard hoping to find a latch.

"I'm sorry, but I don't know how to pop the hood. It's a rental. Maybe you can figure it out," I say like a clueless damsel in distress. I exit the car and open the trunk.

The guard peers inside, lifts the flap where the spare tire is kept, and writes something on his clipboard. With his black ink pen at the ready, he asks me the name and number of "my inmate." I tell him Khristian's name and fumble trying to recall his number.

He looks at me with a blank expression and shuts the hatch. I feel like he's going to ask me to leave because I haven't played the game correctly.

"This is my first time here at the Polunsky Unit. I'm a little nervous."

"It's alright. You're going to go to that first building there. And you can't bring nothing inside but your ID, some money if you want to buy him something, and a smile."

I look towards the flat taupe building standing behind two barbed wire fences and thank him for letting me slide. After finding a parking spot, I scan the rows of cars looking for Khristian's parents. There isn't a soul around—just a giant orange tabby wandering through the maze of cars. I retrieve my driver's license from my wallet and shove my purse under the seat. This is a totally unnecessary move, as I don't think anyone is stupid or desperate enough to break into a car in a prison parking lot. An armed guard surveys the lot from a tower.

I walk towards the entrance. Inside, a male and a female guard, both in their early thirties, stand at the ready. This isn't my first time at the prison rodeo— just the first time in the lone star state of Texas. I know to place my car keys and my ID in a yellow plastic container and walk through the metal detector. In a polite tone of voice, the woman asks me to remove my shoes and to show her the bottoms of my feet.

"Arms out," she instructs. She runs a pointed thumb along my bra line, then pats me down along my side, my stomach and the inside of my legs. Finally, she scans me with a wand. Without a blip or a beep, I pass the contraband test. As I put my shoes back on, I think briefly of my brother, the only other person I've ever visited in a prison. He's now free after serving twenty years for bank robbery.

The male guard tells me to hand my ID to a woman who is seated behind steel and thick bulletproof glass. I place my driver's license in the metal slot and tell her that I'm there to visit Khristian Oliver. In exchange, she deposits a chain necklace with a yellow visitor's card attached. She looks up some information on her computer and fills out a blue piece of paper. She scoots it at me through the metal tunnel, and I study it. *Pamela Skjolsvik FRND.* This puzzles me. What does F-R-N-D stand for? It takes a second for my brain to work. Friend.

She points to the door. "Walk through the outside corridor and head towards the next building."

Once outside, a steel gate buzzes as I approach. I push through it to the outdoor walkway and continue on. The woman's voice booms from the intercom, freezing me in my tracks.

"Close the gate, please."

Oh, shit. I push the heavy gate closed, but it won't latch. I stand there and wait, feeling like a kid being called on in class — the one who doesn't know the answer and picks his nose while he thinks about it. The buzzer sounds, and I slam the door locked.

The sun is blinding. I reach for the neckline of my shirt, but my sunglasses are back in the Vibe, squished under the seat with the contents of my purse. I squint my way towards the prison entrance and enter a regular door. A lone guard sits at a desk. He looks up at me from his newspaper and acknowledges my presence with a nod. There are two restrooms opposite him. I figure this is my last chance, so I zip into the ladies' room to fluff my hair and check my teeth in the reflective thing masquerading as a mirror. For some reason I feel rushed, like if I spend more than three minutes here, I could arouse the guard's suspicion that I'm birthing a balloon of heroin or a small pocket knife. These thoughts don't help my chronic pee anxiety.

I am beyond nervous, but there's no turning back or running away as fast as my sensible shoes will take me. I'm too far in.

"It's just down that hall," the guard says as I exit the restroom.

With the determination to just get it over with, like a scary roller coaster or Band-Aid removal, I tromp down the plaque-lined hallway towards yet another guard station. I flash my lanyard and the door opens automatically into the spacious visiting area. On one side of the room there are several empty visiting tables, while the other side is divided by a long row of individual booths with Plexiglass windows, immobile stools and black phones. In the far corner of the room by the vending machines, a female guard sits at a desk. I walk towards her with my now wilted piece of blue paper.

"Good morning. And how are you today?" she chirps.

Texans are so dang polite. I hand her the piece of paper. "I'm a little nervous," I reply.

She looks at the name on my sheet, then back up at me and stands. Her casual demeanor dissipates: Khristian is set to die tomorrow and she's never seen my face before.

"I think Mr. Whiteside is waiting for Khristian too. Follow me." She leads me to a small windowed room with several chairs and two black phones. Khristian is not behind the glass. Just inside the room stands a white man with salt and pepper hair, a burgundy button-down shirt, and a blue hooded sweatshirt draped over his arm. The guard acts as if I should know who he is.

"Khristian should be here soon," she says and heads back to her desk.

I nod and smile at this complete stranger. He is carrying a brown Bible with gold lettering, so I figure he's got to be some sort of chaplain. For some reason, I envisioned that it would just be me and Khristian: we'd have a quick conversation, then off I'd go to buy the t-shirt and go home. I never expected other people.

"Are you a friend of Khristian's?" he asks with genuine interest.

"No," I say. "I've never even met him. I'm just interviewing him."

We introduce ourselves. Mr. Whiteside is Khristian's spiritual adviser, but not the one appointed by the state. Last month, another inmate told Mr. Whiteside that there was another man on the row who probably needed his guidance more than he did. Whiteside admits that a lot of the men he meets with are just looking to get out of their cell or to use him for a soda or a snack. They're just killing time.

I look towards the still-empty room.

"So, you're in for a tough interview. He can be real shy."

That's exactly what I don't want to hear. As an introvert, it's uncomfortable to engage in a conversation with someone who is equally as reticent. Especially now that the clock is ticking. To add to my anxiety, his parents will be here any minute. They never called me back to arrange our meeting times.

"Does it usually take this long to bring him out?"

"I've waited up to an hour before, but considering the day, I think they should be a little more expedient."

I don't know him, but I like this guy. He knows he's being used by the majority of the men he meets with, yet he shows up anyway. As we wait, he tells me he's surprised that Khristian's parents aren't here yet. I ask if he thinks it's a positive or a negative thing for his parents to be present for his execution. He advises against it if asked.

"It's hard to erase that image from your mind," he says.

"Are you going to be there for Khristian tomorrow?"

"Yes, ma'am. I'll meet him in Huntsville and spend time with him there."

"Are you going to be there for his execution?"

He nods without a word. I wonder if he feels the same sort of compassion about the other death row inmates. Unlike me, he didn't get to pick the least scary man off the TDCJ website. He just helps whoever reaches out to him.

"Have Khristian's parents talked to you about attending?"

"No. They're very private people." He switches the brown Bible to his other hand. "But I'm sure they'll be there for him. They're here almost every week. And it shows."

"What do you mean?"

"It shows in Khristian. He isn't institutionalized like many of the men I encounter in here. He's very shy and gentle and kind. He's like a kitten."

Oh no. Not a kitten. Before I can fathom these endearing words, Khristian enters the room behind the glass. He is dressed in an off-white t-shirt with a white sleeveless jumpsuit over it. After his hand restraints are removed through a slot in the door, he walks towards the glass with a curious expression. I smile and wave at him like I'm standing outside some strange window display. He reciprocates.

"If you don't mind, I just want to say hello to him before you get started."

"Of course."

I stand off to the side. I think about leaving the room to give them some privacy, but Mr. Whiteside directs me to sit in a particular chair. "Have a seat. That's the most comfortable one."

Khristian sits down and wipes the phone with the bottom of his shirt before lifting it to his ear. Germs are the least of his concerns right now, but to me the gesture is an act of hope. As I watch him conversing with his adviser, I realize he looks nothing like his eleven-year-old mug shot. In addition to wearing glasses, he is heavier, and his buzz cut has been replaced with a thick mane of jet-black hair.

As Mr. Whiteside hangs up, I tell him goodbye, and quickly pick up the other black phone without wiping it down.

"Hi Khristian."

He flashes me a look of amazement. I don't think either one of us can believe that we're sitting here face to face.

"Hey there, Pamela."

He speaks slowly, with only a hint of a Texas accent. I tell him that I wasn't allowed to bring any paper or a pen inside, so if he could do me a favor and send me a letter that thoroughly answers the questions we discuss, I'd really appreciate it. He agrees.

I rest my elbow on the green ledge and lean towards the window. This chair is too low and it adds to the awkwardness of the situation. I want to be the fearless death writer, but I feel small and insecure talking to this stranger in a shatterproof box.

"So, Mr. Whitehouse seems really nice," I say to get the conversation going.

"Yeah, he is." He pauses for a moment. "Um, it's Mr. Whiteside."

I slap my forehead and laugh at my stupid mistake. "I'm pretty observant for a writer, huh?"

He smiles at my nervous attempt at levity, but it's not a tooth baring smile—more like a slight upturn of the corners of his mouth. His pupils are fully dilated behind his tinted glasses. His eyes look black. Either he's really happy to see me, or he's loaded up on drugs. I make a mental note to find out if he's on any medication, which wouldn't surprise me. Depression is rampant in penal settings.

I guess my error breaks the ice because he looks at me with raised brows for my next question. He's expecting death questions, but I'm at a loss.

"So, what's your favorite song?"

He answers immediately, like he's been waiting for someone to ask him this exact question. "Orinoco Flow by Enya. Have you heard of her?"

"Oh, yeah. I think I worked at a record store when that album came out. That's an old song. Orinoco Flow?" My questioning tone reflects that I think it's an odd choice, but he stands by his selection. I can't recall any of the lyrics other than, "Sail away, sail away, sail away." It's a new-age type song. Maybe that's why he likes it. It's about traveling and he's stuck in a six-by-nine-foot cell. I would bet money it has significance to his relationship with Sonya, who is also in prison, but I don't ask. It seems too personal.

He maintains eye contact but I find it difficult to meet his gaze. He's a dying man and I'm just here to prove something I can't name. I take a deep breath and look towards the booths just outside the door. "So, I got your letter. By your responses, you seemed like you were okay with what is going to happen. Are you really okay with dying tomorrow?"

"We all have to go sometime. It's a transition from one form of energy to another. You know, like in quantum physics?"

I nod in agreement, but I only have a vague idea of what he's talking about. He tells me he is intrigued by science and studies of the brain and that he discusses these topics with Mr. Whiteside, who in addition to providing spiritual support, also knows a surprising amount about neurology.

"How is your family doing with this?"

He pauses. "My family is really guarded with their emotions, so it's hard to tell. My mom thinks I'm going to get a stay. My dad is more of a realist."

"What about your siblings? You have a brother and sister, right?"

"Yes, ma'am. I don't really know. My brother came to visit me for the first time this week."

"Oh, my gosh. Really? How did that go?"

"It went okay, but when he was leaving, I told him I loved him and he didn't know what to say." He attempts a smile.

This breaks my heart. "I'm sorry. I don't know your brother, but I do know that it's hard to have a sibling in prison. Maybe he didn't want to get too emotional. You know? Like maybe it was a guy thing. My brother was in for over twenty years and it was really hard to go visit him. I felt helpless."

"What did your brother do?"

"Bank robbery." And he shot at a police officer during a high-speed car chase, but I don't go into details. This isn't about me. "So, all your family members are going to attend tomorrow?"

"Yeah. It's gonna be really hard on my mom." He says this with such defeat in his voice that tears well up in my eyes. His poor mother.

I want to change the subject, but they're all difficult. "So have you thought about what you're going to say as your last statement? For me, that's got to be the weirdest aspect of this process." Man am I stupid. It's not a process. It's his death.

"I'm going to recite the 23rd Psalm. Do you know it?"

I do, thanks to my Bible-quoting Grandma Lola. "'Yea, though I walk through the valley of the shadow of death'...is that the one?"

Although he agrees that that's the one, I'm finding it difficult to recall it. Although I want to ask him if he will address the victim's family in his last statement, I don't. I believe that Khristian agreed to speak with me because I didn't want to talk to him about the murder. Bringing that up now would be a betrayal of our tenuous trust. And as odd as it sounds, I want him to like me.

"Have you picked out your last meal?"

"Fried chicken, chocolate ice cream and coffee."

He smiles at the reaction on my face, which screams *is that it?* "You've got to be kidding me. Fried chicken?"

"Yep. It's the only thing they know how to make any good."

Well, I guess that makes sense. It's not like the prison brings in Wolfgang Puck to whip up a steak au-poivre, garlic mashed potatoes, crisp green beans and a molten chocolate cake, which would be my last meal of choice. "So do you have any questions for me?"

He smiles and almost laughs, but catches himself. "How do you pronounce your last name?"

I can't believe it. Here is this mild-mannered kitten on death row, and they're about to put him down like a feral cat—and that's all he wants to ask. This would be ten times easier if he were unlikeable.

"It's pronounced like Dr. Scholls with a 'vik' on the end."

"I would have never guessed that." He laughs.

"Believe me, you wouldn't be the first."

His eyes dart towards the visiting area. "My mom's here."

I spin around in my chair. Mrs. Oliver is the color of caramel, dressed in a pale yellow coat with a silk scarf covering her graying hair—a sunny visual for such a dreary place. She looks towards the room and I whip back towards Khristian. My heart races and my breath shallows. For some reason, I want to drop to the floor.

"I better get going so you can spend time with your mom."

"It's okay. She doesn't mind."

No, it's not okay. I'm caught between a dying man's request and my desire to flee. Maybe it's easier for him to talk to a stranger than to his mother. But he needs to talk to her. This is all she has. "Would it be okay if I came back tomorrow?"

"Sure. You can have a full hour if you want." He says this like it is something I should be excited about.

"Okay." As I stand, he stares up at me with an incredulous expression, as if he's not quite sure he believes that I'll come back. "Well, I guess I'll see you tomorrow, Khristian." I hang up the phone a bit too quickly with a mix of shame and relief that I am free to walk out of here.

It would be easier not to approach Mrs. Oliver, but I have to. Her diminutive size and the way she gently shakes my hand makes me want to kneel down to be on her level, if only to be able to decipher her softly spoken words. If I were her—if one of my kids were going to be executed— I'd be a wreck, like a giant mound of sobbing, raw ground beef, but she is outwardly calm. She thanks me for talking with her son, as if my presence in some way will help him. I want to say I'm just a nobody. Instead I tell her that I will call Rick Perry's office to let him know that I am opposed to this execution and to the death penalty in general.

"Bless you," she says. I'm not quite sure how to respond. I've only heard those words after a sneeze.

"So are you done speaking with Khristian?" she asks.

"Yes."

"You can go talk to him some more if you'd like."

I don't know what to do. I look towards Khristian's room. His eyes are fixated on the two of us. If I don't go in, his mother will think I'm cold and unfeeling. If I do and he doesn't get a stay, she might blame me for taking away the one thing she can never get back: his last hours. It's a no-win situation.

"I'll just be a few more minutes," I say, just a tad syrupy, and sprint back towards the room.

Khristian looks surprised that I'm back.

"So, your mom's nice."

He agrees and tells me that she's more open and outgoing than his father. *Aren't they all?* I ask if she was born in February. He says, "No, she's not an Aquarius. She's a Libra." He leans forward in his chair. "Can you guess what sign I am?"

I should just play along and pretend that I don't know, but I do. I've read his booking card. "I can't guess because I already know. You're a Virgo."

He looks pleased that I've remembered this about him, or maybe that I made the connection in the first place. I blab on that I was also born in August, but that I'm a Leo. I tell him my dad is a Virgo. I feel totally ridiculous for talking with him about astrology. If I'm going to take his visiting time, I need to ask something serious. "So, has the warden gone over the execution process with you?"

"No, they do that tomorrow," he replies in a matter of fact tone.

"Have you ever had surgery?"

"Yes." He nods.

"Well, I think it's like that. It's like falling asleep from the anesthesia."

"I wasn't put under," he says.

"Oh. Well. I've had a couple of surgeries and it's not bad. You just fall asleep."

And never wake up.

CHAPTER NINE

Ask for Help

The bright Texas sun assaults my eyes the minute I step out the front door. I feel like cursing the cloudless smog-filled sky, but I'm not alone and I don't want to look as crazy as I feel. A lone figure stands by the trash receptacle reading a paper. As I pass, I realize that it's Khristian's father. Only two visitors are allowed in at a time and I took his spot. He has no idea who I am and I don't feel like introducing myself in some stilted, weird exchange that will only waste more of his time.

I sprint to my car, grab my purse from under the seat and retrieve the pack of cigarettes. I light one with unsteady hands and the cheap red lighter. It tastes horrible, but I draw it deep into my lungs to help me feel something other than desperation. At the moment, this cigarette is the only thing I have any control over, yet the very act of smoking again is so out of control. The stimulant aspect of nicotine isn't helping my already amped up, sweaty state. I lean against the hood of the rental car to brace myself from a fit of coughing that morphs into a mournful, wounded animal wail. This outflow of emotion surprises me, and the thought that I must look ridiculous to the guard or the random people entering the prison with their Ziploc bags and toothless smiles reins me in. I crush the cigarette into the asphalt and retreat into the safety of the car. I want to write everything down, but I find myself staring up into the sky. A group of large birds—crows perhaps—circle above the prison, taunting the inhabitants of this dreadful place with their effortless flight. They stay in this circular holding pattern for at least twenty-minutes. I wonder if this is what birds do when they hone in on their prey. Do they know that someone is about to die?

I feel immobilized by the circling birds and the monarch butterflies that flit and flutter on their way to Mexico. I don't want to leave. I convince myself to wait for his parents to exit the building at noon when visiting hours are over. I've brought a literary journal that I had an essay in and I want to give it to them. I want them to know that I'm not some morbid weirdo out to meet their child on the day before he dies. The essay is about helping my brother get treated for Hepatitis C while he was in prison. There is a religious undercurrent about what it means to be a Christian. My brother became a fundamentalist during his later years of incarceration and was constantly telling me that I was going to go to Hell if I didn't accept Jesus Christ as my savior. Despite his taunting and questioning, I helped him out anyway.

I sit in my car and exit it every fifteen minutes to smoke. Each cigarette tastes better than the last. I scan the lot for the orange tabby. Two women park next to me and exit their burgundy Buick in a cloud of smoke, cigarettes still dangling from their lips. They're dressed like twins in black leggings and unflattering plaid shirts with white socks bunched at the top of their worn out tennis shoes. Both wear their greasy graying hair pulled back into severe high ponytails, a style befitting a child. I am just as inconspicuous to them as I am to the man in the guard tower.

A faded orange plane flies above us. Its loud engine distracts me from my notebook and I wonder if it is some sort of tourist flight. I picture a tour guide saying, "And if you look directly below us folks you'll see the infamous Polunsky Unit—otherwise known as DEATH ROW—home to the most fiendish, horrible, and dastardly men in Texas." As the plane takes another pass over the prison, I see it—the pale yellow coat. I grab the book and run towards Khristian's parents, leaving my purse on the seat of the unlocked car.

Mrs. Oliver looks happy to see me, despite the fact that I'm winded and clutching a literary journal like a madwoman.

"You're still here. Oh, I'm so glad. You can visit with Khristian again if you'd like."

"He doesn't have any more visitors?"

"No."

I hand her the journal. Mr. Oliver reaches for it, but she takes it from my hands first.

"Listen, there's an essay in there about my brother. I want to give it to you."

Kermit Oliver says thank you in a muffled voice and the two of them shuffle towards the parking lot. His hand rests on the small of his wife's back, almost as if he is gently nudging her to leave. I feel so bad for them—more so than Khristian. I wish I had it in me to embrace them like children—to assure them that I won't let the monster get their son. But I'm not a touchy feely kind of person. They're shy, reclusive people—at least that's what I've read on the Internet—and Mr. Whiteside confirmed it. And it wasn't going to be okay. Things were pretty far from okay.

On my reentry into the prison, I endure the same process of being patted down and searched for concealed weapons and contraband, but I'm now hip to the whole procedure and I rush back into the prison. I look towards Khristian's room. Another man is now behind the glass, chatting with the pony-tailed women from the parking lot. I approach the guard and hand her my blue piece of paper.

"You're back. We'll have to bring Khristian to another room. It will be just be a few minutes." She instructs me where to sit.

Khristian appears much quicker than before, but the privacy of the other room is gone. Not that we need privacy, but it seems like maybe he should be in the special room, considering this is his second to last day on earth. I don't like being surrounded by others, even if they have phones pressed to their ears.

I pick up the black phone after wiping it on my shirt. "Why did your parents leave early?"

"They had to go to Austin to the governor's office."

I confess to him that I feel really weird about being here, which seems so petty in comparison to his concerns. "How are you feeling about tomorrow?"

"It's surreal, but I guess we all have to die at some point."

"You're right. I could get in my rental car after I leave here today and get hit by a mac truck. Nobody really knows when their time is up—but you do. And you're really okay with it?"

He assures me that he is, but I can't believe it. I'm not okay with it and I don't even know him.

"I'm a very spiritual person, Pamela. This isn't the end."

But it's the end to all this. Won't he miss it? I ask him if he has any friends in prison, people that he can talk to about what he's dealing with.

"Pamela, these are not the kind of guys you want to be friends with." He draws this out for comedic effect.

I laugh nervously, but the reality of his situation is not very funny. He is housed in close quarters with a pack of murderers and rapists— a tiny kitten surrounded by growling Rottweilers and pit bulls.

He asks me if I have any kids. I tell him their ages and that Lola is an aspiring artist and that Nik likes to write stories, kind of like their mom and dad. "They're at a good age, where they still love me and they're not yet embarrassed by my presence."

"Just you wait till they're teenagers," he says. He then tells me he has a daughter of his own. This was never mentioned before.

"Oh my God. Really? How is she handling this?"

"I don't know. I haven't met her. Her name is Kittisue." (I find out later that she goes by a different name.)

He tells me that Sonya's sister adopted Kittisue. Sonya is serving a ninety-nine year sentence for sitting in his truck as he burglarized Joe Collins' home. Sonya hasn't seen her daughter since she was a baby.

"So why doesn't the sister bring her here? I mean it's not the greatest place to bring a kid, but..."

"She doesn't like me."

I tell him I'm sorry. I don't know what else to say. To deprive him of meeting his own flesh and blood seems beyond cruel. He tells me that his parents had to sue for visitation, but the last time they saw her was in 2007, over two years ago. His life, or what is left of it, is getting sadder by the minute.

I quickly change the subject to his art. I tell him I'm attending the retrospective art show of his parents' work in Waco. It also includes several of Khristian's pieces. "What medium do you use to make your art?"

"Pencil and you know those water colors that kids use?"

I nod.

"That's what I use."

Now that we're on to a less stressful topic, I tell him that my husband is an artist and that he used to paint backdrops for touring rock bands. Unlike other people, he doesn't inquire about the bands, but I rattle a few of them off anyway. With a hint of pride in his voice, he informs me that all of his artwork sold and that it will help pay for the legal bills he's accrued over the years. The sad reality is that the price of his art will go up after his death.

"How do you spend your time in here?"

He tells me that he gets to go outside two times a week for an hour. His days are spent reading, writing letters and making art—art that can never hang on the walls of his cell. They must remain blank. He says that he does have a calendar hanging on his door. "The guards can't see it." He stops and thinks for a minute. He's searching for a word.

"What do you call it when you don't have anything to look at but white?"

My mind goes equally blank. "Sterile?"

"No, that's not it." He rubs his chin. "Sensory deprivation!" he exclaims. "You can go crazy in here from that."

I don't ask him if he has gone crazy. I ask him if he likes to read. He says he loves science fiction and fantasy.

"What's your favorite book?"

He looks up at the ceiling and contemplates the question. I too would have difficulty answering.

"Probably the Thomas Covenant books."

I am not familiar with these books, but I tell him that I'll check them out.

"So what's the name of your book?" He leans towards the glass.

"I'm thinking *Death Becomes Them*."

He looks perplexed. I explain that my focus has been on people who work in a profession where they have to deal with death. I say it is also a personal narrative about my own fear of death—not the actual act of dying, but the death of people I love. I remind him that I contacted him because only a person who commits suicide or a person scheduled for execution knows the day and time of their death.

"This might relate to your thesis." He pauses for a moment. "I've tried to kill myself three times in here."

My face can't hide the shock. "Really? How?"

"With a shaving razor."

When I worked in a jail, the guards took the razors back after the men were done shaving to prevent them from being used as weapons. I would think death row would be the last place they would allow men to keep their razors.

"They don't take them back after you're done shaving?"

"No."

I find this hard to believe until he extends both arms. His left arm is scarred with stitch marks where the arm bends. Now that he does this, I realize that he's been covering it with his hand the whole time. I am so not observant.

"Thirteen stitches," he says like a soldier proudly displaying his battle scars. He extends his right arm towards the glass. It is less scarred than his left. "This one doesn't look as bad, but it actually bled more." He lifts his chin and points to a scar on his neck. "I had a towel over the window on my door when I did that one. The guard asked what I was doing. I told him I was going to the bathroom."

"Didn't that hurt?"

"No. Once you get past the skin, there aren't any nerves."

I'm speechless. I don't know what to say to a man who wants to end his life. And these were serious attempts, not just surface scratch marks. My eyes well with tears. I'm finding it terribly difficult to remain the impartial observer. "Do you get any kind of counseling in here?"

"No, not in here. When I went to the Jester unit, I got counseling about once a week. They've put me in the death-watch cell. It's got a camera in there to make sure I don't do it again."

"Yeah, because they want to be the ones to do it." This slips out before I can even think about how callous it must sound.

Surprisingly, it makes him laugh. "Yes, I guess they do, don't they?"

"Do you know how ironic that is?"

He nods.

"So why did you do it?"

He looks down at his clasped hands and back up at me. "I've suffered from depression for many years. I'm on meds for both depression and schizophrenia."

Meds. That's why his pupils are so large. Why wasn't this brought up in his trial? Was it? Would it even have made a difference? I tell him that I'm sorry that he's suffered so much and that it must be so hard to live in a cell and rarely see the sunshine. I imagine that all he can do is sit and think about his family, his child that he'll never get to meet, and how little control he has over his life. I'd probably want to exit the world too.

He tells me that after I leave, he has a call from his lawyer.

"Is he the one that advised you not to communicate with me at first?"

"Uh huh."

He says that after the call, Melanie Lawson from ABC is interviewing him. I ask if he gets lots of requests for interviews. He says that he turned down the *Associated Press* and the *Nacogdoches Sentinel*. He also gets a lot of letters from people trying to save his soul.

"I got twenty letters yesterday."

After talk of depression and suicide, I try to lighten the mood. I tell him about my last trip to New York. He tells me that he went to New York and D.C. on a class field trip when he was in high school. He got to see *Phantom of the Opera*, the White House, and the Twin Towers. He said he liked *Phantom of the Opera*. I tell him a story about meeting my dad in New York and going to see *Sunset Boulevard* the day after the OJ Simpson verdict. The story involves meeting my dad and brother for dinner, getting drunk and proceeding to vomit all over myself within the first five minutes of the play.

"What were you drinking?" he asks.

"I started off with wine and then rum and cokes. My dad and I aren't very close so I guess I got drunk because of nerves."

The female guard approaches with splayed fingers and mouths, "five minutes."

I thank Khristian for talking with me again. I wish him luck with his interview and tell him he should say "Go Yankees" — who are playing in the World Series—to endear the public to him, but he says he's not much of a sports fan. He says press isn't always a good idea, but he figures he has nothing to lose by doing the interview. We say goodbye and I exit the many doors of the prison. As I walk towards my car, I reach into the right pocket of my pants. The red lighter is there.

After the morning I've had, I'd like to curl up in bed—my own bed, not the cockroach-infested dung heap at the motel—and sleep for the rest of the day, but I have an appointment to meet Jim Willett at the prison museum. On the drive back to Huntsville, my empty stomach growls and gurgles from too many cigarettes. I've got an hour to kill, so I pull into the local Chili's, which looks like every other Chili's I've ever been to. I guess that's the point of chain restaurants—familiarity in the unfamiliar.

The restaurant is packed with couples, college kids and families. I slink into a booth in the bar section and light up another cigarette. I don't know what else to do. *Kid* by the Pretenders plays on their 80's nostalgic XM feed. I have no idea what this song is about but it's depressing the hell out of me. I stare at the couples and the people of Huntsville on their lunch breaks and want to yell at them for being oblivious to what is about to transpire.

The young attentive waitress refills my Diet Coke three times, while I poke at the most unappetizing cheesesteak sandwich ever. When I pay my bill, I ask her if she knows how to get to the Texas Prison Museum.

"I don't. I just go to school here."

"Oh," I say and stub out my fifth cigarette.

"I can find out for you."

"That's okay. I've got a GPS."

How can someone live in Huntsville, the execution capital of the United States, and not know where to find such a monumental tourist attraction? This is a prison town. It's what they're known for. Men are executed here every month. I would think the residents would try and stay on top of this kind of stuff.

Like a person without kids contemplating the safety of car seats, I didn't give much thought to the death penalty. Until now. With a robotic GPS voice telling me where to turn, I make my way to the Texas Prison Museum to sit and chat with a man who has presided over eighty-nine executions. Even though Jim Willett has been nothing but nice to me, the thought of talking about his former job as Warden of the Walls Unit makes me queasy. The cheesesteak isn't helping.

   The Texas Prison Museum is housed in a pristine brick building with a faux guard tower to convey an air of authenticity. The large parking lot can accommodate busloads of curiosity seekers wanting to take a peek into the closed-off world that the law abiding among us never see. The main attraction at the museum is "Old Sparky," which is advertised on the local highway billboards.

   As I walk inside, Jim Willett is waiting for me at the front counter. Like a helpful tour guide, he leads me to his office and informs me that after our talk, I can look around the museum as much as I want and I don't have to pay. I find this very endearing. He's dressed in jeans and a white button-down shirt that matches what's left of his hair. He has a casual, sort of grandfatherly way about him that immediately puts me at ease, even though I'm in an unfamiliar place with a stranger. After I ask him how he became a warden, he leans back and begins spinning yarn like a natural-born storyteller.

   Like the waitress at Chili's, Jim Willett tells me he attended Sam Houston State University to pursue a degree in business. To make a few bucks, he worked at a service station, but his pals said he really needed to get a job working at the prison. They told him the pay was way better than the minimum wage and 'it wasn't like in the movies.' Convinced, he went into the personnel office the next day to fill out an application. He remembers a sign posted in that room that stated that there were hundreds of applicants ahead of him. Undeterred, he 'bugged them to death,' and within a couple of months was hired as a nightshift guard. He jokes that on his first day he received about fifteen minutes of training and then was stationed at the number one picket outside the wall. It was dark. And he was alone.

   "The first night I was scared to death. I think I prayed all night, *don't anybody go over the wall, don't anybody try to escape tonight.*"

   "Were you armed?"

   "I had a pistol and a shotgun and nobody even said 'we're gonna take you out and show you how to shoot these things.'"

He laughs at how insane it must sound to give a man a gun and not show him how to use it. In a humble 'don't you worry little missy' kind of way, he tells me he already knew how to handle a firearm, having been born and raised in Texas.

"I wasn't the best shot, but I certainly wasn't the worst," he adds.

It didn't matter. There wasn't much use for his gun. Someone had to escape and until that happened, there was nothing for him to do but look at the top of the death house. Radios, books, or any kind of distraction were not allowed. He just had to bide his time. The pay was good, but he had no intention of making guard duty his life's work. No one dreams of growing up to stare out into the night waiting for the sound of hushed voices or men climbing fences.

"So what was your first experience with death at the Walls Unit?"

"My first encounter with death, at least in the prison system, was a hostage situation in 1974. Three inmates got a bunch of ammunition and three pistols smuggled in and they took some people hostage in the education department in the library, which was on the third floor and in the center of the walls. They kept them hostage for eleven days. On the eleventh night, and I was there, they attempted to escape and there was a shootout. When it was over, two of the female employees, a teacher and a librarian were dead, and two of the three inmates were dead. And a priest got shot. I did not see the two women or the priest up close, but I saw the two inmates and one of their heads was split wide open...At that point, I said 'Jim Willett, when you get this degree, you need to get out of here.'" After the incident, the guards were allowed to go home and get some rest, but they were expected to come back and help "shake down" the prison.

Despite his intentions of leaving upon graduation, he didn't. He attributes this to a kind of laziness on his part—the laziness that occurs with a familiar and comfortable situation. He liked the people he worked with, he knew how to do the job, and he was given a promotion. Another soon followed, and with it, the pay and benefits increased. When he started at the Walls Unit in 1971, the death penalty had been abolished, but the death house remained, along with "Old Sparky."

"We took a crew of inmates in there and cleaned it every Wednesday, spick and span."

When they reinstated the death penalty in 1976, he was a captain at the Walls. The warden gave all the guards a duty. Willett was thankful for his periphery assignment. "My job was to escort, to ride with the funeral home vehicle when it came in and stay with it until the execution was over. As many times as I'd been in that room with that electric chair, I'd never really thought about having to deal with an execution. I mean that was something that happened a long time ago to me—I was just a kid. In '64 when they quit, my God, I was only fourteen years old. I can remember very little about that night... As midnight approached—they were at midnight at that time—standing there at the back of that vehicle, and thinking my gosh, we're really going to kill somebody in that room in a little bit...I came from a little country town, raised on a farm. This was really different. I mean prison was different, but this was really different."

My stomach growls loudly. "Sorry, I ate at Chili's," I laugh.

He flashes me a smile. He's so kind and willing that I don't feel weird inquiring about the execution process. I ask who works on the medical team.

The term 'medical team' makes him lean forward in his chair. "And when we say medical people, um, define medical people."

I laugh again, but a bit more nervously. "See, I don't know."

"Let's just throw this out here. You might, and I'm just saying—I don't know that I ever saw anybody like this—but you might find somebody that's retired, a nurse for instance or even a doctor. I don't know. But you also may find someone who was a medic in Viet Nam. That kind of thing. That might be a good person. Particularly because they've done this under pressure before. That would be a good somebody. Somebody like that. To hook the IVs up, we're talking. Okay? But I don't know that maybe somebody that is good at veterinary type stuff might make one. I don't know. They might. But I'm guessing. I'm just saying this to you to say that they don't have to have a medical degree."

"Are they employed by the prison?"

"Could be, could not be. Doesn't have to be. The people these days don't want people to know who they are."

In the past, the name of the executioner was printed in the paper. I ask him if they use a double blind system in Texas so no one really knows who gives the lethal dose.

He shakes his head emphatically. "Everybody who's back there knows who is doing everything. The guy is standing there and he knows exactly what he's doing. That person may or may not be a medical person, okay."

The way he's hinting at the medical issue, it appears to me that anyone can take part in an execution if they're willing to do so—desire being more important than credentials. I ask him about what it's like being in the death chamber.

"Once the inmate is completely hooked up, and I'm talking about strapped down and hooked up with the IVs, at that very point when you're waiting for the witnesses to be brought in, the warden and the chaplain are the only people in the death chamber with that inmate."

"So how is that?"

"Typically the first time I see these guys is when they come to the walls that afternoon."

"But you talk to them, right? Like explain the procedure. What's their biggest concern?"

"If it was gonna hurt. And I was honest with them. Nobody really knows because everybody is dead. I can tell you what I've witnessed and what it looks like to me and it looks like you're gonna go to sleep and you're gonna die very quickly." He sounds sad. He's probably had to repeat those words to many very scared men.

I ask him about removing his glasses, which I'd read was the official signal that the warden gave to the executioner to start the lethal injection.

"There were two wardens ahead of me that did executions in Texas, lethal injection executions. And that's what the first one did and the second one did the same thing. I don't wear these except to read, but it had worked for everybody else, so conveniently I just put them on before the witnesses came in and I took them off to do that."

Now it's a remote device, like a car remote that signals the executioner.

"So how did it feel to witness so many executions?"

"I would say to anybody that has the opportunity ... I would suggest you don't do it. You'll never get it out of your mind."

"Was that what it was like for your first one?"

"The first one was unbelievable. For me personally, I never witnessed an execution so to be the person in charge at one ... It would have been a whole lot better if I'd been able to watch one or two. There's got to be a word that means the same thing as awesome but lets you know that it's really a bad thing also. You know what I'm saying? That is the feeling it is. The feeling I had, that my gosh, this man is alive with no physical disabilities and we're fixin' to put him to death and it's gonna happen because I'm gonna take these glasses off. I can't make it sound as big as it was to me that night. I just can't. And there wasn't anything good about it. Nothing. Everything that was happening was bad."

I almost feel as if he's confessing to me. I know he's been interviewed before and he's probably shared the same things with others, but it feels like what he really wants me to take away from this is how horrible and taxing his job was.

"I remember going home that night and my mind was racing a hundred miles an hour... I mean, just imagine it—not everyone in the world experiences something like that. I mean you just go home and you get in there and you think, what just happened up there and I was a part of it? That first one was just unbelievable."

He took part in eighty-eight more before retiring. "After that?"

"It got easier, but it never got easy."

I tell him about meeting Khristian Oliver earlier in the day. His voice changes as if he's interviewing me.

"How was that? What do you say to a man who is being executed tomorrow? Did you say good luck when you left? I'm not trying to mess with you. That must be a strange thing to sit down in front of somebody and you'll ask me later what it's like. I tell you what it's like: it's a whole lot like you sitting right there and thinking, 'that man is perfectly healthy and he's going to die tomorrow.'"

And that's exactly what I thought, except I didn't know it for certain like he did. "Do you think an execution provides any resolution to the victims' families?"

"I just always got the feeling that they didn't really get what they hoped to get out of it in the end."

It was a sad note to end on. *So what's the point of an execution, again?* I thank Mr. Willett for his time and hospitality and take him up on his offer to visit the museum. On my way out, I purchase a leather drink cozy that was made by a real Texas inmate, and a copy of Willett's book. He signs it, *I enjoyed our conversation.*

Me too.

When I get back to the motel, I grab my computer from the room and head straight to the lobby. I don't want to be alone.

An older African American man greets me as I enter. "How are you doing this evening?"

It is such a simple question, one that I've answered probably a thousand times with "Fine and you?" but I can't for the life of me utter those words. "Not very well."

"I'm sorry to hear that. Is there anything I can do?"

I walk up to the counter, feeling like a total jerk for burdening this man who probably just wants to finish out his shift in peace. Normally, I wouldn't engage with a stranger, but I have an overwhelming need to feel connected with people right now.

"You wouldn't happen to be friends with the governor, would you?"

"No, ma'am. I can't say that I am."

"I'm sorry. I'm just messing with you. I've had a tough day." I tell him about the prison and the museum. He listens to my every word without interruption or questions. He just nods and looks sad about my very odd tale of woe for a man he's never heard of. I then cap it off that my room is filled with cockroaches and that I can't sleep when I think there might be a bug crawling on me.

"Well, now, there's something I can help you with." He steps over to his computer. "There's a room right up front here. It's a little nicer than what they put you in." He grabs a key and writes my room number down on the cardholder.

"Thank you so much."

He hands me the key and looks directly in my eyes.

"You really a writer?"

"Yeah, but not for a newspaper or anything."

He smiles. "You're somebody."

It's such an odd exchange. Yes, I am somebody, but not anyone who can change the course of events. God, I feel alone.

CHAPTER TEN

Bear Witness

I arrive at the Polunsky Unit at 7:30 am on November 5th. I want to get all the patting down and checking in done before 8:00 so that I can see Khristian for a full hour. I stop at the little kiosk at the turn-in to the lot. The guard today is different. He asks me to pop the hood and the trunk. I give him the same helpless monologue that I delivered yesterday, but he isn't impressed. He asks me to step out of the vehicle. He finds the latch and determines that it's broken. He searches the car more thoroughly than his co-worker. After I sign in on the clipboard, he tells me that I have to stay here until 8:00. So much for showing up early.

I stand outside my car and smoke. Two elderly women with snow-white hair pull up behind me in a gray Ford Taurus. They look like a couple of God-fearing, church-going women ready to entice the congregation with a roll of quarters. Mr. Whiteside pulls up behind them and steps out of his vehicle. Grateful to see a familiar face, I approach him. He immediately diverts the conversation away from Khristian by telling me about another death row inmate that he visits in Mississippi. He says this young man likes to write and would be thrilled to correspond with a writer. I don't know if I'm up for another round of befriending a dying person, but I write down my contact information and agree to send Larry Matthew Puckett a letter. Before I know it, the guard tells us we can go in. I rush to my car and pull in to the lot.

The check-in procedure is quick. I sprint to the visiting area, acutely aware of the time. When Khristian finally enters, Mr. Whiteside asks if he can say a quick hello. He tells Khristian that a really nice woman in Louisiana is praying for him. Then he recites Psalm 46 and tells him that he'll see him later this afternoon. They knock knuckles on the glass.

The first thing Khristian says to me is that he wrote me a letter last night to answer all of my questions. "Hopefully that will be okay."

"Thank you for taking the time to do that. I'm sure it's fine."

A guard knocks on the door that leads back into the prison. Khristian turns to the person and says, "No, thank you."

"What was that about?"

"She wanted to know if I wanted my lunch tray."

"Now? What time is breakfast, one in the morning?"

"It's actually at three."

"You've got to be kidding me. You mean they wake you up at three in the morning for breakfast?"

He nods.

"I'd be like, 'I'll take about five more hours of sleep for breakfast.'" I lift my Zip-Loc bag filled with coins for him to see. "Can I get you something tasty from the vending machine?"

"No, thank you." He seems despondent.

"How was the call with your lawyer?"

"It was kind of depressing." In a somber voice, he tells me that he has lost all of his appeals and that his only hope now is Rick Perry, the governor.

"Khristian. Let's say your sentence was commuted and you had to spend the rest of your natural life in here. After what you told me yesterday about your depression and trying to end your life, how would that sit with you?"

"I'd at least get to meet my daughter. When she gets older, she can make up her own mind to come visit me."

This changes everything. He wants to live. I meet his depression with anger. "Sonya's sister really pisses me off. To keep your daughter away from you is cruel. Where does she live?"

He tells me that they're moving to another part of Texas. I have no idea what transpired between the two of them, but I can't comprehend how she could deny him from seeing his only child. This is his dying wish. I want to find this woman and talk some sense into her. This is so unlike me.

"How do you want to be remembered, Khristian?"

"I don't care what the public thinks about me. But I'd like for my daughter to know that I love her."

He tells me that he and Sonya wrote and illustrated six books for Kittisue. He says that some of them are on display at the art show in Waco. I don't know how to respond. There are absolutely no words in the English language that will make his day less painful or scary. That's what Mr. Whiteside is for.

Khristian's eyes light up and he looks out towards the visiting area. "That's my sister."

I turn to look. "Really? Well, I guess we're done. You need to talk with her way more than you need to talk with me."

Khristian's sister walks directly to the room and enters. Her eyes are red as if she's been crying. I ask Khristian if I can get a picture taken with him before I go.

"Sure." He smiles.

I leave the room and approach the guard, who is not the same woman as yesterday. I ask if I can get my picture taken with Khristian.

"I have to go get the camera. Who is that woman with him?" she asks.

"That's his sister."

"She didn't give me her paper. I need that."

"I'll go get it."

"And tell Khristian to get ready."

I have no idea what she means. I walk back to the room and collect his sister's paper. She is holding a man's ID. I pick up the phone.

"The lady told me to tell you to get ready, whatever than means. Maybe to smile?" I smile at him and return to the guard with the blue paper. She is talking on the phone with someone about the ID. I hand her the paper and we walk back to the room. Khristian's sister steps off to the side. I stand next to the glass and Khristian does the same. The female guard keeps looking in the camera and complaining about the glare. She takes a shot and looks at it.

"Move closer to the glass." She takes another and inspects it. "That one's no good." She raises the camera to her face and moves to Khristian's other side. She inspects and deletes another photo. This is a giant waste of his precious time.

"Whatever you take is fine. Don't worry about the glare." I say.

I lean into the glass and smile.

She looks at it and lowers the camera. "It'll just take a minute to print." She exits the room.

This is it. I pick up the black phone. We are both still standing, so I look directly into his eyes. "Thank you so much for taking the time to share with me, Khristian. It meant a lot."

He flashes me half a smile and looks towards the corner where his sister is waiting. "You're welcome. Take care, Pamela."

I can't say goodbye. I can't bring myself to utter that word. Instead I say "thank you," and leave the room. I approach the guard, who is bent over a small printer. I'm about to lose it. Without looking at me she says, "This is going to take another minute."

Tears stream down my face. A man standing near the vending machines looks at me and I want to hide under a table.

"Do you have any Kleenex?" I ask in a lowered voice.

The guard looks at me as if I'm contagious. "No, but there's toilet paper in the bathroom."

I run to the women's restroom, slam the door and lock it. My eyes are burning. I begin to cry like a faucet on full blast. Helpless and hopeless, I clutch the sink to steady myself. I splash my face with cool water and pat it dry with a brown paper towel.

After composing myself, I sneak out of the bathroom and approach the guard. She hands me the photo.

"It's a good picture. You look nice," she says.

I thank her. She asks me to return Khristian's sister's ID to her husband, who is waiting in the first building. As I walk through the main visiting room, I'm unable to look at Khristian one last time. I put my sunglasses on and trek back out of the maze.

When I get to the first building, I hand the ID over without a word and leave. I'm going to start bawling any minute, and I need to do it in the safety of my car with the doors closed and the windows rolled up. A prison parking lot is not an ideal place to lose control, but I can't help it. I have to make it to the safety of my car without running into his parents. Once I see them, it's over, and my emotional breakdown is the last thing in the world they need to witness. I trot to my car and grab a cigarette.

My phone is beeping. Two messages. I smoke, listen and sob. I don't care what the guard in the tower thinks. The first call is from Katie. The compassion in her voice as she asks whether I'm okay only makes things worse. The second message is from Audra, a school friend who makes me laugh like no one else. I immediately call her to distract me. She answers on the first ring.

She knows I'm at the prison, but she tells me about a ridiculous gang website she found and has me laughing and crying at the same time. Khristian's parents pull into the lot and park three spots away. I walk to the other side of my car and listen intently as Audra rambles on about her love for the band Journey. Listening to her is all I can do to keep it together. I can't look either of his parents in the eye right now. So for now I'm engrossed in a very important conversation about the vocal talent of Steve Perry.

Somehow I manage to pull it together for the drive back to Huntsville and my last interview—the one I've been dreading. Since I've got time to spare, I swing by the motel to change clothes and attempt to change faces. My reflection in the bathroom is horrific. My pale face is streaked with black mascara, my eyes are Rocky-in-his-final-fight puffy, and my hair looks like it was styled by an angry toddler. This is not the impression I want to present to Richard Lopez, a chaplain employed by the Texas Department of Criminal Justice. Out of everyone I've attempted to contact, Mr. Lopez is probably the most hesitant to meet with me. In twenty years as a chaplain, he has only granted two media interviews — as he's reminded me twice now.

The pressure is on, and for the first time in my adult life, I am late. Neither my GPS nor I can find his office. Reluctantly, I call his cell phone, feeling like a helpless woman who still can't exit a fire truck during a fire without someone holding her hand. In a calm, soothing voice, Mr. Lopez reassures me that I'm not far — a welcome change from the Tom-Tom's repetitive monotone "Turn around when possible." In less than a minute, I pull into the parking lot of the TDCJ Chaplaincy Department.

Lopez, a stout man with a full head of salt and pepper hair, greets me warmly and leads me through a maze of cubicles to his office at the back of the building. Unlike Mr. Whiteside, Lopez is dressed for a Sunday sermon in his neatly-pressed gray suit and shiny shoes. As I take a seat in front of his desk, he offers to get me a glass of water. Normally I would decline, but I feel needy and alone. I think I need God. Actually, I know I need God, and Richard Lopez might be the closest I'm going to get right now.

Before I turn my recorder on, he looks me square in the eye and says he doesn't trust journalists. I assure him that I'm not out to expose him or make him look bad, and that I'm really not a journalist: I simply want to know about his job. I rattle off all the people I've met and followed around, and when I tell him that I'm a hospice volunteer, he says "Oh, bless you," as if I'm some kind of angel. I don't reveal the real truth—that I stick to office work because I'm too afraid to actually face a dying person.

Mr. Lopez's slow, hypnotic speech, while probably very sooth-ing to those facing death, is making me want to curl up on his office floor and take a nap. I'm so tired. I open my silly notebook and the first question is from Roger Haney, a coworker friend who happens to be a minister. I don't have any sort of plan or strategy for this interview, so I just go with it.

"Okay, so my first question is, how do you prepare the inmate for their spiritual needs for what they're going to face?"

Lopez thinks for a moment.

"I've been through a lot of these, Pamela, and everyone is different in terms of my approach...I try to help the individual stay calm. I begin with simple questions like, how was your trip here? How was the weather? Just those simple things to start a conversation. I remind them for the duration of the afternoon I will be there at their side, that I can answer their questions. I can listen to them. If everything is exhausted in the courts, the execution begins at six."

He also reminds them that they can make phone calls to loved ones and family members. Most men don't want to talk about scripture or God or life after death at first, so he starts out small, like two people standing over a punch bowl trying to break the ice. By execution day, they've only met twice. Now that I think about it, Khristian is most likely chatting with a stranger about the weather right now.

He mentions discussing the witness list as a way to get the conversation going. And with those words, I want to drop to the floor again. In four hours, Khristian's mother is going to watch him die. My voice falters.

"So, what do you think about the family being there? Isn't it hard for both parties?"

"I think for the most part, it is support for both the inmate and the family...the parents being there is showing support for the individual in those last minutes of his or her life."

"So can the person actually see their family?"

"The inmate can move his head to the right. There are two witness rooms to his right. One for his family and one for the victims."

"He can see both?"

"Yes. He can see them from the waist up…I tell the individual that they will hear him, but he will not hear them. So a lot of times, they will speak but he has to look at their mouth in order to see what they're saying. For example, I love you or goodbye or whatever it may be. They will look at each other."

In other words, the silent film from hell. The inmate is lying on a gurney. He is not standing like in the movies to deliver his final words. His eyes are the only part of his body that can move, and he has to look up in probably his most fearful moment and what does he see? His parents mouthing words that he can't discern.

"For a lot of reasons, they don't look towards the victims…Sometimes they do turn over to the victims and apologize."

"Do they ask you about their last statement?"

"As we begin to talk about their past, I say, 'tell me about your upbringing'—what was it like?— and they tell me their stories, many horror stories. In no way am I defending, in no way am I expressing sides in what I do. I'm simply trying to help the individual get rid of stuff that that individual may be carrying for a long time, years and years. And so I allow them to talk about whatever they choose…And along the way, if I don't know, and even if I do know, I'll ask them, 'do you believe in God, do you have faith in a higher power?'"

He is so passionate that I feel as if he's preaching to me.

"If it is in your heart that you truly repent for what you've done to offend God, to break the commandments of God, we as human beings know what sin is and you have the opportunity to ask God for forgiveness." He pauses and then adds, "It's amazing how they begin to feel some difference in knowing and hearing that they can be forgiven."

I reveal that my brother was in prison for over twenty-years and that several Christian people helped him, on the inside and even after he got out. I don't know why I do this. Lopez leans towards me and repeats "wonderful, wonderful." He's a good listener, but we're not here to talk about me. I ask if there is spiritual support on the row other than at the last minute. He tells me yes, and that they have staff chaplains, but ultimately, it is the choice of the offender to be ministered to.

"No one is going to force themselves on the prisoner." He crosses his arms and leans back in his chair.

"Do you consider a death row inmate a dying person?

"Absolutely. Just like every one of us. We're all dying." We both laugh. I laugh a little more nervously.

"Do most inmates retain hope till the end, or have they surrendered to the idea that their life is going to end?"

"Hope for a lot of them is there." He further explains that attorneys are to blame for creating this sense of hope. "They have a way of misrepresenting and making mountains out of molehills."

And families shell out tons of money on these tiny shreds of hope. "For many of them, they're buying time, but ultimately after all possibilities have been exhausted, they're still holding on because of what their attorneys have said."

"So why did you choose to get into this line of work?

He leans forward and places his elbows on the desk and clasps his hands as if in prayer. "Very long story, but from the very beginning, I didn't choose to do this. This was a calling from God."

He initially worked on death row as a chaplain. "I began to experience, and I want to emphasize a God/Christ relationship with these men. I earned respect. I earned appreciation. I earned love from those men and a few of those women like never before in my life. As a minister, I found God using me for a very good reason to bring people to him. So it was God who chose me."

"Have you found that people can't handle this job? That it's too difficult?"

He sips from his own water. "Oh, yes. It's not for everybody...It stresses the individual. Because I've been there, there are days at the end of the day of an execution where I'm exhausted—I'm drained mentally, emotionally. So other people have experienced the stress and found it's not for them."

"So how long have you been doing this?"

"Twenty years."

"And how many people do your job?

"There's only two of us. We alternate...It's too much for one person to be there time after time after time."

I mention Khristian and Mr. Whiteside and he tells me that Mr. Whiteside can't be in the chamber during the execution. He can only be present in the witness room.

"His spiritual adviser can come visit him for 20 to 30 minutes at the death watch cell in the Walls Unit."

My stomach growls loudly and I tell him I have stomach issues whenever I travel.

"Do you want some more water?" he asks.

I decline. "So what is the most challenging part of your job? Ministering to a man with no faith, or being present at the execution?"

"An offender who is in denial or an offender who doesn't want to talk or hear about God. That's the most difficult part of what I do or what I'm there for. Because in my faith belief, there is an opportunity for salvation...God gives us many opportunities for us to get ready."

"So what do you do if they don't want to talk about it?"

"I'm not their judge. I'm not going to force my faith or my religion on anybody. I'm just there as an enabler to help that individual. So if that individual chooses not to talk about it or focus on God, I will communicate, I will talk to him about anything he wants to talk about. It's amazing how much they want to say and what they want to talk about...I listen and we do engage in non-religious conversation."

"How do you take care of yourself after an execution?"

"That's a very good question. A very good question." He leans back and contemplates his response. "I spend quiet alone time in my faith belief of the presence and spirit of God."

"Do you have anybody here you can talk with?"

He initially says no, but then adds, "I have some interaction with my partner here who relates to what I go through, and I relate to what he goes through...It's important for us to process that with one another and move on."

I tell him that I don't know how he does it, but I'm glad that he does. He's glad that I've said that. *That I'm on his side,* I think.

"It's the most difficult thing I've done in my life. Because of the exhaustion, energy, emotion, so many things I deal with. Because in essence when I'm interacting with this individual the clock is literally ticking. Time is running out. So I always wear a watch. I don't ever wear a watch unless I'm doing an execution. I'm literally looking at the clock. The prisoner often asks me, 'Chaplain what time is it?' Because there is no clock. We're working against the clock. In that span of time, as it gets closer to six o'clock, knowing that he or she has already gotten that call from their attorney, sorry everything is over, you have been completely turned down by the Supreme Court, then everything is over. So I know literally that we've run out of time...There still needs to be some closing, some preparation because of what is going to happen."

"What is the inmate's fear? Is it pain? That the actual act of dying is going to hurt? Or is it the fear of going to Hell or the afterlife or what's going to happen after they've ceased living in their body?"

"That's a very tough question. And the only way I can answer is that a number of things are going on—their mom, wife, son, daughter seeing them in this situation, totally helpless. There's a lot that enters into what that person goes through."

"What do you tell them to lessen their fear when it's 6 o'clock and they're going to that room?"

He responds slowly and carefully. "I say to them, in your own life, whatever fear you may be going through, whatever uncertainty you may be going through, right now at this time, if you will allow me to pray with you and ask the spirit, the presence of God to bring to you reassurance that you are in God's hands, He will see you through this."

I interrupt him. "And does that work?"

"Sometimes it does and sometimes there's no response."

I ask if he has contact with the inmate's family. He tells me that in the afternoon of the execution, after he's met with the inmate, he'll cross the street to a holding place where the family stays. He'll give them an update to let them know what's going on with their loved one, and offer counseling.

"The mom must be the hardest to deal with," I say.

He shakes his head mournfully and mutters under his breath. "Absolutely. Very difficult. Very difficult."

"Are you a mom?" he asks.

I laugh, as if he's got me figured out. "Yes, I am." My recorder clicks off at this point. I fumble with it and tell him offhandedly that I don't know whether I could be there if it was my son. Once the recorder is situated, I ask about grief counseling for the family. I want some reassurance that Khristian's parents will be given some sort of help.

He tells me that there is a pamphlet that they give out, a crisis intervention sort of thing, but he seems somewhat dismissive of it.

"Can I see it?"

"Um, well, I don't think I have one. They have them at the Polunsky Unit." He searches through his desk drawers.

"Not here at the Walls Unit?" Which would make more sense to me.

He finds one and hands it to me.

It suddenly hits me that I'm going to the Walls Unit. I look at the brochure, which looks like it was printed on regular old copy paper in this very office. It's titled, "Critical Incident Stress Management," with a black and white picture of lilies on the front. On the second page, I see the stages of grief.

"Kubler Ross!" I say as if I know her.

He stares at me for a moment, as if my questioning of psychology diminishes the healing power of God. I awkwardly tell him that I plan on going to the Walls Unit today for the execution.

"What's your part in this?" he asks, with just a hint of accusation in his tone.

I speak of Khristian, but to deflect the fact that I have feelings for him, and would be willing to hug him without God acting through me, I bring up the logistical aspects of parking. I hand him my printed directions to the Walls Unit.

His demeanor returns to warm and helping. He points to Avenue I and says that on the corner is a big parking lot. "That's where I suggest you park." With his pen, he circles places of interest on the map. "The people who stand here are against the death penalty and over here are the ones for it. If I were you, I would be somewhere in the parking lot, but you'll be fine wherever you stand."

"Can't I just stand in the middle?"

He laughs at what is probably a ridiculous statement, but doesn't comment.

"So when should I get there?"

"Around 5:30 is when they start gathering."

I look at my cell phone—3:15. I need to wrap this up.

"Do you feel there is any sort of misconception about what you do? What do people think? In your experience."

"People see me there as being against the death penalty, and others think that I'm for it. And I want you to respect that. I never talk about where I stand. I am there as the presence of God."

For a brief moment, I entertain the idea of asking him what side of the street God stands on, but I vowed not to press him—as a human being or as the presence of God—and I should probably stick to that. "Not to mention, you are the only source of comfort for that person in their final moments—the only person to touch him. Do you touch?"

"Through the bars, we can hold hands, and we do hold hands, and we pray. And sometimes it's amazing, because when I go back at the end to take the property to the family, the loved one will want to touch my hands, because I had touched their loved one."

"Do they want to hug you?"

"Oh yes."

"That's so sad."

I reach for my recorder and he quickly interjects "Some do, some don't," as if to minimize the power of hugs.

"Pamela."

I look up at him. He rises from his chair, a man in his Sunday best, standing at his desk as if it were his own private pulpit.

"I'm not there representing the attorneys. I'm not there representing the state. I'm there representing God. I thank the state of Texas for allowing us to do what we do. Because we're talking about religion here. We're talking about spirituality. We're talking about God."

Thank God.

I drive to the Walls Unit and park in the lot, just as I was told. The prison is made of brick and sits in the midst of houses and a gas station with an adjoining Subway sandwich shop. It is literally in the middle of town in a heavy traffic area. At each corner there is an elevated guard tower. I exit my car.

A Waco news van is parked with reporter and driver inside. The reporter, Donna McCollum, is speaking with Christy Wooten, a reporter from the *Nacogdoches Daily Sentinel* who is parked next to her. I hesitantly approach them by walking in between the two vehicles. I awkwardly ask Ms. Wooten if she is going to be a media witness at the execution. She says she is. I tell her that I was initially going to interview Mike Graczyk, but the AP office said he was at Fort Hood because of the shooting. I ask if I can interview her after the execution.

"Will it take long? Cause I have to drive to Dallas afterwards."

"No. It shouldn't. I just want to know what the experience was like for you. Have you done this before?"

"No."

"Are you nervous?"

"Nah. I cover worse stuff like murders, so this isn't so bad."

Donna McCollum seems annoyed by my presence. Neither one of them introduce themselves to me. They remain seated in their vehicles with their windows rolled down.

As Ms. McCollum discusses the witness list, I interject that I interviewed Khristian. Ms. Wooten says, "Huh. That punk turned down my request for an interview." I recognize this false bravado from the female deputies when I worked in a jail. I walk away without another word. No wonder Khristian turned down her interview request. She views him as a punk. The sad reality is that an article about a monster sells more copies than one about a kitten.

I take a seat on a low wall around the lot. A man approaches the news team and they follow him inside. A group of prison employees is seated at a picnic table on the lawn. I ask them where people gather and one of the uniformed men replies, "That corner down there, ma'am." Everyone is so polite in Texas— except reporters.

I walk back to the lot. A woman is seated in a green car a few spaces from my Vibe. She watches as I take a seat on the wall and open my notebook for comfort. I try to write, but words fail me. This is too surreal. Why am I not at home eating dinner with my husband and kids? I feel like I'm in an alternate universe or on drugs or both. I think about Khristian. He's in that brick building right now. Did he see Lake Livingston or the grocery store or the orange tabby that wanders the lot at the Polunsky Unit? He's probably sitting with a state chaplain right now, a man he met just a couple of days ago. Maybe he's still eating that chocolate ice cream or drinking another cup of coffee. Does he drink it black or does he ask politely for a little cream and sugar? I wonder what he's talking about. Who is he going to call? What will he say? *I love you Mom. You'll be okay. I'm sorry for all the pain I've caused you. We'll see each other again in heaven. Well, they've told me I got to hang up. I love you too. Bye.*

In just an hour and a half, or maybe less, he will be led into the death chamber, strapped down to a gurney, hooked up to a pair of IVs, and then the curtains will be pulled back for the worst show on earth.

As I stare at the picture of us in my notebook, a tiny white feather drifts into my line of vision and lands at my feet.

It could be a molting bird, or a down jacket with a tear, but I interpret it as my guardian angel giving me a sign. *It's okay, Pamela. You are supposed to be here. You'll be all right.*

I don't feel like approaching the woman in her car after the frosty reception I received from the reporters. Two guards set up a "Do Not Cross" tape, sealing off the road directly in front of the prison. They just stand there facing my corner of the lot. Occasionally they lift the tape for a car to exit the street. There is constant traffic. Many of the cars have their windows rolled down, with hip-hop booming out into the fading sunlight.

My phone rings. It is a number from my hometown. I answer it.

"Hi Pamela, this is Natalie from Salon del Sol and I was wondering if we could change your appointment time with Heather on the thirteenth?"

I don't miss a beat. "I'm actually sitting outside a prison in Texas where a man I know is being executed, so I'm going to have to call you back on Monday when I get home."

"Oh. Ohhhhhhhhh! I'm so sorry. Okay."

"Bye."

A tall man with a long gray beard arrives and takes his place at the corner facing the guards. He obviously knows what he's doing.

A young woman in her twenties takes a seat on the wall by the street corner. She must have come for the execution. Why else would she be here? I decide to get my ass up and approach her. "Hi, um. Do you know which side this is? I was told there is a side for people who are against the death penalty and one for those who are for it."

"I don't know, sorry."

"So, which side are you on?"

Her face scrunches up, but she can't help it. Tears run down her face as she relays that she was Khristian's pen pal for nine years. I also cry. Seeing another person in pain is all it takes today. This woman, Amber, cared for him, and here she is waiting outside a building where he will die. I look away, embarrassed by my own emotion. She actually knew him and witnessed his progression from young man to adult. *Who am I to feel this way?*

I turn back to her and ask if she needs a hug. She nods. And we do. I don't feel awkward. For the first time in my adult life, I feel that embracing this total stranger is the most natural, appropriate thing to do. I hand her a Kleenex and we wipe our tears. I show her my picture with Khristian and she whips out a Polaroid from her purse. In it, he looks skinny and young. He's hopeful as he poses for the camera in the visiting area cell. She tells me of their relationship. That they never met. How he painted a picture for her to hang in her new apartment when she went away to college. How he stopped writing to her after his appeals had been lost.

As two women arrive in anti-death penalty t-shirts, we realize we've been on the right side of the street all along. One sets up a lawn chair at the entrance to the parking lot. The other posts signs along the fence. Cars whiz by and their occupants stare at us like we're putting on a show. Maybe we are. I tell the two women why I'm there and that I met Khristian. I want to make him real so this nonsense will stop. Governor Perry is going to call the prison, halt the execution, and we can all go home. Right?

"If you see the media witnesses cross the street, that means that the execution is going to take place," one of the women informs me.

I never check the time. I simply stand on the corner as if in a hypnotic trance as the light fades around us. More guards take their place at the tape, facing us, as if we pose a threat. Maybe we do. One particularly beefy guy walks to the front of the tape. He crosses his arms and the stern expression on his unflinching face warns us not to make any sudden moves. I try not to look at him. Instead, I focus my attention to the corner of the building, the death house.

I relay to Gloria, one of the anti-death penalty protesters, that the saddest thing—besides the obvious—is that Khristian will not be allowed to hug his family.

"The only time his family gets to touch him is when he's dead on a gurney," she says. Her words hit me like a slap. With that, Gloria marches into the middle of the street and positions herself in front of the guards. She turns on a microphone attached to a large speaker system. It squeaks and squeals. Her voice booms into the silent night. She's mad as hell and she isn't going to take it anymore. Midway through her speech, her microphone dies.

I am relieved by the return to silence, as her words are not a comfort. I assume they are intended for the guards, not for the people on the corner who already agree with her. A group of college students join us. Their attendance is part of a class at Sam Houston. Amber and I remain quiet, transfixed by the street and any pedestrians that might cross as it gets closer to six. There is nothing more to say.

As the media witnesses cross the street, the gray-bearded man beside me points at them. "That's Graczyk right there. He's the first one climbing up the stairs. Trust me. You don't want to talk to him. The man is numb."

They all look blurry to me without my glasses, but after the media disappears inside the building, I see Mrs. Oliver's yellow coat in the fading November light. My stomach flips. Khristian's mother is about to witness her beloved son die right before her eyes and there is nothing any of us can do about it. The last time she will see him alive, he will be on display, like a fish in an empty tank—strapped down, helpless and struggling for breath. She won't be able to rush to him, comfort him or hold his hand.

Six bells toll on the prison clock.

Don't be afraid. Even as I mentally repeat the words, I don't know who they're intended for. Amber is crying on the edge of the street. I dig for another tissue in my purse and hand it to her. I feel numb, like I'm stuck inside a vacuum with whooshing and whirring all around me. At 6:15 my phone rings, startling me and breaking the silence of our vigil. I answer it quickly to stop the ridiculous sound. It's my sister.

"I can't talk right now," I say and hang up the phone.

Within five minutes, the witnesses and the media exit the prison. I watch as Khristian's parents and siblings cross the street.

"Oh, my God. His poor family," I say to no one, to everyone.

Gloria gathers up her belongings. As she passes, she mutters, "God, I hate this place," and loads the signs and her recorder into the back of her Jeep. I feel the same way. This place is the biggest pink elephant I've ever seen— smack in the middle of town. As the residents of Huntsville sit down to dinner, or click on the evening news, most are probably oblivious to the fact that a man's life has just ended. And for what? Revenge? Is the world a safer place without Khristian in it? Did the victim's family feel vindicated now that the state has ended his life? Has their sorrow and anger dissipated?

I have no answers. All I know is that I need something. It isn't a cigarette or a drink or even a hug. I can't walk away from this moment, this THING, and go back to my motel room, surf the internet or numb myself further with the boob tube. I turn to the bearded man.

"Does his family get to take his body back to Waco tonight?"

"No. They take everyone to a funeral home right around the corner. The prison's got a pretty sweet deal with the state. Everyone, regardless of where they end up, has to go there. That's where his family is probably headed right now. You can go too if you want."

"Are you serious? I can?" After all the patting down, security measures, thick glass walls and telephoned conversations, it's hard to believe I can just walk into a funeral home and see Khristian without some sort of bureaucratic barrier.

"You probably want to get there when his family walks in."

Gloria interjects. "Yeah, but sometimes the funeral home employees can be real assholes."

"Well, I can be a real bitch when I want to."

Gloria laughs. "Me too."

I turn to Amber, who looks like a lost little girl. "Do you want to go too?" I ask.

"Yes."

We take my rental car and follow the bearded man to the funeral home. As we pull up, the Oliver family is exiting their car. I say a quick thanks to the man and we dash towards the building, hoping to sneak in with the family.

I am not thinking at this point. Something greater is pushing me towards the funeral home, and I can feel it. I see Mr. Whiteside exit his car. As he walks towards the entrance, I greet him and stick as close as possible to his side. A tall older man in a dark suit blocks the entrance. He looks at Amber and me with a dour expression.

Mr. Whiteside addresses him. "This is Pamela, a friend of Khristian's and this is…"

"Amber," I say.

"She is also a friend." Mr. Whiteside has no idea who Amber is, but she is with me and he covers for us without explanation or awkwardness.

We enter the funeral home. Khristian's parents, a man and woman I don't know, and his brother and sister with their spouses stand at the front of the room. Amber and I take a seat on the first pew. Khristian's lifeless body lies on a gurney at the front. A burgundy blanket is pulled up to his collarbone, as if he's just been tucked in for the night. There is a box of Kleenex sitting at the end of the pew. I grab a handful and sob into the mound of tissue.

Katie and Kermit Oliver stand near their son's lifeless body in the overly bright room. Kermit's arm rests on the small of his wife's back, just like at the prison. They look like they are in shock. Katie Oliver turns towards the sounds of my sobbing. Her eyes are wide and sad. She recognizes me and nods, acknowledging my presence.

"I'm so sorry," I say and wipe my face with the tissue. She turns back to her son. The small group parts and I can see his body clearly. Mrs. Oliver steps up to the gurney, gently touches Khristian's face, and strokes his black hair. This vision is more than I can take. I doubt if I will ever be able to erase it from my mind—the mother and son reunion fifteen minutes too late.

An employee enters a room off to the side. A Muzak version of *Let There Be Peace on Earth* begins to play. To me, it sounds cheesy and cheery. I don't know if this is an attempt to drown out the sound of my sobbing, or if he is trying to comfort the family members. It is an odd choice. Here, a perfectly healthy young man lies dead on a gurney, and to comfort his grieving family members, he plays a Christmas song. He returns to the room and stands at the end of our pew. He looks at me again and I want to tell him to buzz off, but I'm too busy trying to control my own sobbing. Suddenly, I remember that my phone is still on. It plays a loud jingle as it powers off and I feel like a jackass.

Kermit and Katie Oliver approach the funeral home worker. He leads them to the back of the room to discuss something. I ask Amber to hand me more tissue. Another employee tells us that when we exit, we need to use that door.

Realizing that our time is limited, Mr. Whiteside asks everyone to join hands in a prayer. He motions for us to join him. I take Mr. Whiteside's and Amber's hands and we form a circle with Khristian's family. He says a prayer I can't remember. My nose runs at an alarming rate. I sniff the snot back, since I am unable to wipe it. When the prayer ends with "amen," I walk back towards the pew.

Katie and Kermit Oliver approach me. "Thank you so much for coming," she says.

I hug her. "I'm so sorry."

"Bless you."

Kermit says, "Thank you," and they return to their son's body.

Each member of his family stops and spends a moment with him. I am the last to leave. I walk up to Khristian and look at his face. I place my left hand on his shoulder. His body still feels warm. I say, "Goodbye, Khristian," and walk out the door.

The family is gathered at their cars. Amber and I walk slowly to mine. I look at her tear-stained face and say, "I don't think I can go back to my motel. Do you want to go get something to eat?"

Neither of us can believe that we were able to say goodbye to him and to grieve with his family. If Mr. Whiteside hadn't been there at the right moment, we would never have been let in. I wanted to thank him for that, but he was gone, the poor man. I think Khristian's death really affects him. I wonder if he will drive home tonight or stay another dreadful night in Huntsville. I wonder who will lift him up.

Amber and I drive to IHOP. The fluorescent lighting and the buzz of families with small children running around the restaurant adds to the unreality of the night. Time hasn't stopped, even though it feels like it has. I try to cheer Amber with talk of Khristian, but it is no use. The waiter approaches our table and asks how we're doing. We say "fine" in unison. We both order the special—pumpkin pancakes. When they arrive, I take three bites. Even though they are warm and I've drenched them in maple syrup, my taste buds interpret them as soft, fluffy cardboard.

After I drop Amber back at the prison parking lot, we agree to meet the following morning to attend the art show in Waco. When I return to my motel room, I can't sleep. Nor can I express to Erik the magnitude of what I just went through. Like Jim Willett, I feel there has to be a word that means the same thing as awesome, but lets you know that it's a bad thing also.

CHAPTER ELVEN

Hold the Baby

K hristian's last letter to me arrives on Monday, November 9, 2009. He has been dead for four days. I almost don't want to open it, knowing that this is his last correspondence. Unlike his other letters, it is written on graph paper.

Well, here's my letter to detail my answers to your questions—I hope I will be thorough enough for what you need, so here we go! Having been locked up over 10 years I've grown complacent over the years and my execution date seems surreal to pop up what seems so suddenly. I try to distract myself but it's rather hard to do so with something as profound as death looming over me. I seem to be growing more nervous as the hour approaches but I doubt I'll lose any sleep over it—I'm pretty tired and it's only 4:12pm as I write this. I received a call from my attorney saying I lost my appeal in the state court and in the court of criminal appeals, so they very likely will execute me in 26 hours.

Is there any peace with this process? I don't find peace outside my spirituality—my beliefe in the Lord is the sole source of my peace and tranquility. I hate to think of this as a process—it makes it sound so cold and clinical. I of course believe in an afterlife—death is merely a transition from one state of existence to another. Mr. Whiteside, my spiritual advisor, comes to pull me out early so my family doesn't have to wait on me to be escorted out. The best way to deal with this situation (or what works for me anyway) is both Hope and Surrender. Hope that relief will be given but surrender to the reality of the situation. Never give up hope though.My family has been handling this situation very reserved and humble. We're not a family that wears our emotions on our sleeves so you would be hard pressed to know anything was wrong. Both me and my family are accepting of what will be however my mom refuses to contemplate my execution. I think all this will be hardest on her. I've told my family that it's up to them if they want to be present. I've put my parents, my brother, my sister, and her husband on my list of witnesses. We're not allowed contact visits for any reason. My last goodbyes will be by phone at Huntsville.

I don't know what (if anything) I'll say to the victim's family but my last words will be the 23rd Psalm. I have thought about my funeral and decided to leave it up to my family if they want to do anything. They probably will have me buried—I'm not concerned what's done to my body. I did decide against donating my body to science—seems kinda gruesome. My funeral will likely be a solemn affair—again my family doesn't really show their emotions. My parents asked what kind of things I wanted done, funeral-wise, but again I've left that to them.

There are a couple of reasons I keep to myself in here—first because a lot of people here are looking to use you for their own ends. Some try to learn as much about you as they can so that they can testify against you if you receive relief from the courts—others are just looking for someone to support their eating habits. Secondly the majority of the people here are very easy to anger. They think you're weak if you help someone out, they say you're scared if you don't join a gang—just aggressive machoism. A lot of the guys here deserve very much to be locked up (Not neces-sarily on Death Row—I really don't believe in the Death Penalty).

Well, I hope this letter is sufficient—I have a long day ahead of me so I'll close here. Thank you for choosing me for your the-sis.P.S. Oh, I attempted suicide 3 times, each time I was simply overwhelmed by depression over my situation. I'm on medication for depression and schizophrenia—it helps. I've suffered depres-sion for many years before being locked up. I treated it with drugs and that likely made the situation worse.

Sincerely,
Khristian Oliver

I am thoroughly depressed. When I share the letter with Erik, he tells me that he heard about a grief support group that starts tomorrow night. I contemplate that for about a second. What would I say to the people who have lost their spouse, their par-ent, or their child? *Hi, my name is Pamela and I'm here because I went to Texas last week and met a death row inmate that I found very sweet and honest and they killed him, just like they were fixin' to do. Oh, and I only knew him for two days.*

They would kick me out and call me loony. But I am grieving. The only way I can make any sense out of it is to imagine that Khristian and I were like a couple of people who meet at an air-port bar. We both had a three-hour layover and we knew we'd never see each other again. Because of that freedom, our ex-change was honest and intimate. I go on my way and he goes on his.

Since the world doesn't stop when someone dies, I still have to help at a Thanksgiving party for my son's kindergarten class. When I show up at the festively-decorated school, I feel like the walking dead. I don't know what to say to the other parents dur-ing the introductory chitchat, so I hide in the school's kitchen to bake chocolate cupcakes. Nik's teacher, a young woman who initially had a difficult time handling his exuberance, wanders in, startling me as I remove a pan from the oven.

"How was your trip to Texas?"

I've had several interactions with Nik's teacher about his behavior. I must have mentioned my Texas plans, or else my outspoken son blurted it out during show and tell: "My mom went to death row!"

"Oh, uh. It was pretty horrible." *Shouldn't you be out there with the kids and all the normal parents?*

"Was he executed?"

"Yeah. He was." I attempt to remove the cupcakes from the pan without burning my fingers. I feel like a car accident she won't stop looking at.

"Did you witness it?"

"No. I didn't. Thank God." She's not moving. "I don't think I could have handled it. I ended up meeting his family and his pen pal and then I went to the funeral home where they took his body and it was just horrible. And now there's a whole new set of victims."

She nods compassionately, like she understands, which I totally don't expect from a woman who used to call me daily to report the various ways in which my son was behaving like a five-year-old.

"I don't know if you know this, but when I was Nik's age, my parents were murdered."

"What?" I shout in disbelief. No, I didn't know that —and her revelation is so out there that I feel like someone is going to pop out of the pantry with a video camera and say it's all a joke. "Oh, my God, I'm so sorry." I touch her arm briefly. "What happened, if you don't mind me asking?"

And I'm getting the distinct impression that she doesn't. "We lived out in the country and my dad saw a man walking around with a gun on our property. My dad went out there to see what he was doing and the man killed him. Then he came in the house and killed my mom."

I don't know what to say. This is the strangest conversation—and I've had a few of those lately. I feel like this one is my fault. I look down at the cupcakes for possible responses, other than 'what did the man do to you in the house?' "Was he arrested?"

"Yeah."

We spend a good twenty-minutes talking about my trip and my newly-solidified stance on the death penalty. She seems very interested in what I have to say. If I hadn't learned it from the people I've already met, it is now obvious with a capital 'O' that listening is one of the greatest gifts you can give to someone who wants to talk about death or is grieving.

I walk to my car in a daze. My phone rings. It's Heather. I contemplate not answering, but I do. She wants to know how I'm doing. Since she's never called me before, I feel like she psychically knew that I'd gone back for a cut with Lisa Marie. I tell her about the trip to Texas and that I felt sad and overwhelmed by grief. I also relay all the trips to dermatologists and doctors to figure out why my hair is falling out. When there is nothing left to say, I pause for a moment and jump right in to what I really want: "I know this sounds totally off the wall, but I was wondering if I could be present when you give birth?"

Heather is silent, so I jabber on.

"I've been following you and Dan around for a while and I'd kind of like to write about something happy. You know what I mean? I really need to be in the presence of something happy."

"Okay."

"What?" I shout like a bartender in a crowded bar.

"Yes. I have a friend who wanted to be present, but I don't think I could handle her personality when I'm in labor. But I think you would be okay. Yeah. I think you would be okay."

"Are you serious?" Even I doubt her decision. She barely knows me—just six or seven haircuts and an interview over tea—and birthing a baby is a pretty darn intimate moment. There's nakedness, pain, screaming, crying and poop with a chance of vomit as well. It's kind of traumatic for all involved.

I take another deep breath and remind myself that this isn't about me. It's about Dan and Heather—and if she doesn't mind my presence, then I guess I should just roll with it.

"Well, okay. Cool. I guess call me when you're in labor, then."

*   *   *

Like most people with anxiety, I am not patient. I want to know when things are going to happen so that I can busy myself with plans. You can't do that for babies. They get here when they get here. As Heather's due date approaches, I call her daily for updates, but every call is the same. She is having contractions, but they aren't that bad. Finally, on January 19th, there is talk of induction in the next day or so. I clear my schedule for the next few days and step away from the pot so that it can boil.

Just when everything seems to be neatly put in place and planned like a Martha Stewart dinner party, the National Weather Service announces that a snowstorm is headed towards Colorado. Stephen King didn't set *The Shining* here without good reason. We get enormous amounts of snow, and there isn't much that I hate more than driving in it. It fills me with white-knuckled, sweaty-armpit anxiety bordering on outright terror to navigate my tiny Toyota onto a snow-packed highway with ginormous GMCs and Ford F-250s careening by me without a care in the world. Erik works at a body shop, so I know what can happen, and it's usually the egos behind those gigantic vehicles that cause the mayhem.

The snow is falling hard on January 20th. My plan is to drive in to work, put in a couple of hours to give Heather and Dan some alone time, and then head on over to the hospital. But the roads are icy and the white-out conditions during my morning commute change those plans. I turn in to the hospital, park my car in the Birthing Center's parking lot, and trot on over to the coffee kiosk. I really don't want to show up in their room at this exact moment, as I already feel like a unwanted party guest showing up two hours early.

So with coffee in hand, I enter the hospice office on the second floor. The regular receptionist has been replaced with a less chipper, visibly pregnant woman. She greets with me with a surprised "Hello."

"Hi. I'm a volunteer here, but I haven't been here for a while. I decided to come in to assemble some packets, if that's okay."

"Oh, okay."

She follows me into the office. Because of the snowstorm, the office is lacking the usual traffic. I approach the office manager.

"Well, hello there." There is an awkward pause, as if she doesn't remember my name.

"Pamela," I say. "I'm a bad hospice volunteer. I've been really busy lately." She smiles and pats me on the shoulder. "You're not a bad volunteer. There's no such thing. We just wondered what happened to you."

"School, life, kids. My friend is being induced today and she's allowing me to be at the birth, so I thought I'd come up here for a bit."

"How exciting."

It's weird referring to Heather as my friend. I mean, I can count my friends—the ones I could call at 2 in the morning in a drunken stupor and ask for a ride home—on one hand. The last person I told about being present at the birth said, "She must be a really close friend to let you do that." Bingo! And that is the problem. I am not close to Heather at all. I don't know her favorite color, what kind of music she likes, her birthday, nothing. All I know is that she cuts and colors my hair on occasion and now she's having a baby.

After a few hours of nurse packet assembly, I leave and find Kati Bachman, the grief counselor, chatting outside the front door. I nod and smile as I pass, but she grabs my arm and abruptly ends her conversation. She stays glued to my side as we walk towards the elevators, barraging me with questions of how I'm doing and where I've been. I tell her about Heather, Dan, and Tommy, and why I am at the hospital.

"I get to witness the happy ending," I say with a smile, and push the elevator button.

She looks at me quizzically. "You mean the full circle of life?'

"Kind of. I mean, these two people had the worst thing happen and now they're having another baby, and..."

"But you know that isn't necessarily a happy ending. Grief and loss is normal. You know, if you've loved a lot in this life, you're going to grieve a lot too."

Damn, damn, damn, damn, damn! I want to stomp my feet, drop to the floor and have a full blown tantrum smack dab in the middle of the hospital. The door opens.

"Yeah, you're right. It isn't the happy ending, but it's still happy." I laugh nervously. "I better go before that baby is born."

"Call me," she says, and I escape into the elevator. This baby is supposed to fix everything, to erase the grief, to make them forget and to help them move forward. But that's not the case and now I'm exasperated that Kati Bachman is right.

When I return to the maternity ward, I am directed to Room Six. I find Heather, dressed in a red fuzzy robe that barely covers her standard issue hospital gown, seated on a silver exercise ball. She smiles up at me, as calm and cool as the Mona Lisa. This is not the vision I was hoping for. I expected full-blown labor, so I could avoid awkward small talk.

I set my stuff down and take a seat in the corner of the room. While Dan surfs the Internet, Heather gyrates on the ball, producing loud flatulent sounds into the dimly lit room. I try not to giggle like a teenage boy. In the distance, I hear a woman scream. I gingerly pick up Heather's copy of *What to Expect When You're Expecting* and read the labor section to pass the time. My stomach gurgles at regular intervals, so I decide to grab some lunch—with the caveat that they call me if delivery is imminent.

After no calls and a mediocre sandwich from the hospital cafeteria, I return to Room Six. Heather's friend is massaging her feet and legs. Heather remains calm and quiet, but her grimace indicates otherwise. After a few minutes, she props herself up on the bed and tells Dan that she wants to get in the tub. He helps her up from the bed, and they shuffle into the bathroom like an elderly couple. I continue to stare at the pages of my book while the massage therapist just sits there. I really don't feel like striking up a conversation with a stranger.

After about an hour, Heather and Dan emerge from the bathroom. Heather paces the room like a caged animal at the zoo, then stops to lean on the counter during a contraction. She moans in pain. Carefully she makes her way back into bed and the nurse affixes a monitor around her belly. Dan studies the monitor as Heather softly says, "Oweee," over the baby's heartbeat. Her contractions are now coming on strong every two minutes. I hope she doesn't feel awkward or obliged to keep things PG-13 for my sake.

Heather's grunts and groans intermingle with the jingling rings of different cell phones.

"Shut those phones off," she commands.

Dan looks at the caller ID.

"It's your mom," he says. "Hello. Yep. She's in a lot of pain right now. That's why we're not answering. Uh, huh. Bye."

Right after the call, Heather decides that she would really like some drugs. The nurse checks Heather's cervix again and happily announces that she has "dilated to a five or six." This is good news.

"This Stadol is going to go right to your head and knock you out for about fifteen minutes. It'll give you another centimeter." The nurse prepares the dose.

Drugs were not in Heather's plan. "Is it going to make the pain worse when I wake up?" she asks sheepishly, knowing full well what the answer will be.

"Honey, you're in labor. That's why it's called Mercy Labor and Delivery and not Mercy Health Spa."

After the injection, Heather mumbles, "It still fucking hurts." We've moved into R rated territory—and then she's out.

Dan sits by her side as she sleeps, periodically checking the monitor. The baby's heartbeat sounds like a galloping horse.

Heather lifts her hand drunkenly and mumbles something. Dan and I look at each other and smile. We both know that when she wakes up from her narcotic slumber, things are going to progress quickly. Earlier in the day, Heather predicted she would deliver at 3pm. Dan predicted 4:30. Having a nineteen-hour labor with both of my children, not to mention a pessimistic worldview, I predict midnight.

As Heather groggily awakens, she tells her midwife—the same woman who delivered my son—that she feels a lot of pressure. The midwife checks her and announces that she has made it to seven centimeters. The drugs have worked. Heather's water breaks at 4:20.

"The fluid is nice and clear, which is great," the midwife says. She removes her gloves and tells Heather and Dan that she has to leave to assist with a cesarean delivery. She assures them that she'll be back the minute Heather is ready to deliver.

Literally five minutes after the midwife leaves the room, Heather says in a wee little voice, "It's time. I need to push. Oweeeeeeeeee."

Calmly, the nurse calls the midwife.

As Dan holds one of Heather's legs, he turns towards me with a pleading expression. "Can you get me a cold washcloth?"

I dart to the bathroom, feeling like Butterfly McQueen in *Gone With The Wind*. *I don't know nothin' bout birthin' no babies, Miss Scarlett.* There isn't a washcloth in sight. I feel totally stupid and inadequate. I haven't done a damn thing this whole day, and the minute I am asked to do something, I can't deliver. I look into the still-filled tub and spot a washcloth floating on the bottom. I push up my sleeves, grab it and wring it out. I hand it to Dan as if I'm passing a relay baton. The baby is crowning, yet Heather has barely made a peep. This is the most calm and quiet birth ever.

Three minutes of silent pushing pass. It is 4:32 when baby Marion Grace enters the world. As she is placed on Heather's chest, Dan looks back at me. His eyes are wet with tears. Goose bumps shiver up my arm. The silence breaks as baby Marion cries from the nurse's rubbing and scrubbing. I sit silently, in awe of this new beginning. This child is hope materialized, and I don't want to spoil the moment by saying something stupid like, "Way to go, Heather!"

Outside, the sun is setting. It has been snowing intermittently all day and I'm afraid to drive the icy roads in the dark. I ask Dan if he wants me to get him anything to eat before I leave.

"I'm fine," he says, cradling his new daughter. And at this moment, he is. Dan reaches for the camera in his overnight bag.

"Here," he says.

I think he's going to let me hold Marion, so I take a seat in the chair. I'm wrong. He hands me the camera. I take pictures of all three of them. And then I leave, almost as unceremoniously as I'd arrived.

As I crunch through the snow-packed parking lot towards my car, I want to kick myself for not holding the baby. What is wrong with me?

✳   ✳   ✳

When I arrive home from the hospital, there is a letter in my mailbox. It's from Sonya Reed—Khristian's girlfriend.

1/17/2010

Dear Ms. Skjolsvik,

Please forgive me if I am imposing on you. I asked Mama (Katie Oliver) for your address. She had sent me a copy of the letter you wrote to her and Papa after Kit died. I want to express my gratitude for your kindness to him, and for being there for him during his darkest time. I was moved to tears by what you wrote, and my heart is comforted that someone as kind and sensitive as yourself was there for him on his last day.

He told me about you, both in a letter beforehand and on the phone the day of. You are obviously special, as he had refused many offers for interviews in the past. (He didn't like the media voraciously capitalizing on people's pain.)

Thank you for choosing Kit for your research. I'm sure you know now you couldn't have selected a better person for what you are writing about. I hope to be able to read what you write, and if you're interested, share with you his thoughts and feelings to me. We weren't legally married, but as he put it, we were in our hearts. It has been my honor and my joy to glean, and now carry with me his deepest secrets, hopes, fears, dreams and thoughts. Our daughter will one day need to know she came from someone with an identity other than just a death row prisoner. I have made it my life's work these past eleven or so years to provide that for her. If you're interested, or curious as to who that man is, I would love to show you. He was the most beautiful, caring, attentive person I've ever known. Ironically, he was also the most wounded. It was those wounds which allowed him the propensity for such deep sensitivity to other's needs.

Amber and I have been writing, and she shared with me how you and she were able to comfort one another. I know you are busy, but I can't help but beg of you to share with me your time with him. To not be there with him was torture for me, and not knowing how it was for him only adds torment to the torture. I know it was for the best that I not be there—I'd have tried to take his place, or thrown my body over his to protect him, but I also know I was the one he wanted to see as he left this world, and to not be able to give that to him was agony.

I was struck by the importance of making him laugh. I did, too, on the phone that day, and that's the one thing I hang on to in my darkest hours. It was a beautiful sound, wasn't it? I had forgotten the sound of his voice, so to hear the melody of his laughter was a gift I'll cherish forever. He always maintained I was the only one who ever made him laugh (and he didn't laugh often) so I know you made a difference for him.

I will be indebted to you forever for that alone.

Gratefully yours,

Sonya Reed

Just when I thought I was moving towards my own happy ending, I am pulled back into tragedy.

*   *   *

"If you've loved a lot, you're going to grieve a lot." Kati Bachman's words haunt me as I think about Dan, Heather, Tommy and Marion. At the moment we acknowledge a life, we simultaneously acknowledge that it will end. We can either cherish it while we have it, or we can remain distant, simply going through the motions in order to save ourselves from the inevitable pain of loss. For most of my own life, I've done the latter, either by keeping people at a distance or beating them to the departure punch. I'm an adult now, and at some point I'm going to have to learn how to engage in life without the assistance of a notebook.

I can't get it out of my head that I didn't hold Marion. Was I scared that I'd drop her, or give her some sort of germ from my hands? Did I feel that it wasn't my place? I honestly don't know. I could have asked them. I could have. But I didn't. I just did the same damn practical thing I always do. I walked away. I am such an emotionally stilted ignoramus. Have I not learned anything? I've got to go hold that baby.

I call Heather with an almost panicked urgency. "Can I come over and hold Marion?"

"Of course. We're home if you want to come over now."

I do. I zip on over to their house and clomp through mountains of snow to their front door. Heather is seated in a chair with Marion asleep on her elevated legs. I quietly take a seat on the couch next to her and she hands me Marion, who remains asleep as I maneuver her pink-clad body into a comfortable position. As I hold her in the crook of my arm, she lets one rip. I love babies.

As I stare into her sleeping face, Heather and I talk about baby pictures, newborn diapers, pink clothes and the enormous amount of snow that has fallen since the day of Marion's birth. Dan shuffles into the living room from the kitchen and hands Heather a plate of food. He plops down on the ottoman in front of her and takes a bite from his burrito. They both look exhausted.

Marion's tiny face twitches and relaxes in my arms. I forgot how tender it makes me feel to hold a baby. Marion is so tiny and new and beautiful. I know on a rational level that she will never replace Tommy or erase the pain that Dan and Heather went through after his death, but I'm hoping she can somehow minimize it.

When she wakes with a turn towards my chest, I hand her over to Heather. "I'll call you," I say. This time, I mean it.

I return to the reminders of the dead and pen a response to Sonya Reed, and an introductory letter to Larry Matthew Puckett. Both are painfully difficult to compose. I don't know what to say to Sonya other than that I'm sorry for her loss and will get that last picture of Khristian copied and mailed to her. With Mr. Puckett, I keep things simple and straightforward. I basically tell him that I'd be happy to critique his writing if he wants to send it my way. It's difficult to believe that my life has veered in this direction. There are now two convicted felons, one sentenced for life, and one awaiting death with my home address, and if either have mob/gang/psycho connections on the outside, they will know where to find me.

For now.

CHAPTER TWELVE

Mess With Texas

In 2010, seven days after receiving my MFA, I officially turn the corner into middle age. On the day of my birth, Erik and I move to Texas—for good. Or bad, depending on how you view the Lone Star State. Even though I've spent many holidays and summer vacations visiting Erik's family in the town he grew up in, I never thought I'd mess with the state on a permanent basis. But the phone book was dying, the recession hit us hard, and moving closer to family seemed like a good idea. With the exception of my friend in Austin, my only real friend in Texas is Sonya Reed. We write to each other weekly.

I also write a monthly letter to Larry Matthew Puckett. Unlike Khristian, I don't question Matt about being on death row or how he feels about dying. It's all about the writing. After a few introductory chit-chat letters, I ask him to pen a short essay, which he does on unlined copy paper. His response makes me laugh.

"Wow! Did you read Pamela's letter?" asked Super Ego.
"Yes, of course, at the same time you did," replied Ego.

Super Ego ignored the sarcasm. "She sure is an interesting woman. But look at that name! How do your pronounce it?"

"I have no idea, but it has to be Polish or maybe from the Baltic region."

"Russian, even," Super Ego added.

"What gets me is that I can't tell what's more morbid, that she researched all that death or that she's a proofreader for the phone book."

"Be nice. Someone has to do it."

"She enjoys watching movies, but doesn't watch TV."

"We liked Schindler's List. Wonder if she did?"

"We can't really talk about our favorite TV show, House, and how we are drawn to his incredible wit and genius."

"No, but I am interested to see what Creative Nonfiction means," Super Ego said.

"If it's anything like what Edward Humes does, that guy that wrote Mississippi Mud, then we definitely want to write to her."

"I like that she enjoys coffee!"

"That's cool! A coffeeholic like us. Warms the heart like a good cup of Maxwell."

"She'll think we're crazy if we tell her that we eat it by the spoonful a lot of the time."

"Well, it was your idea."

"Hmmm. Her favorite flavor of ice cream is rocky road?"

"Makes me think bootleg ice cream. Like someone cooked that stuff up in the mountains."

"Or at the end of a gravel road."

"Doesn't matter what it is because vanilla is the best ice cream."

"Ooooh, especially with some root beer!"

"I wonder what that means that she is not religious but spiritual."

"Maybe she is new age?"

"Uh, oh. She's a registered Democrat."

"Hold up. Be nice."

"Yeah, all right, whatever."
"You'll have plenty of time to ask her about politics."
"You bet," Ego replied with enthusiasm.
"She does like to make people laugh."
"Oh, that's a good one. Slide that one right in there. And you're supposed to be the moral one."

After reading this piece, I ask him to write me an essay that starts with the line, "It was another gritty Maxwell House morning." I find out that Matt has many people that he corresponds with and that he's super regimented about it. Right around the 17th of each month, a handwritten envelope graces my mailbox.

Now that I am done with my thesis, I naively think that I am done with death—but it only takes twelve days for it to ring my doorbell at an ungodly early hour. Crazy as it sounds, hearing a doorbell totally freaks me out. For the past ten years, I lived on top of a Colorado mountain where the only people athletic or determined enough to trek up my seriously steep driveway were two young Mormon men on a mission. I don't think we even had a doorbell for them to ring.

Instead of answering the door like a normal person, I dart to the bathroom and peer out the window through the Venetian blinds. An ABC News van is parked out front. I quickly check my reflection to make sure I don't look as crazy as I feel. The bell rings again, startling me. I fast-walk it out of the bathroom and crack open the front door. A brunette woman in business attire asks if I'm related to Tonya Page, who she insists lives in my house.

"Um, no. We just rented this house about two weeks ago."

The woman explains a little too eagerly that Ms. Page was walking alone on the highway in the middle of the night and was killed. This was her last known address.

"You wouldn't happen to know her new address?" she asks.

"No."

She hands me her business card. "Well, if you could have your landlord give me a call, I'd really appreciate it."

In the next few hours, two more reporting teams show up at my house to speak to the family of Tonya Page. They all seem so downtrodden when I tell them that I have no idea who she is or where she calls home.

Welcome to Texas!

In addition to renting a creepy house with a possible ghost haunting the hallways, I can't seem to find a job, which is one of the main reasons we moved here. The death blog that I began in July of 2009 now pops up after Googling my name. On this blog, I interview people about their own experience with death, as well as folks who work in death professions. Despite the normalcy of death and grief, potential employers probably view the morbid focus of my blog and think I'm a wannabe Morticia Adams. If only they knew the truth.

I spend the first few months sending out my resumé, but the only interview I land is for a receptionist position at a chiropractor's office. The middle-aged chiropractor gives me a timed personality test and then asks me about the organizational status of my sock drawer. It is over ninety degrees outside. I never unpacked my box of thick wool socks.

"I don't really have a sock drawer." I confess like I'm guilty of something terribly embarrassing. I look down at my feet, bare in a pair of sensible black flats. This is not the answer she is looking for.

"Really?" She stares at me in disbelief.

"Well, the few socks I do have are stored in my underwear drawer," I lie.

"Are they organized by color or size or are they just thrown in there?"

I shift in my chair, fully aware that my ability to answer the phone and schedule chiropractic adjustments hinges on the coordination and storage of my undergarments.

"They're on one side of the drawer and they're all black, so it's kind of difficult to arrange them in any kind of order."

I don't get the job.

Each day, I feel more like a failure, cloistered behind closed Venetian blinds. Almost daily, some sweaty stranger rings my doorbell to sell me the paper, cleaning supplies, magazines to support the high school football team, frozen meat, curb painting services, carpet cleaning, and the like. I don't imagine anyone particularly enjoys the interruption of solicitors, but I interpret the person on the other side of the door as an axe-wielding maniac. I know I have a problem when I peer out the peephole at a couple of Boy Scouts shilling bags of popcorn and want to cower under the covers.

After three months of looking, I give up on finding a job and veer over into the volunteer section of Craigslist, which is a cornucopia of market research studies, calls for egg donation, and amateur 'modeling'. Buried in this nonsensical list is a posting for a paid treatment study of social anxiety. I answer a long series of questions and within an hour, a research assistant from Southern Methodist University calls to invite me into the study. I don't know if this is a good thing or not, kind of like Groucho Marx's old quote, "I don't want to belong to any club that will accept me as a member."

Erik's mom, Lovina, agrees to watch Nik and Lola so I can learn how to relax in social situations. The first therapy session is on a Tuesday night, and as usual, I show up early—as does everyone else. We may be anxious, but at least we're punctual. In the waiting area, the five other study participants stare at their smartphones while I leaf through an old copy of *Vogue*. Of course nobody says a word.

After the initial intake with a million different forms to fill out, our two therapists explain that we will be doing weekly "exposures" based on our own personal list of fears. They further explain that with each successive week in the four months of therapy, these exposures will become increasingly difficult. Everyone at the table looks like their puppy just died. Faces flush, feet tap and pens click against the faux cherry wood table. The anxiety is so thick, you couldn't cut it with an industrial strength Xanax.

That night, our first exposure is to stand up and introduce ourselves. It is painful to watch, yet even more painful to wait my turn. It never occurred to me that there were other people whose body reacted as if a tiger wanted to rip their throat out whenever they were required to stand in front of a group of people and move their lips. The next session, our exposure is to give an impromptu speech on a topic chosen by the therapist. By week three, the first person drops out of the study. The day after we have to give a speech on a controversial subject, I finally get called in for a job interview. I am hired as a cashier in a high-end clothing store making eleven bucks an hour. For the first time in years, I am not nervous during my interview. I don't know if I can attribute my calmer state to the therapy or to desperation. Maybe a combination of both.

In addition to the weekly exposure sessions with the therapists, I have homework. *Use public restrooms. Make eye contact. Talk to people I don't know. Try on clothes in a dressing room. Eat by myself in a restaurant.* Lovina finds it difficult to believe that I'm communicating with another death row inmate, yet I'm unable to converse about the weather with a stranger. But each week it gets easier. I simply have to run towards the fear and nullify the thought patterns that immediately dart towards the catastrophic.

As our exposures became increasingly difficult, the other participants drop out. Only two of us remain till the bitter end. By my fourth month, I have performed a series of seriously ridiculous exposures out in public. I've stood up in the middle of a Starbucks and read from a book. I try on ill-fitting clothes at an Ann Taylor and wander through the busy store asking strangers what they think of the dress I'm wearing. During my last exposure, I approach a group of men at a crowded bar and ask if I can read them three pages from my thesis. In my head, I concoct all sorts of worst-case scenarios—but the funny thing is, I don't suffer a heart attack or sweat to death in front of any of these people. By making myself a guinea pig, I am gaining confidence with the discovery that most people don't give a hoot if you read to them in a bar or speak to them in a public restroom.

CHAPTER THIRTEEN

Save the Cat

hortly after moving to Texas, I drive to the Mountain View
Unit—the women's death row facility in Gatesville, Texas—to
finally meet Sonya Reed. As in her weekly letters, I find her
intelligent, kind and courageous. Physically, she reminds me of the
painting, "The Martyr of Solway," by John Everett Millais, with
lengthy tendrils of strawberry blonde hair that cascade down her
bleached white prison uniform. With a plate of glass and a mesh
wire between us, we spend four hours eating copious amounts of
chocolate from the vending machine while she tearfully shares stories about her love for Khristian—a love that deepened despite
incarceration—her life in prison, and Kittisue, the daughter she gave
birth to in jail. She hasn't seen her daughter since she was a baby.

I don't know how she endures day to day, but during our
weekly correspondence, I learn one of her secrets. Despite the
consequences of love and loss and potential disciplinary action
from the guards, Sonya is attempting to tame a feral cat, Violet,
that lives in a culvert near her dorm. In subsequent letters, I learn
of their growing bond.

It's a lot of stress transporting my own serving of food from the chow hall and sneaking it past the pat-searches, but I do it, twice a day, every day. I have to constantly fend off the cat haters and bullies in my dorm who just need something to direct their anger at. When I defend Violet against these women, it makes me appear more fearsome than I really am, but I would do anything to keep her from harm, which is hard to do when only one of us is in a cage.

I've watched in agony when her belly grew round with kittens, then worried myself silly over every scratch and cut as she fought off the tomcats, opossums and skunks who tried to get at her babies. I grieved with her as she paced and cried for days after the well-intentioned but misguided yard crew took them away at only four weeks. I too lost a child to this place, and while I never got to mother the baby girl who was taken from me, through Violet, I'm getting a taste of what motherhood feels like.

A year after her relationship with Violet began; Sonya is threatened with major disciplinary action if she continues to feed the tiny feral cat that is now pregnant with her second round of kittens. The idea of trapping the cats for euthanization is bandied about among the guards and inmates. Sonya knew this day would eventually come, but the heart wants what the heart wants. As a cat lover myself, I feel her pain. I don't want my friend to hurt. I email PETA and the Texas A&M feral cat trap-neuter-release program, hoping they can rescue this little cat from imminent death. Two weeks later, I receive a laughable form letter from PETA, and nothing at all from the college. From this, I can only gather that prison cats are regarded no differently from their human counterparts: they are a menace, their lives don't matter, and they aren't worth saving.

In October of 2011, Sonya informs me that the prison has agreed to let one of her visitors take Violet. She figures her friend Scott will take her if we can somehow come up with a pet deposit for his apartment. I know I can't take her. I already have a cat, and without a decent income, the last thing I need is another mouth to feed.

With great hesitation, I call the prison to confirm that I can indeed pick up Violet. It seems so 'out there,' but for Sonya's sake, I figure I can at least make the trip to Gatesville and take Violet to a pet shelter for adoption, if and when she is caught. The woman I speak with at the prison has never heard of such a thing, which doesn't surprise me. I send Sonya a letter to relay the bad news. Within days, she replies that I need to speak with the assistant warden.

I feel beyond ridiculous calling the assistant warden to inquire about a cat, but she immediately puts me at ease by asking how soon I can get there.

"Well, I live about two and a half hours away, so as soon as you call me, I'll be there as fast as I can."

"Do you have other cats?" Her tone becomes serious.

"Yes."

"You'll want to get the cat tested for Feline Leukemia and AIDS before you bring her home. She'll be contagious."

Oh, great.

She further explains that many of the feral cats are stricken with these diseases, and that most shelters will put her down immediately if she tests positive. Unbelievably, she offers to bring her own carrier to the prison so that Sonya can capture Violet. I press my luck and ask if maybe one of the guards can drop Violet off at a local vet, with the promise that I'll prepay for the tests. She agrees and we have a deal.

In the meantime, I send e-mails to several of Sonya's friends on the outside, informing them that Violet needs a home. Within an hour, Andrea, one of Sonya's old pals from Nacogdoches, agrees to adopt her. I seriously doubt I'll have to take her up on her offer because the idea of capturing this wild animal seems so far out of the realm of possibility. I can barely manage to catch my own snuggly little snoozer of a cat when it comes time to go to the vet: faced with entrapment, Judy can be quite cunning. I can't imagine a cat raised in the wild would be an easier target. But the irony is, if you don't know what a cage is, you'll never see it coming.

It is Kittisue's thirteenth birthday when the assistant warden calls to inform me that Violet has been captured. I thank her and then quickly call the vet's office to let them know that Violet is on her way, and to call me as soon as the test results come back. Excitedly, I send Andrea an email to update her on Violet's status. Andrea responds that although she wants Violet, she is in a financial bind and that her other cat just had kittens. My heart sinks. I've read that taming a feral cat is a long, arduous process. You can't just dump them in the middle of a house with other cats and expect them to thrive. It would be like dropping a human raised by wolves off at Harvard. I know right then that this cat will either be euthanized or end up in my care.

Later that morning, I find a letter from Sonya in my mailbox, begging me not to take Violet to a humane society. There is a frightened desperation in her words, like a mother defending her child. I feel immense guilt that she hasn't heard that her friend Andrea was going to take Violet, but now that news is wrong too. Letters have an archaic sort of sweetness about them—but when time is of the essence, I want to scream at the U.S. Postal Service for its inefficiency.

I watch the clock and worry why the vet is taking so long. They told me the tests would be quick response. Something has to have gone wrong. Either Violet is raising hell and they are hesitant to come near her with a needle, or worse, she has already been euthanized. I decide to call.

"Oh, we're just real busy this morning," Sherry, the receptionist, assures me. "They haven't even run the tests."

"Oh. Okay." I want to prepare them, but also humanize this cat so they'll show her compassion. "So what does Violet look like?"

"You haven't seen her?"

"No."

"Well, she's a gray and white tabby. She's a tiny little thing, but she's all muscle."

Oh, great: a Napoleonic feline who's probably sharpening her claws as I speak.

"Is she hissing or mad? She's feral, you know."

"Oh no, she's real sweet. Somebody tamed her. I picked her up and she buried her face in the crook of my arm."

"Are you serious?"

Sonya really did tame Violet, just as she said.

After we hang up, I pace the room like an expectant father. Sherry calls me back within the hour.

"I've got good news!" she chirps. "Violet doesn't have either disease!"

"Really?" I squeal.

"Do you want to get her vaccinated while she's here?"

I of course say yes and ask if they can board her till Saturday, so I can visit Sonya while I'm in Gatesville.

"Since you're going to keep her here a couple of days, do you want to get her spayed?"

Again, yes. This cat is mine, and now that she knows what it's like to be caged, I doubt I'll ever be able to get her in one again.

On Saturday, I briefly visit with Sonya. The visitation room is half full. A pair of red-haired girls play with germ-infested building blocks on the dirty floor as two women chat with their foul-mouthed mother. The woman prances and preens inside her solitary cage, the sleeves of her prison uniform bunched up at the shoulders. Every other word out of her mouth rhymes with duck. I purchase some beef jerky and various chocolate treats from the vending machine and wait for Sonya, weighed down by the depression-inducing funk of the place.

It takes about twenty minutes, but Sonya finally appears. Her hair is tied back in a matronly bun, and she looks thinner than usual. She sits down and smiles.

"Pamela, are you an angel?" Coming from another person's lips, this question would seem ridiculous or schmaltzy, but from Sonya it just seems normal.

The answer is no. My wings were clipped a long time ago.

"Oh, Pamela. You are going to love her. She is the sweetest cat. I'm just so thrilled that you're taking her. Promise to send me pictures."

I can't help but think of Violet and Judy's first meeting and hope there is no hissing, scratching or bloodshed. "I will. Promise."

"She's been eating scrambled eggs and mackerel, but I'm sure she'll love tuna or whatever kind of food you end up giving her. Just make sure it's not the really cheap stuff that's full of grain. Cats need meat." Sonya leans in closer to the mesh wire. "And be sure and talk to her in a baby voice. She really responds to that."

I feel like a babysitter, and Sonya is the worried mother entrusting me with her newborn. I nod and smile and move closer to the small wire rectangle. "It's going to be okay, Sonya. I'll give her the same dry food as Judy. It's Iams. I even bought some wet food and a bunch of treats."

With a bit of guilt behind her smile, Sonya admits that there are two other cats that she's been feeding. Although I'm thrilled she has animals to love and care for, I want to inform her that the Skjolsvik cat condo is at capacity, but I don't. She seems so happy.

On my way out, one of the guards stops me. "Are you the lady that's taking Violet?"

This seems like such a strange question. Usually the staff is cold or indifferent to my presence. "Yep. I'm on my way to get her now."

"I just wanted to let you know that that cat saved Sonya Reed's life. She was a mess after they executed her boyfriend. She didn't eat, she slept all the time—but when Violet came around, it gave her a reason to get up in the morning. I thought you should know that."

The pressure is on.

When I finally arrive at the vet's office, one of the vet techs has a large bandage on her face, as if she's been attacked by one of the animals in her care. Despite what I've been told about her sweet demeanor, my mind wanders straight to Violet.

"Can I see her?" I ask the receptionist.

"Sure—she's right back there in that room."

My heart races as I peer into the metal cage. Violet, the cat I've heard about in countless letters, is crouched in a corner, looking smaller than I ever imagined. Her amber eyes widen in fear as I poke a solitary finger between the wires.

"Come here, Violet," I coo in my most come-hither kitty speak.

She remains immobile, with wild eyes fixated on my face. This is not the introduction I was hoping for.

The stare down doesn't last long. With a blue towel and one deft move, the burly vet tech lifts Violet from the cage and deposits her into my carrier. Nobody pets her or tells her she is a pretty kitty to ease the transition. It is more like, *here's your cat, what's your hurry?* Without a ceremony to commemorate this strange adoption, I pay for the vaccinations, the tests and the spaying and we leave like a couple of improperly introduced strangers. Violet doesn't meow or hiss or do much of anything on the two and a half hour drive back home. I try to entice her with a piece of my chicken sandwich from a McDonald's in Waco, but she remains frozen in place in the corner of the carrier. I play classical music. I talk baby talk. I place my hand next to the opening in the hopes that she'll interact, but she wants none of it.

Despite the pleading of Nik and Lola, who want to see the newest addition to our family, I deposit Violet into the seclusion of my bathroom for a little decompression time. I have a litter box, food, water, toys and her own little private kitty cubby ready for her, but she chooses to stay in the enclosed plastic safety of the carrier. While speaking in a high-pitched baby voice, I hand feed her salmon-flavored kitty treats. At first she doesn't trust my intrusive hand in her personal space, but the allure of food wins out.

The next morning, I find the food and water bowls empty and the litter box untouched. The room is pungent with the smell of urine. I carefully remove the top from the carrier. Sensing her world is about to become bigger, Violet darts behind the toilet. Inside the carrier, a corner of the brown towel is soaked. On hands and knees, I cajole her from her hiding place and set her tiny squirming body into the box while attempting to scratch her paws into the litter. She leaps from the box in a flurry of sand and runs straight into the red cubby. I notice that her fur is jumping with fleas.

I give up. If someone had told me a year ago that I'd be living in Texas, pen-palling with two inmates and adopting a feral prison cat, I would have said they were crazy. Well, who is the crazy one now?

While Violet immediately takes a shine to Judy, treating her like one of the kittens she lost, her first few days with me are spent running under the bed whenever I come near. It takes about three weeks for her to finally lick the hand that delivers Savory Salmon Fancy Feast. In late November, just as Violet and I are beginning to bond, she disappears. I panic, haunted by the thought that she might have dashed out the door as I thoughtlessly lugged my groceries inside the house. I search everywhere—behind the dressers, in the closets, inside kitchen cabinets, under the bed and the couch and every single chair. I even check inside the oven and the washer and dryer for good measure. I comb the neighborhood calling her name, but I know in my heart that she will never come running and leap into my arms as a tear-jerking Hollywood movie score swells in the background. If she did manage to escape, she won't linger between neatly-manicured suburban lawns: she is headed back to the wilds of Gatesville. I envision the dangers of her journey—the cars, the raccoons, coyotes, vicious dogs, or worse, well-meaning people who might capture her and drop her off at the Humane Society. Hours crawl by. I debate whether or not to send Sonya a letter.

Dear Sonya: I lost Violet. You trusted me with your beloved cat, the one that gave you so much joy, and I messed up and left the damn door open.

As I sit down at my desk to compose this thoroughly depressing letter, I hear the crunching of chicken-flavored kibble coming from the bathroom. I creep towards the open door, half expecting to find Judy. But she's there as if she'd never left—hope.

*   *   *

But as much as I think of Violet as Sonya's baby, she has a real child, too—one she must miss even more, now that Violet's not there for company. Kittisue's adoptive parents were court-ordered to allow Sonya visitation with her daughter. That never happened. And now Sonya wants contact. Kittisue deserves to know that her mother is out there, thinking of her and loving her—and while I still don't think of myself as an angel, guardian or otherwise, Sonya's chosen me to be the bearer of this news.

With two letters and a surprisingly beautiful painting of roses that Sonya made with a set of children's watercolors, I drive the two and a half hours to a small Texas town. My original plan was to bring Erik and the kids, but I have to be on the road at 6:30 to make it to the church before the service starts, and it doesn't seem fair to subject them to this crazy mission on a Sunday morning. Besides, this is a solitary task that must be completed fast and efficiently. If I linger too long, I will stand out among the Pentecostal crowd. With their long, pulled back hair, ankle length skirts and long sleeves, I look like a short-cropped, towering infidel dressed for a Johnny Cash concert.

I stop at a McDonald's to use the restroom and buy a mocha latte out of guilt. Not a wise choice, considering I'm already jittery. Sweat is trickling down the inside of my black cardigan, and my hands are visibly shaking. I don't know why I'm so worked up. It's just a church and I'm just the messenger. I don't even have to talk if I don't want to. I just have to hand over the envelopes and the painting and leave. That's it.

But, really, who am I kidding? I'm a stranger in a strange land, delivering a message that no one wants to hear.

The church is at the end of a long residential road, and consists of two adjacent brown buildings that aren't particularly ornate or church-like. I pull in and park in the designated 'visitor' spot. I watch as a man in a black suit walks in with his two young children. I try calling my mom for a pep talk, but she doesn't answer. Nor does Erik, who is probably still sound asleep. I'm unsure as to which building to enter—the one with the people or the one without the people. I don't know if it's because I'm scared or because it's Sunday or because I'm about to enter a house of worship, but I say "God, help me" and exit my car.

I tuck the envelopes inside my roomy black purse and clutch the painting and coffee in both hands, which makes opening the door to the empty building problematic. I walk in, not expecting a soul, but three adolescent girls standing at a counter greet me. One of them is Khristian and Sonya's daughter.

Kittisue's long brown hair is free from the secured braid that I've seen in every picture of her; it cascades in long, dark waves down the back of her floor-length purple dress. My heart feels as if it is going to pop right out of my mouth. The three girls look at me as if I were a short-haired, black-clad alien.

"Hi. Um, I'm looking for Veronica. Is she here?" My voice quivers.

Kittisue steps out from behind the counter. I want to tell her so much—that her dad loved her and wanted nothing more than to meet her, and that her mom is a lovely, intelligent woman stuck behind prison walls, dying to reach out to her.

She points towards the hall. "She's down that hallway in the kids' room."

"Okay." I take two steps forward and then freeze in place. This is it—carpe fucking diem and all that. She has moved behind the counter with the two other girls. I hurry back over, unsure of what to say. Meeting her without one of her parents glued to her side wasn't how I envisioned this.

"Are you Kittisue?"

"Yes."

"Hi. I have something for you." I hand her the painting. She gently takes it from my hands and holds it by the outside edges, like one would hold a photograph to keep from smudging it. She studies the words on it: "My Daughter, My Heart."

"It's from your mother. Your biological mother," I clarify, hoping to impart some sort of understanding.

One of the girls yelps, "What?" as if this was the craziest thing she'd ever heard.

Oh God, what have I done? I dig through my purse. "This is a letter from her to you."

"Thank you," she says, and takes it from my trembling hands.

"I'm sorry. I'm really nervous. I'm going to go talk to Veronica."

I hightail it to the hallway, leaving these three sheltered girls in the fallout of my verbal bomb. I don't even have three seconds to compose myself. Veronica and an older woman with a black bun eye me suspiciously as I approach. I can't catch my breath.

"Hi, um, my name is Pamela Skjolsvik, uh, and I'm a friend of your sister's.' My voice sounds as if I've just finished a relay race. As if in exposure therapy, I remind myself that I'm not going to die. It just feels that way. I try to slow my breathing.

Veronica's strawberry blonde hair is piled into a bun, with a few loose curls framing her makeup-free face. It's definitely Sonya's sister. She looks at me quizzically. "Sister?"

"Sonya."

Veronica's facial expression changes from perplexed to pure anger. The black-haired woman, steps in to block my entrance.

"I have a letter from her to you. I just need to get it out of my purse."

I walk between them, deeper into the room, and plop my purse and coffee onto a low table to rifle through my bag. They stare at me with icy silence—probably thinking I have a lot of gall to invade their space—but if they could only listen to the sound of my pounding heart, they'd realize how afraid I am.

"Here," I hand her the letter. "Sonya wants visitation with her daughter."

"Uh huh." Veronica backs away as if I have horns and a tail.

"That's it," I say. *No big deal.* I sling the bulky purse over my shoulder and step out into the hallway. Then I turn back.

"I also gave a letter to Kittisue."

Both women sprint from the room in different directions, like some sort of folk family swat team. When I leave, I find that Kittisue and her two friends have disappeared from behind the counter. The black-haired woman follows me out into the courtyard with the man I saw earlier. They stand on the steps of their church and watch me—the bumbling messenger of doom—as I search through every nook and cranny of my purse to find my keys.

Once inside the safety of my car, I lock the doors and call Erik. The man and woman stare in my direction with stern expressions, their arms folded firmly across their chests. Part of me wants them to feel a bit of my panic. I just sit there, taunting them with my inactivity—until Erik answers. Then a flood of suppressed emotion gushes out of me, something I don't want them to see: I'm human and I'm scared. But I'm riding it out. My therapists would be so proud. I pull out of the lot, one hand on my phone and the other on the wheel. No matter how justified I am, I feel reckless as if I walked into a house of worship brandishing a gun.

✳   ✳   ✳

At the beginning of March, I learn that Matt will be executed by the state of Mississippi at the end of the month. From the moment I agreed to write him in November of 2009, I knew this day would come, so it's not particularly shocking to see it in print. His friends and family don't share my 'been there, done that' sentiment. I can understand that. This ritualized countdown to state-sanctioned murder is all new and fresh to them. It's unreal in its stark, cold reality. I wish I could spare them all a bunch of heart ache and trouble and tell them to prepare for Matt's death—to say what they need to say and get right with each other. Instead, I keep mum and watch as the cavalry rushes in at the eleventh hour.

Although Matt has had a Facebook page for months, once he gets a public, definitive, we're-actually-gonna-do-it date, its membership grows. Everyone is caught up in the drama and religious fervor of the ticking clock. The possibility of his guilt is never questioned. I rarely comment. I've never spoken with Matt regarding the reason for his incarceration, and I intend to keep it that way.

I do however, contact Mrs. Puckett and encourage her to speak with Mr. Whiteside. I feel it's imperative that she speak with someone compassionate, not to mention experienced, to prepare her for the awfulness of it all. Although I know in my heart that no one can really steel her for what is about to happen to her son, they can at least let their presence be known. Sometimes the walk is a little less scary if you have someone at your side.

About a week and a half before Matt's date, Therese Apel, a Mississippi crime reporter with the *Clarion Ledger* contacts me. A blog I wrote about Matt piques her interest, and she wants to interview me for a story. Since no one in the death penalty movement seems to trust journalists, I ask Mrs. Puckett first. Mrs. Puckett agrees, and says it would be okay to send Ms. Apel some of Matt's essays.

His stories are all that will remain of him.

* * *

MARCH 20, 2012—EXECUTION DAY

Surprisingly, Mr. Whiteside is in constant contact with me throughout the day. He is driving from Louisiana to Mississippi to be there for Matt, and apparently he likes to talk while he's driving. In a weird way, I feel like maybe I'm helping him— caring for the caregiver, if you will. After relaying an awkward story about being patted down by a female guard at Parchmann, he informs me that Matt requested no family members be present at his execution. In one of my recent letters, I advised him not to let his family watch him die. He responds that he couldn't keep his mother away, even if he tried. I quickly write back that out of everyone, it would torment her the most.

> *Matt, she will walk into a tiny room with a glass window. You will already be strapped down on a gurney with IVs in both of your arms. The lethal concoction will start, you'll close your eyes and your mother will feel nothing but helplessness and anger that she can't comfort you in your last moments. If you were dying a natural death by cancer or some other terminal illness, you would want her there, but when it's your execution, you're inviting the one person who loves you the most to witness your very calm and clinical murder.*

At 5:25, Mary Puckett posts an announcement on Matt's Face-book page.

> *We have heard from the governor and he has declined Matt's clemency application. We have talked to Matt and he is calm and at peace. He asked that we not worry about him. We prayed that God would free Matt, but God has a different definition for free. Matt will finally be free. I told him that he was put on this earth for a purpose and that was to teach us lessons. He asked that we*

not squander what we had learned, and that if we can't love our neighbor, then we cannot get right with God. We want to thank each and every one of you who joined us in this fight. We appreciate the petition signatures, the prayers and all the encouragement we as a family have received.

As the clock ticks past six, I witness the hope on his page deflate into anger and sadness. People can't believe the state of Mississippi is really going to kill him.

Mr. Whiteside texts me the time of Matt's death. I call him. "What were his last words?" I ask.

"No."

"No?" That's it? I can't believe that Matt didn't say anything. He's a writer. Why wouldn't he take the time to write his last words? Not many people get the opportunity to actually write the last words they will ever speak. But maybe he didn't want to take part in the ritual.

On March 22, I receive Matt's last letter.

3/17/12

Dear Pamela,

Hello! Well, I never wanted to go through this. And it sucks that you are doing it again. We humans are kinda crappy to one another.

I went through a round of letters to as many churches and organizations that I could. Something like 80 stamps worth. Don't know if there was any good done or all a bust. Thursday was the last mail call day—the last day we could send mail out—so I couldn't write more. I fell back to writing to everyone on my monthly schedule. Got a lot done so far. About 12 more to go.

They aren't that long. I have to thank everyone. There have been so many good people that supported me. I couldn't have found a better group of people. So, thank you for all the love and kindness. I so hate that we couldn't keep the correspondence going.

It's technically not over with but I've had nothing but bad news for so long I do not expect it to change. I'm tired anyway. Hell one minute I'm up hoo-rahing, the next I'm just out of it.

I'm still at 29 Jay. I actually expected them to come today at four-o'clock to pick me up. Usually when the date is a Wednesday they come on a Sunday to get them. Since mine is a Tuesday I figured a Saturday. I thought that despite the fact that Sparkmann told me they would come Sunday. So about four o'clock tomorrow they will come get me and take me to unit 17. I try to get some hope drummed up and then viciously close it off. Once you go to 17 it is rare that they make a trip back. Only twice out of 12 executions.

I'll be the only prisoner in the whole unit. Constant guard from then on out. When I go I can't take anything with me. I pleaded with Sparkmann to let me take my journal. It's my ca-tharsis. And it would suck so much to record all those years and not be able to describe the last 48 hours. He let me take that and some stationary. I don't want to take that so I am trying to get the letters done here at 29. Get that task done and I will get the last four essays in final draft.

I laugh at myself because I had not done much writing. And when that ball is rolling, I have been on a tear. Wish I had that motivation all the time.

I've given most of my stuff away. A couple of items left—a fan, hygiene items, bed linen, clothes, basic shit. When I first got locked up all I had was a spoon and a cup. I'm almost full circle.

I gave it all away. TV, radio, dictionary—these possessions had been in my cell for years. They'd been packed up and moved to other cells. They made the trip from 32 to 29.

That's my day. Write letters. Give items away. Met a couple preachers today. Less and less activity, like a pendulum slowing down. I used to be rabid about activity. I had to do something. I reasoned there was no minute of the day when something couldn't be done. My energy has me shaking my leg, you know like people do—bounce on the toes while sitting. I hate idle. I hate not being able to do something. Cleaning the showers was a bitch, but it took work that I loved.

Shoot, I've rambled on enough. With deep sincerity I thank you for being my friend. Thank you for the kindness and love. Keep at the cause. Only when people care can something be done.

Make them care.

Matt

On Friday morning I send Mary Puckett a Facebook message to let her know I'll be attending Matt's memorial service. By the end of the day, I haven't received a response, so I interpret her silence to mean she doesn't want me there. Even though my mind automatically ventures to the worst case scenario, it doesn't deter me from my plan. I am facing my fear and attending Matt's service. Not counting Khristian's viewing after his execution, this will be the second funeral service I've ever attended.

In the early hours of Saturday, I see Mrs. Puckett's response.

"Pamela: I am so glad you are coming but hate that it is such a long drive. I hope you will be able to stay for a while after the service so you can meet the other boys and we can talk for a bit. Bless you..."

Bless you. I've heard these words before from Mrs. Oliver, but it still makes me feel weird to hear them. I breathe a sigh of relief as we embark on our six-hour trip to Vicksburg, Mississippi. Erik is pooped, so I gladly take the first driving shift, while Nik and Lola fight over the snack bag in the back seat. I'm usually jittery and sweaty upon entering into new situations or even new states, but this morning I am filled with peace. I will be present. That is all.

Ten miles into our trip, the emergency tire light blinks its yellow warning. Erik assures me everything is fine with the tires, and I let it go. As the sun appears, dappling rays of light onto the green pastures and blooming trees, I realize I've driven this way before. For a brief, fleeting moment I consider swinging by the church to give Sonya's sister a good scare, but I don't think I have it in me. I need to stop thinking I can save the world.

We pull into Glenwood Funeral Home at 1:17. The parking lot looks like a new car dealership. A sheriff's patrol car is parked prominently near the entrance. I hope it's just a precautionary measure to ward off any pro-death penalty folks who might show up at Matt's funeral. That's all the Puckett family needs after the hell they've been through—more drama.

Yesterday I called Mr. Whiteside to see if there would be an open casket, because I thought that might freak out Nik and Lola, but he informed me that Matt was cremated. Good choice. Mr. and Mrs. Oliver had to bury Khristian's body in an unmarked grave to prevent vandalism. For the life of me I can't understand why the state of Mississippi would inform the public of the funeral home's name and location in one of their press releases. It's like they wanted to make it as difficult as possible for the Puckett family to grieve.

I wander into the packed funeral home as Erik and the kids follow me around like I'm some sort of tour guide. Almost everyone I pass looks at me quizzically. I don't know if I'm getting this reaction because they fear the unknown, or if they're expressing kindness to a stranger who looks kind of lost. I'm not freaked out by the attention, but I do need to find Mr. Whiteside so that he can introduce me to Matt's mom. I approach a lone priest near the entrance.

"Do you happen to know where Mr. Whiteside is?"

"Brother Whiteside?" he asks.

I nod yes, even though I've never heard him called that before.

"I think he went to the restroom."

"Thanks." I position myself at the end of the bathroom hallway like a stalker. When "Brother" Whiteside appears, I barely recognize the man I met two years ago. Not only is he dressed in a suit, he is considerably thinner, with more gray sprinkled through his hair. We greet each other with a hug.

Nik and Lola stand to my right, quiet and unsure. Mr. Whiteside asks them their ages. Nik, normally outgoing and loud, says "eight" as if he's in the library and needs to use his quiet voice. Lola is just as quiet with a bit of added shakiness, which adds to my guilt for bringing them. They don't know Matt. Only I know Matt. But it's important to me that they see a funeral so that the next one that they attend—be it a grandparent or aunt or uncle or, God forbid, a parent—isn't so foreign. Death is all around us. The more experience we get with it, the less alien it becomes.

"Can you introduce me to Matt's mom?" I ask Mr. Whiteside.

"Certainly."

We walk into the main room. Flowers, pictures and mementos from Matt's life adorn every surface. The room is elbow-to-elbow with people. I never imagined so many at a funeral. I navigate to the front of the room behind Mr. Whiteside. Mary Puckett, dressed in a sparkling black shirt and slacks, is surrounded. I've never met her before, but I'm not feeling weird about approaching her.

Mr. Whiteside sidles up beside her and tells her who I am. She looks up at me, clasps my hands, and thanks me for making the trip. Many people are waiting to speak with her, so I step back. Erik, Nik and Lola are seated on a bench behind me, taking the scene in. A man in his early thirties with teary eyes approaches me.

"Pamela Skjolsvik?" He pronounces it correctly. "Trey Puckett. I just wanted to thank you for being Matt's friend." With these words he chokes up, steps in and embraces me. I hug him back. It's all I can do.

"You're welcome. I'm quite impressed that you pronounced my name correctly."

"Matt told us how to say it."

"Yeah, it's a doozy. I'm glad I was able to be here for the service."

Even more than Matt's mom, it seems his brother is looking for someone, anyone, to help him make sense of this. He is shell-shocked, like a man coming home from war. I have no words to ease his pain. He just has to go through it.

We all do.

EPILOGUE

Like Thanksgiving leftovers that never quite leave the fridge, my dad sits at my kitchen table like a cold lump of mashed potatoes, playing his millionth game of solitaire. Erik and I prepare a huge feast of scrambled eggs, bacon and fried potatoes for his farewell breakfast.

As I scrape the eggs onto the plates, Erik's phone rings. He covers the potatoes and turns off the burner.

"Who is it?" I ask, slightly annoyed by the interruption.

"Hey, Karen," he says and presses speakerphone. There is a moment of silence and then a gasp.

"She's gone," his oldest sister sobs.

"Karen. What is going on?" he asks, his eyes widening.

"Mom. She's gone. She's dead, Erik. I just found her."

In the middle of a normal Saturday morning, it begins—the 'thing' I've dreaded for so long.

My dad looks at me with a panic in his eyes. "I should probably go," he says, standing.

"No," I protest. "I need you. I can't take the kids over there right now. Can you watch them?"

Like my former self, my father is uncomfortable around emotions such as grief. He wants to avoid discomfort—but for now he reluctantly agrees to stay an extra day.

I don't know what to expect when I dash out the door and rush towards my greatest fear, but it isn't what I find. Fully dressed for bed, with slippers still secure on her feet, my mother-in-law's body is curled into a fetal position in the middle of her living room floor. From the couch, my sister-in-law Stacey looks up at me and cries into her cupped hands. I bury my face into Erik's neck and we embrace as if it's the end of the world. Right now, it certainly feels that way.

Karen and Jason, two of Erik's older siblings, wander over with lost looks in their teary eyes.

"Do you by chance know if she has some sort of will?" Jason asks.

"I don't know," I say, "but I do know that she wants to be buried. She said she was afraid of being cremated. Plus, she's Catholic, so I think burial is the way to go." At least that's what she told me when I brought the subject up a few months ago at her kitchen table.

"Did she have any of this in writing?"

"I have no idea. I told her she needed an advance directive and a will, but I don't know if she ever did it. I do remember her telling me she didn't want an open casket. When I told her about the embalming process, she said she didn't like the idea of a bunch of people touching her body or staring at her when she was dead."

And here we all are, lost and directionless, peering down at her while frantically searching for answers throughout the house. If anything, I'm grateful I knew at least some of her end-of-life wishes. If she ever made them official, she never told anyone. I check the top of her fridge, just in case. After scouring her desk drawers, Erik finds a business card from a local cemetery with an account written on the back. She'd made a down payment on a crypt space, but kept this information to herself.

Despite her wishes to the contrary, I know I have to look at her before the funeral home comes and takes her away. I crouch down on the floor and stare at her face. Her eyes are closed and her mouth is slightly open, as if she is simply taking a nap on the floor, but her pale gray skin belies this notion. A part of me expects her to open her grey-blue eyes and admonish me with, "Take a picture, it lasts longer." She was a photographer.

Was.

After a police officer determines that her death was a result of natural causes, an older woman and a younger man in black polyester pant suits arrive with a gurney, a quilt, and solemn expressions. We all stand around, staring down at Lovina on the floor. This might be the last time any of us will see her face again, and nobody really knows how to act. I kneel down, place my hand on her shoulder and say goodbye. I don't feel as if I'm going to lose it until Erik offers to help the funeral workers lift his mother's body onto the gurney. I excuse myself to the kitchen.

The night before Lovina's funeral, we attend a rosary service at the funeral home across the street from the local Target. I shop there weekly, but I'd never noticed the funeral home before. The four of us plant ourselves in a front pew, feeling vulnerable.

"Why are they playing this sad music, Mom?" Lola whispers into my ear. Her tears land on my shoulder.

"I think they want to help people get their feelings out. Here's a tissue."

Lola hiccups and sobs into an endless series of Kleenex, while Nik fetches them from various locations throughout the room.

As all of Lovina's nine siblings, five children and their spouses settle into their wooden seats, two men from the funeral home remove the flowers from atop her expensive Pecan wood coffin and open the lid. This is not what Lovina wanted. But since she never made any of her wishes official, her relatives were allowed to 'see' her one last time. Nik looks up at me with wet eyes. I hug him closer and squeeze Erik's hand.

"I'm not going to go up there," Erik says under his breath.

Two of his mother's siblings approach the coffin. They touch her hand and lean in to kiss her face. My heart races at the idea of touching what used to be her. I don't want to go up there either.

"We don't have to," I say, and pat Erik's leg as if I am being the brave one. I tell myself that I want to honor her wishes of not being looked at when she's dead, but as I watch each family member step up to her coffin to say their final goodbye, I begin to think that maybe I am rationalizing this because I'm anxious. Erik places a sweaty palm on my leg, bracing himself as he silently debates whether he will make that walk. After everyone has taken a turn, Erik buckles under the pressure. He squeezes my hand and we stand.

"Let's go say goodbye to Grandma," I say to the kids.

The four of us walk slowly towards the front of the room. I brought a coffee mug from San Francisco to place in her coffin. Lola brought a small handmade doll that was proudly displayed in her grandma's house for years, and Erik brought a pencil that he had written on. He places our items carefully into the coffin, without disturbing his mother's body. We just stand there and cry with heaving shoulders and dripping noses. I no longer feel ashamed to show my emotions. This is perfectly normal. Someone we love is in a box. It is a nice four-thousand-dollar box, but it's still a box.

A week after the siblings divide their mother's personal property, which was an exercise in patience and post-it notes, the female members of Erik's family return to the almost-empty home to decorate Christmas cookies. Despite the mounting tension between Karen, who has taken on the role of executor, and Valerie, her younger sister, we agree to continue on with a family tradition for the sake of everyone's holly-jolly sanity.

Erik and I arrive early, and I do my best to be happy and elf-like as I clear the two remaining tables in the kitchen and dining area. When Karen arrives, she presents me with a box of Fancy Feast, since I took on the responsibility of caring for Lovina's outdoor cat, Sally. While I appreciate Karen's thoughtfulness and the contribution to the cat's care, I find it sort of ironic that no one placed their color-coded post-it note on Lovina's most cherished possession—her cat. Since there's no such thing as a free cat and Sally requires more maintenance than a mid-century credenza, I guess I can see why.

Valerie arrives in a cheerful mood, and as an added bonus, her son Chris tags along to share in the festivities. I make bowls and baggies of frosting while everyone takes a seat and cherry-picks their favorite sugar cookie shapes from the giant stacks that litter the tables. Two hours fly by without so much as one disgruntled, emotionally displaced dig about who got what. Plates and platters of decorated cookies rest on every usable surface of the house. I deem it a red-and-green-sprinkled success—until the focus turns to Lovina's kitchen cabinets.

As I wipe down the kitchen table to appease everyone's fear that no one will help with the cleanup, Karen opens one of the knotty pine cabinets. It is full of empty jars. She opens another, possibly hoping to find some hidden treasure from her mother's past, but all she finds are more jars.

"What was she thinking? Geez," Karen says and closes the cabinet.

"She used them," Valerie retorts with just a smidgeon of anger in her voice.

"But look at all of them! What's the point of having so many?" Karen huffs back.

The hair on the back of my neck rises and I wipe the counters as fast as humanly possible. I too have seen the jars and wondered the exact same thing. There is nothing extraordinary about them, other than that they inhabit eight whole cabinets. At one time, they probably contained pickles or spaghetti sauce or olives, but now that the woman who emptied them and scrubbed them clean is dead, the jars have been elevated to glorified non-recyclable relics.

A screaming match ensues. Loud, angry words are slung like rotten eggs throughout the house.

"Why do I always have to be the bigger person?" Karen shouts.

"You're putting down Mom!" Valerie wails.

Doors slam.

Feet stomp.

I feel embarrassed to witness it. I know it isn't really about the jars. It is about loss and love and questioning who we are without this person in our lives. I usher Nik and Lola outside and we wait for Erik in the car.

"Why are they so mad?" Nik asks.

"They're just mad that there is so much stuff they have to get rid of. They'll get over it."

My answer appeases Nik's nine-year-old sense of the world. I sit quietly in the freezing front seat, knowing that the day will come when I too will argue with a sibling over some knick-knack or bauble stuffed away in the back of a drawer. Rationally, I know that that the thing is not the person, that possessing the thing won't return the person—but death and the contemplation of it creates a temporary insanity in all of us. We can choose to acknowledge its presence or stay blind until it's in our face and there's no turning away.

Each has its own consequences.

AFTERWORD

"Do one thing every day that scares you."
—Eleanor Roosevelt

This journey began with a wrong number and a fear of death. With a little self-examination, it turns out that what I really feared was engaging in life. With cognitive behavioral therapy, my repeated exposure to death workers, blogging about death, and writing this book, I have learned how to run towards my fears, and to live a more full and gratifying life. I make small talk. I visit Sonya in prison. I smile more. I open the door. I buy popcorn from strange kids. I hold babies. I adopt problematic dogs. If this day is all I'm guaranteed, I want to make it something worth writing about.

Naturally, I've given a lot of thought to my own death. While I can't say that I drafted a will to disperse the slim pickings of my bank account, my vast array of knick-knacks, or my cat-scratched furniture, I do have an Advanced Directive, and my immediate family is hip to my end-of-life wishes, including who gets the dog, the cats and the kids if both Erik and I get hit by a bus.

In case you were wondering, here they are. No burial for me. I do not want anyone 'working' my face or attempting to style my unruly hair. With my luck, they'd flat-iron it and people wouldn't recognize me. I'd also probably end up wearing something that

237

has been sitting in the back of my closet for years, like my prom dress. For the record, I want to be cremated. I do not want any of my family members to place my ashes in an overpriced urn or even an empty Folger's can for home storage. I want them dumped in an outdoor ashtray at the Ritz Carlton in San Francisco. I like the idea of a Ritz employee stamping a big fancy "R" on my ashes, while the nicotine addicted folks, banished to smoke outside, will unwittingly extinguish their butts in my cremated remains. If anything, my kids will get to take a trip to the city where their parents met, and they'll have a wacky story to tell.

You wouldn't think it, but death is a great conversation starter.

ACKNOWLEDGEMENTS

I am overflowing with gratitude towards the many—and I'm talking a LOT, so bear with me—lovely people who have helped me on this journey. First and foremost, I'd like to thank my mom for her generosity of spirit, and for always being my biggest cheerleader. Erik, Lola and Nik, for tolerating my erratic behavior and the long periods I spent planted in front of a computer screen. I love you guys the most, and I'm proud of the people you are becoming. And that includes, you too, Erik, even though you're already all growed up.

Writing peeps in no particular order: Kim Brittingham, Beth Walker, Wini McMichael, Margaret Luevano, Amy Hartman, Carrie Hagen, Susan Olier-Hatfield, Robyn Barberry, Christine Steele and Audra Conway. At one time or another, we've shared our work. We've laughed, we've cried, and maybe at one time or another we've hurled—crumpled paper into the trashcan, that is.

Paula Rose, I thank you for your pushy encouragement. You're like my biggest fan and I'm so grateful that you encourage me to send you more pages. Jenny Felkner, I really appreciate your friendship, especially during the really dark year. I am totally going to take you to Chili's the next time I see you—and I'm buying. A BIG shout out to all the men and women of the Al Anon worldwide fellowship. I can't thank you enough for just showing up and sitting your buns in a chair to share your experience, strength and hope.

A Texas-size shout out for all the faithful members of the DFW Writers' Workshop who have listened to and critiqued my writing over the past four years, but most especially: Trayce Primm, Brooke Martin Fossey, Alex Martinez, Jenny Martin, Rosemary Clement, Harry Hall, Larry Enmon and Emily Nichter. Even though I'm still too anxious for the after-hours socializing at IHOP, I've learned how to read in front of real, live people without passing out or sounding like a complete goober. (At least I don't think I do. Do I?)

At Goucher, I'd like to thank Patsy Sims and my wonderful mentors, Diana Hume-George (you're the bomb), Susannah Lessard, Tom French and Jacob Levenson. You were probably all as perplexed as I was during the formation of my thesis, so I am deeply indebted to each of you for your help and encouragement as I tried to figure out what the hell I was doing.

Tex Thompson. How I love thee! Let me count the ways. You're like the smartest, kindest, wittiest gal I know. You almost make me want to figure out the rules of grammar. (Not really.) Seriously, I can't thank you enough for helping me deliver the baby. You made it way less scary.

To all the people who have allowed me to interview them or share their writing on my blog—there is a special place in my heart for you! I have learned so much about grief and death from your stories. You are all courageous and bad-ass in the best way possible.

Last, but certainly not least, I would like to thank each and every person that allowed me into their lives for this book. It took guts and trust, and if it hadn't been for you saying "yes," I wouldn't have had this life-altering experience. Or this book. Thank you.

LINKS

My blog:
http://thedeathwriter.blogspot.com/

Death with Dignity:
http://www.deathwithdignity.org/

Death Over Dinner:

http://deathoverdinner.org/

The Conversation Project:
http://theconversationproject.org/

The Innocence Project:
http://www.innocenceproject.org/

The Texas Coalition to Abolish the Death Penalty:
http://tcadp.org/

Five Wishes:
https://agingwithdignity.org/

The Neptune Society:
http://www.neptunesociety.com/

The Order of the Good Death:
http://www.orderofthegooddeath.com/

Made in the USA
Charleston, SC
06 April 2016